Praise for *The Soprano State*

"This book makes me proud as a New Jersey citizen. Not only are we first in highway cloverleafs, first in gas stations named after historic figures and football coaches, first in waste management companies, but also first in corruption. Eat your heart out, Louisiana. As a scholar of misfeasance, malfeasance, and no feasance in government, even I was amazed by Ingle and McClure's hilarious story about our state's achievement. Read it and laugh—or cry."

—Marvin Kitman, media pathologist,
HuffingtonPost.com

"Should be required reading for every budding journalist. It shows just how far the egotists we keep electing and entrusting with government coffers will go to advance themselves. It's a delightful read even if politicians aren't that bad in your state . . . you think. The two authors have done a masterful job in capturing the laughter and larceny that abounds in the state house and its environs."

—Barbara Knowles, news editor, *Newton Citizen*
(Covington, Georgia)

"I couldn't put it down . . . reads like fiction. I live in California and feared it might only be of interest to those who live in New Jersey. Boy, was I wrong."

—Cissie Cooper, San Francisco, California

"As the writers say, 'You can't make this stuff up.'"

—*Asbury Park Press*

THE
SOPRANO STATE

ALSO BY SANDY McCLURE

Christie Whitman: A Political Biography

THE
SOPRANO STATE

New Jersey's Culture of Corruption

Bob Ingle and
Sandy McClure

ST. MARTIN'S GRIFFIN
New York

www.stmartins.com

The Library of Congress has catalogued the hardcover edition as follows:

Ingle, Bob.
    The Soprano state : New Jersey's culture of corruption / Bob Ingle and
Sandy McClure.—1st ed.
        p. cm.
    ISBN 978-0-312-36894-4
    1. Political corruption—New Jersey. 2. Scandals—New Jersey. 3. Political
culture—New Jersey. I. McClure, Sandy. II. Title.

    JK3545.I64 2008
    364.1'32309749—dc22

                                                            2007040919

ISBN 978-0-312-60257-4 (trade paperback)

Second St. Martin's Griffin Edition: November 2010

10 9 8 7 6 5 4 3 2 1

For taxpayers everywhere

CONTENTS

ACKNOWLEDGMENTS

The authors say thanks to JB and to our family and friends for their love and support; to Phil Revzin, our St. Martin's Press editor, for his editing and belief in this project; to Edward Knappman, our New England Publishing Associates agent, who initiated the idea and was our advocate, and to his wife, Elizabeth; to India Cooper, an incredible copy editor; to Ellis Levine for his thoughtful guidance; to Mike Symons, our friend and colleague, who has the patience of a saint and the memory of an elephant, and to his wife, Lisa, our Web chief; to Colley Charpentier who originated the job of State Bureau news editor; to Gannett New Jersey, especially our colleagues at the State Bureau in Trenton and Skip Hidlay, *Asbury Park Press* editor; to Bob Collins, former *Asbury Park Press* publisher, who encouraged us to report without fear or favor; to the *Trentonian* and its 1990s staffers Gale Baldwin, Paul Mickle, Dave Neese, and Phyllis Plitch; to John Torok who knows things about Trenton no one else does, and to his wife, Enid; to Joe Potena and Ken Connolly for their whistle-blowing courage; to Chris Christie, who took on the bad guys; to Dick Hughes who knew a good news story when he saw one; to

Ev Landers, veteran journalist and idea man; to Craig Carton of WFAN; and Ray Rossi and Casey Bartholomew of 101.5 FM; to New Jersey journalists who work to keep the state honest, and to New Jersey's taxpayers whose suffering seems without end.

FOREWORD

A s I sat to write this foreword, I did something I rarely do. I called up the Web site of the Central New Jersey newspaper where I was editor for several years.

It was worth the trip.

The former director of New Brunswick's neighborhood preservation was arrested on charges of taking $112,500 in bribes from contractors in exchange for work orders worth millions.

On the same day, a former clerk in the office of Planning, Community, and Economic Development pleaded guilty to taking $3,000 in bribes to expedite payments to contractors.

Jeez, I thought, even those in supposedly do-good agencies are on the take. No surprise here, said an FBI agent: "Corruption is rampant at high levels and at low levels and all levels in between."

How well do Bob Ingle and Sandy McClure know the truth of that!

To play on a discarded New Jersey slogan, Ingle and McClure are perfect together to provide the tough-as-nails reporting (McClure) and the populist outrage (Ingle) in this chronicle of the criminal culture of New Jersey politics.

They've been chasing the people, politics, and plundering for years in the best Ben Hecht "Front Page" style. Investigative jour-nalism in New Jersey is not for the faint at heart, the lazy, or the impatient.

These characters in political Sopranoland are clever, and they have lots of protection from like-minded citizens, not all, of course, just enough.

All of which grows a tough breed of reporters in the Garden State, where hard news, well reported and supported, lives, even now as some newspapers elsewhere (think Washington) buy into the administration line of the day, withhold transgressions for forthcom-ing books, and share luncheon tables with influence-peddlers.

Ingle and McClure and the many other aggressive New Jersey journalists tracking down corruption "at high levels and at low lev-els and all levels in between" don't get asked to lunch, which is a fine thing.

As journalists for Gannett New Jersey, they brought down their share of political wiseguys (and gals) to be sure, but *The Soprano State* credits all the many other newspaper journalists who pull weeds in the thicket of the Garden State. There's enough corrup-tion to go around.

When the record is compiled, as it is here, the reader will rec-ognize the treasure trove that joke writers so love and even will see material for an original one-liner or two. But at the end of the com-edy routine, one has to get dead serious about the state of democ-racy when so many are ripping off so many with so few caring.

However apathetic, the public is well-served by journalists like Ingle and McClure who are true believers in journalism's watchdog role in exposing the corruption that drains taxpayers' dollars and trust, even as it provides a laugh line.

Read all about it here.

—Dick Hughes

(Dick Hughes spent fifteen years as reporter and editor with UPI and twenty-two years at the *Home News Tribune* of East Brunswick, New Jersey, where he was editor for seventeen years. In post-retirement, he was managing editor of the *Moorefield Examiner,* a weekly in West Virginia, where he hounded politicians in the courthouse and meth dealers in the hollers.)

PROLOGUE

In travels near home and on the road, we are often asked if we embellish the incredibly wacky stories about New Jersey crime and corruption published in news reports and columns under our bylines.

The answer is a cliché, but so true: You couldn't make this stuff up. In fact, for newspapers we sometimes tone it down. It's hilarious, outrageous, maddening—and true, really. No flourishes needed. It's not a coincidence the TV show *The Sopranos* is based in Jersey. Its creator grew up in the state hearing the same kinds of stories.

Newspaper readers ask us why we don't write a book so relatives, colleagues, and friends across the nation can be shocked and awed and drop to the floor laughing, too.

That's the genesis of this project—why should such a wealth of lunacy and depravity be enjoyed by a state with just 8.7 million people? It's real. But it reads like fiction.

THE
SOPRANO STATE

INTRODUCTION

The legendary comedy team of Bob and Ray once performed a skit in which they pretended to be New Jersey mayors bragging about whose administration was the most crooked. One claimed he had the nation's only corrupt visiting-nurse program.

The skit came true in 2005 when U.S. Attorney Chris Christie gave the board of the University of Medicine and Dentistry of New Jersey a choice: It could be taken over by an appointed federal guardian or face indictment for $4.9 million in Medicare fraud. UMDNJ may well have been the country's most crooked institution for training doctors, dentists—and, yes, nurses.[1]

Alleged Medicare fraud was just the tip of an operation that demonstrated the tried and true nature of things government-related in Jersey—take care of your friends and allies no matter what the mission statement says about what we're here to do.

And it wasn't just nurses. At UMDNJ's hospital, the federal monitor who took over the hospital launched a probe in 2006 into whether doctors traded referrals to a failing cardiac surgery program in exchange for no-show university jobs.[2] And it wasn't just doctors. The monitor found dental students getting credit for classes they skipped on root canals, extractions, and crowns. Ouch![3]

In grade school when they go over the states and discuss what each contributes to the country, New Jersey's could very well be that it's the national comedic bull's-eye. *Why are New Yorkers so depressed? The light at the end of the tunnel is Jersey.* It's a staple of late-night TV.

Peculiar politicians and corrupt government have been constants since New Jersey was created, but something inexplicable happened in the early 1990s that speeded up the process. It's almost as if the people who run the place wanted to see how far they could push the envelope, how much they could get away with.

Until recently there was no commercial statewide media, and that's a part of how things got to be as bad as they are. North Jersey depends on New York stations for its TV news. Philadelphia network affiliates handle it for the south. Considering that newspaper circulation is falling and local TV news covers mostly fires, traffic accidents, and alley stabbings—it's no wonder overburdened New Jersey taxpayers can't name their legislators. New Jersey's statewide TV is public television, which is owned by the State of New Jersey. Thus, everyone from the news anchor to the cameraman's assistant gets a paycheck from the same place as the governor. This creates at least the appearance of a conflict.

To an outsider it looks like crime and political corruption are the fabric from which the Garden State's government is woven. This fabric is woven so tightly that no institution or individual could ever reverse the flow of taxpayer money into the pockets of the politically connected. Read on and we think you'll agree.

It starts, of course, at the top. There is only one statewide elected official, the governor. New Jersey has had, shall we say, some *interesting* governors recently, some of whom have managed to interest prosecutors as well as voters.

Perhaps the most interesting recent denizen of Drumthwacket, the governor's mansion in Princeton Township, was Jim McGreevey, who among other things named a young Israeli with no appropriate experience to the job of homeland security adviser just months after 9/11. With a straight face, McGreevey talked of Golan Cipel's many qualifications. Well, maybe "straight face" is not appropriate. When McGreevey stepped down, telling us at age forty-seven he suddenly realized he is gay, his staff said that Cipel was someone with whom the twice-married McGreevey, who has two daughters, had an affair. Cipel was threatening a sexual harassment lawsuit, the aides said.

Before McGreevey, Donald DiFrancesco was acting governor because he was president of the state senate, the position that steps in for a missing New Jersey chief executive. DiFrancesco was going to seek a full term but suddenly pulled out of the race after a series of stories by coauthor Sandy McClure and others centered on questionable land deals and loans and alleged unethical conduct.

DiFrancesco became acting governor when Christie Whitman left to be head of the Environmental Protection Agency under President George W. Bush. She promptly made a fool of herself by insisting the Manhattan air in the aftermath of the 9/11 attacks was clean and pure.[4] Not even by New Jersey standards was that so. Rescue workers will undergo medical monitoring for the rest of their lives. Six years later, in June 2007, Whitman was called before a Congressional committee to explain herself. Basically, she blamed the terrorists.[5]

Whitman, who had served only in a county post and as head of the state utilities board, came to office after defeating in 1993 one-termer Jim Florio, whose chief of staff, Joe Salema, was sentenced to a halfway house, home detention, and a $10,000 fine for a role in a $200,000-plus kickback scheme involving a Camden County authority.[6]

But that's just the governor. No one gets that job without the backing of powerful party bosses spread across the state and kissing the butts of special interest groups. These guys make the old days of Chicago look like Sesame Street. The bosses' strength is raising campaign money, the mother's milk of politics. The unions are good for turning out the vote on Election Day. In return, the legislature is more than happy to do the unions' bidding.

Lower down the food chain, corruption thrives on unchecked conflicts of interest. A New Jersey mayor can also be a member of the state legislature and a partner in a law firm that benefits from legislation he writes. In New Jersey pretty much nothing becomes law unless it benefits somebody financially.[7] Hardly anything happens solely because it is the right thing to do. The public's welfare is often the last thing on the agenda. Unions and other special interest groups call the shots. Everybody else pays for it.

But, you ask, doesn't that violate ethics laws? In other places, definitely. Think of the Garden State's ethics laws as what banking regulations would be like if Bonnie and Clyde made them. Government creates agencies to keep mobsters out, and politicians find ways around them. What about the justice system and the courts? You guessed it: Scandal regularly engulfs judges and the attorney general's office.

In New Jersey, government is not about taking care of what people can't do for themselves. It's about jobs. There is entirely too much government. Smallest of the Middle Atlantic states and forty-sixth among the fifty in land area,[8] New Jersey has 566 municipal governments and 615 school districts, some of which don't have students but collect millions of dollars in local taxes and state aid and *do* have *paid* administrations.[9] New Jersey has more school superintendents than do the states of Maryland, Virginia, and Delaware combined. Add to that 187 fire districts, 486 local authorities, 92 special taxing districts, and 21 counties, all of which can add taxes—1,969 taxing entities in total when counting the state, with its taxing arms, as only one—and the picture of a state with its hand perpetually in taxpayers' pockets comes into focus.

The number of elected officeholders in local government is 19,119. Each is a part of a political fiefdom, a power base for politicians who employ supporters and ensure their loyalty with good pay and pensions out of line with the real world. The workers, in turn, get out the vote to keep the pols in office and themselves on the payroll. State government has 154,500 workers, and local government employs 444,000, for an average of about 81 government workers per square mile. The national average, according to the Census Bureau, is six government workers per square mile. New Jersey is the most densely populated of the fifty states, but even so the difference between it and the rest of the country is striking.

Even less visible are the fifty state authorities—unelected, unaccountable independent bodies with the power to float billions of dollars' worth of bonds without being subject to the vote of the people or supervision by elected officials. Authorities are a useful way to get around the state constitution's requirement that voters must approve borrowing. They're dumping grounds for political deadwood, relatives, and boy- or girlfriends, as well as a dandy way to reward allies with fat contracts.

The New Jersey Turnpike, for example, opened in 1951, and it is commonly believed that the Turnpike Authority was supposed to remove tolls when the road was paid for. That should have been decades ago, but the tolls are still there because politicians found out what a gold mine an independent authority is. In most states the highway department is responsible for roads because they are, after all, just strips of concrete. In New Jersey it takes a huge bureaucracy in the form of an isolated authority to administer that concrete. And they keep the tolls because when they float bonds, they have to guarantee tolls will stay in place to pay off the bonds.

It's an endless cycle, one the political trough-swillers created to keep themselves fat and happy.

Should someone complain about raising the tolls, the response will be that most of the people paying them are just passing through. The three most frequent excuses for government waste and excess are: *People from out of town will bear the brunt of it. It's for the seniors. It's for the children.* Taxpayers buy it every time.

Politicians want to keep the status quo, so they have New Jerseyans believing they drive on the best roads in the nation. That's another thing about Jerseyans. They seldom go anywhere—probably because, thanks to the outrageous cost of living, they can't afford to travel farther than the state's beaches, which are, by the way, overcrowded and expensive. Unlike most beaches in the world, Jersey's are not free. To get onto most of them, people have to buy beach tags. You can't lie in the sun without some obnoxious badge monitor asking to see yours.

And then there's the mob. Mobsters, of course, are as much a part of state lore as the legendary Jersey Devil who supposedly roams the very Garden State swamps the Mafia used to dispatch the competition and plant turncoat comrades. From Camden on the Delaware River to Atlantic City by the ocean, mob influence is in the air. Teamsters Union boss Jimmy Hoffa is famously rumored to be enshrined in the cement of Giants Stadium at the Meadowlands in the north. Atlantic City deserves its own chapter, and will get one.

In Jersey, it's not just the Sopranos who make news. Real mobsters do, too. One wiseguy, Angelo Prisco, was serving prison time for arson for hire when he was paroled under unusual circumstances, reportedly after a call from the governor's office.[10]

The place is a comedian's paradise and a journalist's dream. Even the state's Societies for the Prevention of Cruelty to Animals were investigated in 2000, and the State Commission of Investigation found widespread corruption among certain societies. In typical New Jersey style, money intended for animal protection was diverted for personal use.[11] More recently, the state's Emergency Medical Services were found in shambles.

One group of New Jerseyans has actually done something about this mess: Twenty-four percent of the people on New Jersey's government retirement rolls get their checks sent out of state, the *Asbury Park Press* reported, based on pension data.[12] That means the people who helped make the state the disaster it is can't stand to live in the environment they helped create.

An increasing number flee Jersey's kleptocracy, a culture of government stealing, for retirement in Florida, Delaware, or Arkansas, where the taxes are lower and the politicians at least seem more honest—and it makes the natives in other states nervous. A journalist's mother who lives in North Carolina used to introduce her son in the grocery with, "This is my son. He lives in New Jersey." Because the growing number of exiles to the Tar Heel State concerns folks who worry the immigrants could bring their corrupt government with them, the grocery introduction has changed. Now she says, "This is my son. He lives in New Jersey. But he's only visiting."

We're often asked by people elsewhere if New Jersey residents are aware of what the rest of the country thinks and why they don't do something about it. The answer to the first question is, they know. The second is harder. Do they like being the national butt of jokes? Do they wait for the day when they can get their share of graft? Are they too busy working more than one job to afford the extraordinary cost of living? Have they given up?

The latter probably fits best. They go to the polls, and no matter who gets elected, it doesn't make a difference. Politicians of all stripes kowtow to special interests while seeing how many relatives they can pack onto the payroll. What would be unacceptable or illegal in most states is par for the course. Reform is, of course, easy to champion during political campaigns, but much harder to put into practice.

But if reform is hard, public relations should be easier. A state agency recently paid $260,000 to an outside company to create a slogan encouraging people to visit New Jersey. It chose "We Will Win You Over." It sounded like people with a negative view of the state had to be convinced. Senate President Dick Codey, who became chief executive briefly when McGreevey resigned, hated the choice and rejected it.[13] He made it a contest open to all New Jerseyans. Even that was not without controversy. Entries included "New Jersey: Not All Our Elected Officials Have Been Indicted" and "New Jersey: We Hate You, Too." The winner, "Come See for Yourself," was submitted by a guy whose job was, among other things, writing slogans for the state's mass transit agency.[14] The winning entry was first published in a newspaper story quoting someone else, but the winner, who was the first to officially submit it, said he never read the article.[15] Many thought slogan No. 2 was inviting visitors to check out the state as if to prove all the rotten things they heard were true and, like the rejected No. 1, played off the negative.

So the bureaucratic slugs went back to the drawing board for the third slogan, one they hope oozes warm and fuzzy and will draw 'em in like a giant magnet. They're still waiting for that one.

Fuggedaboutit! We've got the winner, a slogan people from the California Redwoods to Mississippi's Gulf Shore can identify with and respond to, one that can be factually justified and guaranteed to bring 'em here by the planeload—the bada-bing of slogans:

New Jersey: The Soprano State

1

Deep in the Pits They Strike Gold

In New Jersey's super-corrupt atmosphere, nothing is sacred or beyond conversion to a patronage pit. Seemingly everything Jersey politicians do is designed to help themselves or their friends. Little is done because it is the right thing to do. Sometimes it can be the right thing, but in that case, it's a coincidence.

The University of Medicine and Dentistry of New Jersey (UMDNJ) is a microcosm for corruption in the rest of the Garden State. Appropriately for an institution of higher learning, UMDNJ made a science out of corruption. It created a system that assigned numbers—1, 2, or 3—to job applicants based on their political connections. If a person with a 1 rating—highly connected to a political patron—showed up at the school's human resources department, personnel staff would search the campus to secure No. 1 a job, qualifications notwithstanding.

UMDNJ employs fifteen thousand at its five campuses across the state, has five thousand students, and spends $1.5 billion a year.

It has been a patronage pit for decades, but not until a *Newark Star-Ledger* team led by reporter Josh Margolin tore away the layers of corruption was there a full disclosure of just how bad things were.[1]

Among those whose recommendations ranked a 1 were U.S. Sen. Robert Menendez and State Sen. and former Newark mayor Sharpe James. State Sen. Wayne Bryant must have had a huge 1 circled in red because he was chairman of the senate budget committee and could steer millions of dollars the school's way. He personally went on UMDNJ's payroll in March 2003 as a part-time consultant for $38,200. Shortly thereafter, Bryant lobbied to get UMDNJ's School of Osteopathic Medicine in his Camden County more money. On one occasion he inserted a $2.7 million budget line item for the school, sources told Margolin and colleague Ted Sherman.

In 2005, U.S. Attorney Chris Christie gave UMDNJ a choice: be prosecuted for federal Medicare fraud or accept Herbert J. Stern, a former federal prosecutor and federal judge, as monitor. Thus was ushered in another of those "firsts" in which Jersey can take no pride—the first medical school in the nation to go under federal supervision. That put the state's medical university right up there with mobbed-up labor unions. Stern's subsequent report cited "potentially illegal activities" including skewed profit reports and a Newark city councilman using his influence for political gain. (The school's main campus is in Newark, the state's largest city.)

R. Michael Gallagher, who later resigned as dean of the School of Osteopathic Medicine, was accused of doctoring financial statements to qualify himself for a bonus. Newark Councilman Donald Bradley was said to have used UMDNJ's Black History Month celebration as entertainment for political backers with costs escalating from a planned $5,000 to $22,000. Gannett State Bureau reporter Gregory J. Volpe explained:[2]

The report also says Gallagher charged the university thousands for expensive restaurants, upscale hotels and his drink of choice—18- to 21-year-old Glenlivet, which costs about $20 per glass.

He used petty cash, reimbursement requests and direct billing to the university to avoid the scrutiny of expense reports, the report says. He spent more than $180,000 in fancy restaurants and country clubs. He also used his UMDNJ car and driver for personal use.

Meanwhile, Bradley, a UMDNJ trustee and Newark council president, is under fire for negotiating a sublease of a UMDNJ space to a political donor vying for a contract with the city.

In 2003, according to the report, Bradley got a $1 per year sublease of office space for Dr. Chandrakant Patel—whose doctor's license [at one point] was suspended for operating an illegal laboratory—and his son, Dr. Saurabh C. Patel. The family and practice have donated $6,415 to Bradley, including $700 that was refunded because it exceeded contribution amounts.

Stern's report claimed the Patels owed UMDNJ about $75,000 in property taxes—and $3 in back rent because for three years they didn't even pay the $1 a year.

The Medicaid fraud probe at UMDNJ spawned at least a hundred investigations. One of them, the Bryant probe, revealed what U.S. Attorney Christie called one of the most brazen examples of public corruption he had ever prosecuted. In March 2007, he indicted Byrant and Gallagher.[3]

The twenty-count indictment charged the two with an illegal scheme in which Gallagher created the bogus $38,200-a-year job for Bryant in exchange for Bryant using his role as a state senator to get money for the university. "You have to wonder why this guy was in charge of giving out taxpayer money," Christie said of

Bryant. "And you have to wonder why no one was watching the store." Christie also charged Gallagher with cooking the university books, showing a profit instead of a loss, to collect $50,000 in bonus money. If the books did not show a profit, he would not have qualified for the bonuses. Ironically, the bonuses were for the good performance of the university's Headache Center, where Gallagher diverted money, at a time when both Gallagher and Bryant were creating headaches for taxpayers.

As if Gallagher wasn't earning enough money with a base pay of $340,000, Bryant, who talked Gallagher up among high-ranking New Jersey officials, is accused of helping him appear to shine in the job, resulting in nearly $99,000 in incentive bonuses in 2003 and 2004.

The U.S. attorney in the indictment classified Bryant's UMDNJ job as a bribe. The indictment said Gallagher created the job, described as improving university communications, when the university already had someone on staff with those identical duties. Gallagher held interviews for the post, but Christie said they were staged. When the interviews were held, Gallagher had already circulated administrative forms indicating Bryant had been selected, the indictment said. Bryant and Gallagher were on trial at the time of this writing.

On the student front, revelations flowed from the federal monitor who said the associate dean for academic and student affairs at UMDNJ's Camden campus, Paul Mehne, pressured directors at the school to give passing grades to some medical students who failed standardized tests, the *Courier-Post* reported. These students were about to start specialty rotations and some are now practicing doctors. Mehne, who denied violating the university's grading policy, was placed on administrative leave. If that wasn't enough to worry New Jersey's patients, the *Star-Ledger* reported that Deborah Johnson resigned as an associate dean for clinical enterprise after the monitor said she signed medical charts and billing documents for patients she had not examined. Johnson, who told the monitor she believed she was permitted to sign for another doctor within the same practice, was still on the faculty.[4]

After Stern started digging, university president John J. Petillo agreed to cooperate and, New Jersey style, was given a $600,000 severance package. In the wake of the probe, some individuals at the university were fired and others quit. One who was removed was Warren Wallace, a $166,234-a-year senior dean at UMDNJ's School of Osteopathic Medicine.[5] Typical of so many in Jersey politics, $166,234 wasn't enough; in addition to his duties as dean, he was a Gloucester County official and chairman of the bistate Delaware River and Bay Authority, a regional Jersey-Delaware agency that wields a lot of influence in South Jersey.

A monitor's report indicated Wallace engaged in activities that benefited friends, family, and, naturally, Wallace himself. It told how Wallace's daughter applied to get into the school where her father was a dean and was granted an interview even though she didn't have Medical College Aptitude Test scores, letters of recommendation, or the two required essays. Reportedly, she got the highest possible ranking.[6]

In 2006 Gov. Jon Corzine said Wallace should leave public life and noted he himself would do his part toward that end by not reappointing Wallace to the Bay Authority.[7] Ironically, Gov. Jim McGreevey had appointed Wallace in the first place to help clean up the agency, which was rocked by a financial scandal not unlike the one that Wallace got caught up in at UMDNJ.[8]

Wallace was an ally of Bryant. After being tipped off that documents were being shredded, the FBI raided Wallace's office to halt shredding thought to be related to the Bryant case.[9]

The original UMDNJ Medicare billing fraud was estimated at $4.9 million, but investigators found evidence of another one totaling about $70 million. Looking at the whole picture, monitor Stern identified more than $243 million in waste, fraud, and abuse. The school was forced to put its planned $110 million cancer center on hold, and more than 150 employees were set to get pink slips.[10]

Then the scandal hit the heart unit big-time.

According to the federal monitor, the university, in violation of federal law, had offered high-paying faculty jobs to eighteen cardiologists in exchange for the doctors' referring patients to a failing cardiac surgery program that the state was threatening to shut down because of poor performance, the *Star-Ledger* reported.[11]

Senate President Dick Codey complained, "When a physician refers you to a certain hospital, the assumption is that that hospital is the best hospital for you in that condition. You never think 'Is that physician doing it for his own financial health?' "

The monitor accused cardiologists with referring patients for nearly $36 million in illegal Medicare and Medicaid payments in exchange for the no-show university jobs that cost $5.7 million and paid each doctor more than $150,000 a year for doing nothing. In addition, the university tried to hide the scam from the monitor, failing to disclose a settlement to an employee who blew the whistle on the kickbacks.

The monitor charged that UMDNJ interim president Bruce Vladeck was part of the cover-up. Corzine in 2006 continued to back Vladeck—but told the *Star-Ledger* that if there were ongoing criminal activities, they should certainly cease and desist. Now there is a novel idea for New Jersey.[12]

Petillo and his temporary replacement, Vladeck, were then replaced by William Owen, former chancellor of the Health Science Center at the University of Tennessee, who would be the first African American to head UMDNJ. In breaking the news of Owen's selection, the *Star-Ledger* said Owen had undergone his own scandals in Tennessee, where he had to repay the university $4,500 for unauthorized decorating of his school-owned home.[13] Those who selected Owen for the new post, paying $570,000 a year, plus $25,000 for travel and entertainment, said it was a miscommunication. At first blush, it sounded like Owen would fit in just fine in New Jersey.

With the goodies at UMDNJ getting plenty of publicity, South Jersey political boss George E. Norcross III said he wanted UMDNJ to put a new medical school in Camden. "Given the opportunities for patronage provided by UMDNJ in Newark, it's easy to understand why Norcross is salivating at the prospect of a new medical school," an *Asbury Park Press* editorial said. "The discussion should be a short one, beginning and ending with 'No.' "[14] As of this writing, Norcross's proposal has been shelved but not dismissed totally.

It was clear the poorly run UMDNJ was costing taxpayers an arm and a leg. The behavior of its dental students could also cost taxpayers some teeth. About twenty dental students were implicated in a cheating scheme in which they were given credit for course work not done. Some weren't allowed to graduate with their classmates in May '06; others did community service work, and some had to repeat the requirements. It is not known how long the scam involving false credits for learning how to do root canals, crowns, and extractions had been going on at the dental school.[15]

Not only did UMDNJ students want to skip practicing pulling teeth, they also wanted to skip studying for exams. The *Star-Ledger* reported that dental students set up an elaborate cheating scheme instructing students to memorize a specific question on a dental exam so the information could be e-mailed under a false name and then put on a CD and posted on a Web site for those who had yet to take the test: "Investigators also found detailed instructions calling for each member of the class to contribute questions for upcoming exams," the *Star-Ledger* reported. "The directions were very specific, according to the dean, including the creation of the e-mail accounts." Everyone was supposed to take part. Dean Cecile Feldman said peer pressure played a role.[16]

As if scandal wasn't enough, the bizarre came into play at the school. UMDNJ med student Ahmed Rashed must have been impressed with nude dancer Linda Kay from a club called Hott 22, because he gave her a hand.[17] Literally. It was named Freddy and allegedly was stolen from a cadaver at the medical school in 2002. Both Rashed and Kay were indicted, he for stealing the hand, she for accepting stolen property.

Rashed, a 2005 grad, moved to California and then to Texas before accepting a plea deal that kept him out of prison but could have banned him from practicing medicine in New Jersey, though only for five years.[18]

Superior Court Judge Frederick DeVesa fined Rashed $5,000 but didn't slap him with probation that would have kept him from his medical career. Kay was allowed to enter a pretrial probationary program.[19]

The hand was discovered when police went to Kay's home to answer a report about a man trying to commit suicide with a hammer. Freddy had roommates, six human skulls, but authorities determined the skulls were obtained legally from an outfit called Skulls Unlimited. According to the *Home News Tribune*, officers found the hand "preserved in a foot-tall mason jar of formaldehyde on a basement table." The rest of the cadaver was cremated after being used in UMDNJ classes.[20] Once again: We aren't making any of this up.

And what was the reaction to the various UMDNJ scandals from the school and the state's political establishment?

UMDNJ wanted to run a $2.5 million advertising campaign to polish the school's image even as more waste and corruption was uncovered almost daily. Stu Rabner, Governor Corzine's chief counsel, later his attorney general and chief justice of the state supreme court, and previously an assistant to U. S. Attorney Christie, pointed out what should have been crystal clear: It was inappropriate to run an ad campaign while the school was eliminating jobs and had a $25.5 million deficit at its hospital.[21]

In another only-in-New Jersey development, questions started about whether the more than $9 million billed to the state for the monitor's investigation was excessive. The bill exceeded the original amount of Medicare fraud that started the flood of investigations. "Maybe we need someone to monitor the monitor or at least his expenditures," State Sen. Loretta Weinberg, a Democrat, told the *New York Times*.[22]

U.S. Attorney Christie defended the monitor's expenses as "the greatest return on government dollars anyone's ever seen in the state of New Jersey . . . Taxpayer money was pouring out of that place like an open fire hydrant. We put a stop to that and put in the type of structure they're going to need for long-term reform."[23]

But the corrupt New Jersey system slammed those looking for reform.

Michael Nappe, a billing manager at UMDNJ, said the university moved his office to a lunchroom, demoted him, and wouldn't give him raises after he blew the whistle on a scheme to cover up more than $25 million in padded bills, the *Star-Ledger* reported. In a lawsuit filed in state court, Nappe said he objected to an accounting system aimed at hiding the high cost of telecommunications contracts not competitively bid, as the law requires. Fake invoices billed university departments for services they never received to hide the inflated bills, including $301,660 to remove two computer viruses from a computer and seventy-seven cents a minute for long-distance calling.[24]

Nappe wasn't alone. Carol Caprarola, a former government affairs coordinator at UMDNJ, said she was laid off after she complained the university was making illegal campaign contributions to Essex County lawmakers, Newark council members, and senate Democrats. Rohit Arora, former chief of the Division of Cardiology, said he was forced from the university after he objected to the scheme to trade cardiology referrals for no-show teaching jobs.

UMDNJ paid Arora $2.2 million to settle his lawsuit, the *Star-Ledger* reported.[25]

Kathryn Gibbons, a former senior financial official, sued after she said she was fired in retaliation. Gibbons and former university vice president Adam Henick were the first to tell federal investigators about the overbilling and fraud, the *Star-Ledger* reported. As the whistle-blower lawsuits piled up, Moody's Investors Service downgraded the university's bond rating.

Even with its financial woes, UMDNJ made headlines again in June 2007 when it was revealed that the state university spent more than $450,000 on legal fees related to the firing of its former dean, the indicted Gallagher. UMDNJ trustee chairman Robert Del Tufo, a former state attorney general under Gov. Florio, defended the bill because it included the cost of an investigator.[26]

Federal monitoring of UMDNJ ended December 31, 2007. The investigation, starting with the university's Medicare double billing, uncovered more than $400 million in fraud and waste. Christie said "at this time" lawbreaking has ended at the teaching institution. The issue of ethics, he said, "still needs substantial improvement."

The monitoring ended, but the federal investigation continued. Two cardiologists, Dr. Bakul Desai and Dr. Laxmipathi Garipalli, pleaded guilty to embezzlement—accepting $840,000 for no-work jobs at the university. The feds said the only thing the two did for the money was refer patients to UMDNJ's cardiac unit. That's the scam that was conjured up by administrators after the university failed to perform enough cardiac procedures to keep its state funding and accreditation, Christie said. Later Desai paid $1.4 million and Garipalli $560,000 to resolve civil suits filed by the feds.

Four more cardiologists settled, without any charges being filed, by agreeing to pay back a total of $387,000 in salaries and penalties.

Remember, this is a hospital, where taxpayers are supposed to be healed, not scammed.

2

Lots of Power,
Less Common Sense

New Jersey's constitution grants its governor the most powers of
the fifty state chief executives. Too bad it doesn't guarantee
good judgment or good luck. Recent governors have stretched,
bent, and from time to time broken their mandates with behavior
that would be termed bizarre, if not unethical and potentially criminal, anywhere else but Jersey. They've favored friends and lovers
and family with loans and state jobs, and hired staffers with criminal connections. They've even tried to tax toilet paper and strong-
arm nuns. On the bad luck front they've suffered major personal
injuries while in office: Christie Whitman broke her leg skiing in
Davos, Switzerland; Jim McGreevey mysteriously broke his leg
while walking on the beach; and Jon Corzine sustained horren-
dous injuries in a car crash when he wasn't wearing his seat belt, as
required by state law.

Let's start with Democrat Gov. Jim Florio, who left Congress in
1990 after being elected governor. He was aloof and distant and

said repeatedly while campaigning that he saw no need for a tax increase. Soon after victory in 1989, he proposed a $2.8 billion tax hike, which was understandably not well received. Even so, he might have hung on for a second term, except a part of his proposal called for what was widely known as the Toilet Paper Tax. Not since General George Washington took on the Hessians in what is now the statehouse parking lot have New Jerseyans been so riled. Reminiscent of that famous tea party in Boston, angry protesters threw rolls of bathroom tissue at the statehouse.

Coauthor McClure reported for the *Trentonian*:[1] "Thousands of irate taxpayers gathered stormily at the Statehouse yesterday to protest new taxes and state spending. When the crowd was reminded about the new tax on toilet tissue, toilet tissue rolls were defiantly hurled into the air, leaving tissue streamers in their wake. One roll, hurled at the Statehouse, stuck and flew symbolically from an upper balcony." A week later, the grassroots group Hands Across New Jersey had gathered 350,000 signatures urging the governor to repeal the $2.8 million tax hike.

Florio's career was in the crapper from then on. The legislature turned Republican in the midterm 1991 election. When Florio ran for reelection, FLORIO FREE IN '93 bumper stickers plastered the Garden State, and some motorists still display them proudly.

But taxes weren't the only thing that damaged Florio's single term.

He and his longtime friends and business associates gave taxpayers an example of the ultimate in New Jersey patronage—helping yourself through your public position and boosting the fortune of your friends.

Using sources deep inside the Florio administration and poring over state nursing home records for five months, McClure compiled a five-part series on how Florio's top aides used their jobs to get rich.[2]

"State health policies developed under Gov. Florio will put thousands—and perhaps millions—of dollars in the pockets of two of Florio's closest and highest-ranking aides," McClure wrote for the *Trentonian*. "Florio chief of staff Joe Salema and chief of management and planning Brenda Bacon stand to profit from policies and administrative decisions that will boost their extensive investments in proposed and existing nursing homes for the elderly."

Records showed that nursing home interests owned by Salema and Bacon and placed in blind trusts received special treatment from the state. At the same time, the two top aides secured a chunk of the nursing home market in New Jersey as the state limited nursing home construction, giving advantage to the politically connected and hurting those who lacked clout, such as religion-affiliated nursing homes desperate for new beds.

"State records reveal that requests for rate increases and other changes that would benefit nursing homes owned by Salema and Bacon have consistently bypassed normal procedures and have been rubber-stamped by top Health Department officials, sometimes as quickly as 24 hours after they were submitted," McClure wrote. "In at least two instances, unprecedented verbal approvals were given to requests concerning Salema-Bacon. Health Commissioner Bruce Siegel termed the handling of one Salema-Bacon application an 'oversight' by the Health Department and said the verbal approvals were 'not something I would ever want to tolerate.'" But he denied politics played a role.

Within seven months after Florio was sworn in, the state approved two special requests to increase rates outside the normal schedule at Meadowview Nursing and Convalescent Center in Gloucester County, owned by Salema and Bacon.

Meadowview also was one of only a few nursing homes that got exceptions to a one-year moratorium to halt nursing home development until a long-term state policy on nursing homes could be crafted. And a second nursing home owned by Bacon and Salema, Whiting Health Care Center in Whiting, Ocean County, received approval to make a profitable change in its nursing services just before the moratorium was issued.

"A review of department records indicates that if any one thing illustrates how the department has been used to insure the worth of Bacon and Salema's nursing home investments, it has been its handling of certificates of need [the state certificate needed to construct a nursing home in New Jersey]," the *Trentonian* series said. "Over nearly three years, Health Department regulations have been finagled to make it possible for Bacon and Salema not only to hold on to those permits long after they should have expired but to increase their potential value. State records show that one of the Bacon-Salema certificates should have been canceled because of a change of ownership and another is being continued despite a Health Department staff recommendation that it be terminated."

With nursing homes in Ocean and Gloucester counties and permits to build nursing homes in Union, Hudson, and Bergen counties, Bacon and Salema were set when the administration slapped restrictions on new nursing home beds based on county-by-county estimates that experts said used bad numbers. The advantage as described in the *Trentonian:* "In two of the counties where no new beds will be allowed, Bacon and Salema own state certificates to build about half of the beds already approved and in the pipeline for construction."

The loudest critics of the plan to limit nursing home beds were religious leaders who said they needed beds and their needs crossed county lines. Religion-based nursing homes could no longer afford the state approval process in a field where well-connected companies were competing for limited beds. "Since Florio was elected, the cost of applying to expand or build a nursing home has increased from $1,000 to as much as $100,000," McClure reported. The Rev. Samuel LaPenta of the Reformed Church of America said, "If we are competing with people who have money to invest, they get the certificate of need because by the time we raise the money, they have the certificate."

After the *Trentonian* series, New Jersey pols—for once—did the right thing, if only to stick it to Florio. In June 1993, the legislature overrode a veto by Florio and freed New Jersey's religion-sponsored nursing homes from regulations that limited construction of needed beds.[3]

GOP Sen. Randy Corman said, "One of the things that played to our favor is that the whole certificate of need process has become tainted with regard to Brenda Bacon and Joe Salema." Republican Assemblyman Stephen Mikulak said a message had been sent to Brenda Bacon, who claimed no role in any of the decisions, while Salema was silent. "If you abuse it, you are going to lose it."

Doing what's right doesn't happen often in Trenton. Surprisingly, it was one of Florio's pals, Assemblyman Joe Doria of Hudson County, who cast the fifty-fourth assembly vote to override the governor. Asked why, he said, "I thought it was the right thing to do." Those on the assembly floor said Doria had been lobbied to vote the right way—by relatives of his who are nuns.

A week earlier McClure had reported that state inspectors showed up at a Catholic nursing home three days after a nun from the facility criticized Florio's nursing home policies.[4] "The sister testified on May 24 before a joint meeting of the Senate's Health and Senior Citizens' committees about the Florio administration regulations that have hindered the opening of new nursing home beds at St. Joseph's Seniors Residence. On May 27, four Health Department inspectors arrived on her doorstep."

Corman said the inspection gave GOP lawmakers more reason for the override vote. "When you have people coming forward to testify about a public agency and three days later that agency shows up to harass and intimidate, that's government by goon squad."

The *Trentonian* published a picture of the nun, Sister Mary Louise Kwiatkowski, kneeling in prayer at the nursing home chapel. "Please, God" was her reaction to the pending override vote. Two years earlier, the Florio administration had moved to gut nursing home inspections by eliminating six nursing home inspectors even though federal money paid most of their salaries.[5] And a federal lawsuit accused the administration of using intense pressure to force the Office of the Ombudsman for the Institutionalized Elderly to replace veteran investigators with political cronies.

Political observers really weren't surprised at the nursing home saga because they watched the Florio operation in Camden County before he was elected governor. Florio gained nationwide attention when *Reader's Digest* published an article in 1988 about how newly elected congressmen get rich quick. The magazine—as it is wont to do—condensed a lengthy series by *Courier-Post* reporter Dennis M. Culnan titled "The Florio Kingdom." As sometimes happens in New Jersey, Culnan later took a leap from the news business into the role of Democratic political operative. Here is the *Reader's Digest* condensed version:[6]

"According to Dennis M. Culnan of the southern New Jersey *Courier-Post*, Florio arrived in Camden in 1964 'in a beat-up station wagon loaded with a pregnant wife, a crying baby and all of his worldly goods.' In 1970, Florio was elected to the state Legislature, and four years later to Congress. Today his financial-disclosure form shows assets and outside income in excess of $300,000—a big boost in net worth, helped along by a 15-percent interest in a bank building in Gloucester Township. Florio paid absolutely nothing for his interest in the building, purchased in 1984 for $855,000. Source of the largess: Joseph C. Salema, former chief of Florio's Congressional staff, and Nicholas A. Rudi, a Florio campaign fund-raiser.

The pair, who became very successful financial-management consultants after leaving the public sector, gave Florio his interest in the
building—out of 'friendship.' "

The troubled Continental Bank got a boost from the politically
connected. Florio's spokesman said Salema family sources supplied the initial money to purchase the bank, Dave Neese of the
Trentonian reported.[7] Rudi, as Camden County treasurer, deposited $2 million in county funds in the bank even as he was serv-
ing on the bank's board of directors. Another investor in the bank,
Dr. William Steinberg, a Florio contributor and fund-raiser, had a
million-dollar contract with Camden County to supply doctors to
the county's Lakeland hospital, and it was renewed at an extra cost
to taxpayers.

"The Lakeland contract could have been done by other bidders
for a $200,000 savings this year by doctors with better credentials.
Instead, the Democratic freeholder majority renewed the contract
with a major financial contributor to Florio campaigns who has
also quietly become a business partner with Florio and some of his
key aides," Culnan wrote.[8] "It is an example of a pattern in which
Florio's protégés, in the name of good government, devised effec-
tive public policies, put them on track and then often cash in on
their government-acquired expertise and connections as private
citizens."

Culnan wrote that while Florio went to Congress in the post-
Watergate era and was considered a champion of the environment
and consumer issues, in Camden County he controlled not just
who ran for office, but who got jobs: "In Camden County, if you
flush a toilet, toss a can in the trash, or try to get your uncle committed, chances are someone close to U.S. Rep. James J. Florio will
have a piece of the action."

No wonder that three months after Salema arrived in Trenton,
Florio defended his new chief of staff's ethics in typical Florio-speak.

"I am very pleased and happy with the ethics of everyone I've hired because everyone that I've hired has met the ethical standards I've established."[9]

As a final farewell, Florio billed New Jersey taxpayers for more than a month after leaving office for state troopers who logged in eight hours a day, plus 151 hours of overtime transporting the man who was no longer governor in an unmarked car from his home to a North Jersey law firm halfway across the state.[10]

While Florio was known for his record tax hike, his successor, Christine Todd Whitman, swept into office on a promise to cut income taxes by 30 percent. She kept that pledge, but at a cost of $1.2 billion to the state coffers at a time when property taxes, levied by local government, continued to rise. "Looked at closely, Mrs. Whitman's fiscal practices reflect less of a Republican revolution in downsized government than the same old game of spending now and paying the price later," the *New York Times* wrote.

"A multibillion-dollar transportation program is being funded by new and newly refinanced bonds that are going to drive up the cost of debt service. . . . The governor also paid for the tax cut by inflating tax revenue projections and by optimistically assuming that there will be savings from her privatization program. . . . Those looking for Mrs. Whitman to have a national impact should be watching the economic indicators carefully to see whether the gambles she is taking in taxes and budgeting end up costing taxpayers more money and hurting the state's future financial health."[11]

And that's just what happened. Under Whitman, state debt grew from $7 billion to more than $16 billion.

Both Florio and Whitman raided state workers' pensions to balance their budgets. The practice continued with both Democratic and Republican governors and culminated in 2005 when the state contributed nothing to its pension fund for teachers. "New Jersey has been diverting billions of dollars from its pension fund for state and local workers into other government purposes over the last 15 years using a variety of unorthodox transactions authorized by the Legislature and by governors from both political parties," the *New York Times* reported in April 2007.[12] In the wake of *The New York Times* report, the Securities and Exchange Commission launched an inquiry into the state's handling of its pension funds and was sharing what it found with the U.S. Attorney's Office.[13] Inthelobby.net's Daily Muse said, "Instead of putting money into the fund, our state may have used the money to prop up state budgets, so they could create more programs, and hire more employees, regardless of whether their taxpayers could afford them, or they had enough money in the pension fund to pay for their retirement. And we wonder why people confuse us with the Sopranos."[14]

Whitman also played politics with farmland preservation and a costly emissions testing program that left the state's drivers fuming in long waiting lines while politically connected contractors raked in millions.

Whitman got national attention for her commitment to stop urban sprawl by buying open space for the state. Alas, it was not what it seemed. In 1998, when voters agreed to dedicate a portion of the sales tax to land preservation, Whitman envisioned a million acres would be preserved. Nine years later, 150,000 acres of farmland and 250,000 acres of open space were all the state had amassed. But many connected landowners got rich along the way, and the Garden State Preservation Trust ran out of money two years ahead of time.

Reporter Alan Guenther, then of the Gannett State Bureau, surveyed twenty-three towns in nine counties and found that local elected and appointed officials with influence over how farmland preservation money is spent had their own land in the program.[15]

In New Jersey, land owners are paid to preserve their land from development.

In Republican-leaning Burlington County, Guenther found a proposal to spend $10 million to preserve 2,852 acres in the Pinelands that already had protection. What Guenther also found was that a local zoning official and member of the Pinelands Commission owned property at the proposed site.

Among those who had a preservation proposal but later withdrew it after publicity singled him out was Steve Forbes, the rich magazine publisher and candidate for the Republican nomination for president. He may have realized it was a stretch to think he would need an incentive to keep from selling the property surrounding his estate to shopping center developers.

There also was a peculiar loophole built into the land preservation law. Local and county governments could declare a "hardship" case in the event of "death or incapacitating illness of the owner or other serious hardship or bankruptcy." In New Jersey, that meant they could adjust decisions for political reasons.

Another way New Jersey favors the rich is by granting big tax breaks to owners of farms as small as five acres with revenue as little as $500 a year.

"Some of the biggest abusers are large corporations and developers," Jeff Tittel, director of the New Jersey chapter of the Sierra Club, wrote in an op-ed piece.[16] "The largest 'farmer' in central New Jersey is Thompson Land Company, a land speculator and developer, and the largest 'farmer' in Hunterdon County is Toll Brothers," a huge home construction company.

"The lawns in front of Johnson & Johnson's plant and Roche Pharmaceuticals in Branchburg, Merck's headquarters in Reddington, and Merrill Lynch and Bristol-Myers Squibb in Hopewell are all considered farmland by the farmland assessment program. Then we have," said Tittel, "our more wealthy residents with large lots and McMansions who use the farmland assessment program to dodge their taxes. In order to get a 90 percent tax break on their land, they simply buy a few horses and grow some hay."

Just to show how ridiculous the $500 limit is and how the rich can benefit, consider the tax bill Whitman paid in 1992 for her two properties. Coauthor McClure wrote in her political biography of Whitman:[17] "Because of the farmland assessment, the taxes for the 228 farmland acres surrounding Pontefract were only $4,535, and taxes on the additional 50.8 acres at Twenty Springs were $47." Whitman had a small number of farm animals at Pontefract and harvested wood at Twenty Springs to qualify for the tax exemptions. Her campaign spokesman said, "There is no special privilege." But when Hands Across New Jersey, the organization protesting former governor Jim Florio's $2.8 billion tax hike, endorsed Whitman, Democratic State Committee Chairman Ray Lesniak said, "I find it ironic that the organization founded to protest taxes endorses somebody who doesn't believe in paying her own."

With patronage plaguing the state's preservation system, the Garden State continued to lose farmland even though New Jersey municipalities put millions of dollars a year into the farmland assessment program. New Jersey politicians still take advantage of farmland tax breaks. In October 2007, the *Asbury Park Press* revealed that Senator Ellen Karcher, who ran on an ethics platform, sold Christmas trees and several cords of wood each year to claim 7.4 acres of her property as a farm. Her husband said they had $510 worth of checks to qualify, and the rest of the business was cash. Meanwhile, people who aren't rich and don't own five acres and can't legally keep a horse for a tax break pay the highest property taxes in America.

A great many Jersey patronage pits are related to cars, the cash cow of the Garden State. They never run out of ways to milk it. A state official once testified that if every internal combustion engine in the state—every lawn mower, leaf blower, car, and truck—were switched off for a year, New Jersey still couldn't meet federal pollution standards. That's because the state is the victim of pollution coming from states west and south, especially coal-fired power plants.

So, then, why would Governor Whitman's administration choose to meet federal pollution guidelines by going after auto emissions? Patronage, of course. Whitman began the drive by asking for bids for a new enhanced auto emissions system. Only one company put in a bid. Parsons Infrastructure and Technology of Pasadena, California, bid $63.2 million to build the enhanced system. It also put in a bid to operate it for $400 million.

A State Commission of Investigation (SCI) report said Parsons had the inside track for the work and documented that Parsons-related entities gave $507,950 in political contributions to select Republican candidates and committees in New Jersey between 1997 and 2000.[18] The day before the contract was signed in 1998, the company sent a $5,000 contribution in response to an invitation to attend the Governor's Gala, a Whitman event the Republican State Committee sponsored.

Moreover, the bid included a $15 million contract to the public relations firm employing Carl Golden, Whitman's former press secretary. Golden said his firm would handle a $6.2 million public relations campaign. Presumably that was to get people to inspect their cars, something they had little choice in since state law mandated it.

A dozen subcontractors divided the spoils of the $400 million emissions testing fiasco without ever bidding. "Several political heavy hitters with links to the subcontractors moreover are slurping at the trough of tax dollars which some say could swell to half a billion," McClure reported for the *Trentonian*.[19] "And no one in state government knows how much they are being paid. Department of Transportation Commissioner James Weinstein was the first public relations man for the emissions testing project before assuming his post as commissioner. A firm with longtime ties to powerful GOP lobbyist Hazel Gluck is supplying the equipment. The man helping to get state and federal permits through the process is former state Department of Environmental Protection Commissioner Richard Dewling. Two of the construction and architectural firms [including one co-owned by Anthony Sartor—more about him in a minute] are hefty GOP campaign contributors." The major contract was subject to state bidding rules, but as far as the state treasury was concerned, all Parsons had to do was list its subcontracts on the bidding document and that was the end of it, McClure explained.

It was a disaster. Chronic computer problems and equipment that didn't work in cold weather—apparently the California-based Parsons people never witnessed a Jersey winter—and too few workers resulted in delays and long lines for car owners, which raised tempers to the boiling point, causing Whitman to suspend the exhaust tests at the busiest stations for months to give Parsons time to make things right.

In addition to a cranky system, the SCI discovered Parsons got paid $9.5 million, or $600,000 a month, for one program it never implemented, the "Gasoline Tank Evaporative Pressure Test." A four-month probe by the state agency found top state officials aggravated the situation by ignoring or concealing warnings that Parsons was bungling the auto inspections. The report blamed Whitman and two top aides. Parsons was fined for failure to meet terms of the contract.[20]

The McGreevey administration extended Parsons's contract for two years but exempted newer vehicles from the emissions testing.

Even after a decade of problems with Parsons in New Jersey and new troubles the company faced overseas with controversy over its construction work in Iraq, the Corzine administration stuck with Parsons in 2007, extending its contract beyond an August expiration.[21] Democrats who had bashed the Republicans for bringing the company to New Jersey under questionable circumstances said that despite all the emissions inspection woes, there had not been time to get specifications ready for a new contract. Go figure. The only explanation is that it's New Jersey.

Whitman went to Washington and the EPA in January 2001, and Republican Senate President Donald DiFrancesco became acting governor. When he was senate president, DiFrancesco voiced concern about the state's image. "We want people to know that there is more to the state of New Jersey than 'The Sopranos' and the Turnpike," he quipped in the *Atlantic City Press*'s coverage of a labor union speech.[22] But DiFrancesco did little to boost the state's reputation. Shortly after he became acting governor, he was besieged with questions about a $150,000 loan from longtime friend Anthony Sartor, who had landed a $3 million contract for the state's new auto emissions program.

Coauthor McClure wrote:[23] "Sartor's 1994 loan of $150,000 was repaid with 5 percent interest in 1995.

"Just three years later, Sartor's engineering firm received a $3 million piece of the more than $400 million emissions testing contract the state awarded to Parsons Infrastructure."

The press continued to raise concern after concern about DiFrancesco's business dealings and ethics. David Halbfinger of the *New York Times* reported that lawyers for Scotch Plains Township, where DiFrancesco served for sixteen years as township attorney, believed he had violated ethics rules, and both a Democratic and a Republican lawyer reviewing the matter recommended his firing.[24]

Halbfinger reported: "After 18 months of agonizing internal debate, members of the Township Council had become convinced that Mr. DiFrancesco had, among other things, lobbied township officials to give members of his family a zoning change they wanted while failing to disclose his own financial stake in the project's success; ruled on projects involving a major home builder [K. Hovnanian companies] shortly after receiving $225,000 from that home builder to pay off a judgment against him; and influenced township officials to drop plans for a youth soccer field because his relatives held out hope of developing the property."

The acting governor labeled the Halbfinger report old news, a partisan attack, and "not really true." DiFrancesco also had hoped for a boost when he nominated Isabel Miranda as state treasurer. She would have been the first Hispanic and the second woman to hold the post. But another *New York Times* salvo ruined the day. The newspaper reported Miranda was fired from her job as director of trusts and estates at Citibank because auditors found evidence she used her expense account to fund personal cross-country trips for an extramarital affair with a coworker.[25] Miranda denied the reports but withdrew her name after she was told she would have to sever ties with her new employer who did business with the state.

DiFrancesco's financial disclosure forms, showing he and his wife were millionaires, resulted in more trouble for the man who wanted to make his stay in the governor's seat permanent. McClure wrote:[26] "One of the nation's top experts in hot stock options said yesterday that acting Gov. Donald DiFrancesco appears to have received special treatment during his years as state Senate president in getting initial public offerings of stocks. 'It looks like he has a real friend at Morgan Stanley,' said Jay Ritter, professor of finance at the University of Florida who has researched initial public offerings of stocks for more than 20 years." Despite earnings on ten coveted IPO deals, DiFrancesco said there was no special treatment. But GOP colleagues in the legislature began to lose faith. Political strategist John Torok said pressure also came from the national party.

Republican State Sen. Andrew Ciesla told McClure that fifteen of his senate colleagues wanted DiFrancesco to drop out because of "Clintonesque type rumors" emerging from DiFrancesco's private life: "What else there is potentially out there is key."[27] The Web site PoliticsNJ.com repeated that, then added, "Ciesla's comments are the first public statement of what may be the worst kept secret in New Jersey politics, a potentially explosive story that has had the state's political press corps on their toes for the last two months."

DiFrancesco's campaign manager, Charlie Smith, said the candidate had no intention of dropping out: "The governor has enjoyed great support from his colleagues." That was Friday, April 20, 2001. The following Wednesday, he dropped out of the race.

Former congressman Bob Franks replaced DiFrancesco in the gubernatorial primary, which was won by Bret Schundler, former Jersey City mayor, who went on to lose in the general election to another local politician, Jim McGreevey, the mayor of Woodbridge.

McGreevey took office four months after 9/11 in a colorful ceremony with wife Dina and baby Jacqueline, but he is most remembered for his announcement two and a half years later.

On August 12, 2004, the outer office in the first-floor New Jersey governor's suite was more crowded and loud than usual. Packed with reporters and cameras, the accurate rumor had spread hours before that McGreevey was going to say he was resigning his office because of an adulterous gay affair. The governor, his wife, and his parents, Jack and Ronnie, walked cautiously from the inner office to face the now-hushed gathering, which must have looked to them like lions ready to pounce. Dina wore a pained, painted smile, and McGreevey's dad, a former marine, looked tired and shell-shocked. Mom just seemed sad.

But if you watch it on video and mute the sound, McGreevey himself during the nearly eight-minute talk appears as he did every other time he gave a major speech—stiff, uncomfortable, and unsure anyone will buy what he's selling. There was ample reason. It was political theater, albeit amped up, like most of McGreevey's thirty-four months as governor. He wasn't stepping down because he was gay or because of an affair with his former Israeli aide,

Golan Cipel. He didn't say it, but McGreevey was leaving because his administration was one of the most corrupt in state history and the powerful county party bosses every Jersey politician needs for success had concluded he was unelectable, which must have been like a sharp stick in the eye for a guy who had his sights on the governor's office for as long as anyone could remember. Dina McGreevey explained in her autobiography what happened behind the scenes. She said advisers worked with McGreevey at Drumthwacket "to figure out how to spin the fact that there was a multimillion-dollar lawsuit against him." As for her smile during the announcement, she said, "As we were in the car leaving Drumthwacket, Jim told me again that I had to be Jackie Kennedy. 'You have to smile,' he said." When the moment came, Dina wrote, "He looked over at me and said, 'Make sure you smile a little more when I ask for forgiveness and thank you for bringing joy to my life.'" After the announcement, Dina went to McGreevey's inner office while he was with others in the adjacent office of his chief of staff. That's when Dina said that she heard laughter and applause coming from the group next door.[28]

Fellow politicians joked that McGreevey came out of the womb running for office. A geek in high school, he worked hard for impressive academic credentials, then stepped into politics, where his natural likability and willingness to work nonstop attracted attention from the musty old men who hang around the hallowed halls of government. They were looking for a protégé to nurture as a kind of living legacy. A lifelong Democrat, McGreevey was appointed head of the state parole board by a Republican. When questioned about accomplishments during that period, insiders said he brought in a leather sofa for his office and there were a lot of good-looking young men around. No one drew a conclusion, at least publicly.

McGreevey was elected to the assembly and then, as is New Jersey fashion, served in the senate and as mayor of Woodbridge simultaneously. He might still be in both posts except for the long-standing tradition of handing out jobs to friends and supporters.

At the Democratic National Convention in Los Angeles in 2000, a well-connected Jersey assembly member loosened up over drinks late one night and told coauthor Ingle and reporter Alan Guenther the inside story behind McGreevey's rapid ascension: State Sen. John Lynch was annoyed with McGreevey. They both represented the same general area, and McGreevey wanted to get some of his own people appointed to lucrative jobs. Lynch wanted to get rid of McGreevey so Lynch could control all appointments. Thus the Great Plan was hatched: Lynch would encourage and support a McGreevey run for governor in 1997.

McGreevey was seen as a backbencher, a legislator fellow lawmakers paid little attention to. Everyone thought he would lose the primary against Congressman Rob Andrews, and even if he didn't, he would be a sacrificial lamb against Republican Whitman, who seemed invincible. Who knew, the talkative pol asked, that McGreevey would turn into the Energizer Bunny, beat Andrews, and get close to beating incumbent Whitman. Ironically, Lynch was given credit for it all and seen as a mastermind, bringing along a worthy young man, the epitome of a selfless public servant with a future. Four years later, McGreevey started out as the Democratic front-runner in the governor's race and took on Jersey City Mayor Bret Schundler, whose primary campaign was aimed at the die-hard GOP base, which tends to be ultra conservative and one-issue-related. McGreevey easily beat him in the general election by reminding moderate New Jersey voters, the majority, what right-wing positions Schundler took in the GOP primary campaign, a tactic Jersey Democrats frequently use and Republicans never catch on to.

With magical timing, McGreevey's wife was pregnant for the campaign, giving birth not long after the election. The McGreeveys presented themselves as the typical middle-class family.

On February 1, 2002, just two weeks after he was sworn in, the political drama turned serious as the first of several peculiar McGreevey-era incidents took place in the Victorian town of Cape May, where the southern tip of New Jersey falls into the sea. The official story is right out of a dreamy romantic novel—two star-crossed lovers whose innocent getaway took them into harm's way—if you put aside what was later learned about McGreevey's sexual orientation. The media was told McGreevey and the wife were strolling along a dark, deserted windswept beach around 8:00 P.M. when the governor walked off a four-foot sand dune and broke the largest bone in his body, the femur. Mrs. McGreevey, said to be holding her husband's hand when it happened, was unscathed. There were no state trooper bodyguards present since the governor had dismissed them.

Following the broken-leg incident, McGreevey set about building his administration. The people he chose contributed mightily to his downfall and shifted the political theater from leg-breaking drama to knee-slapping comedy.

Gary Taffet and Paul Levinsohn went from being on McGreevey's election campaign to being chief of staff and chief counsel, respectively. Their tenure was short-lived, however, and they became known as "the Billboard Boys."

Levinsohn and Taffet formed a billboard business three years before McGreevey's inauguration while working for McGreevey's campaign and with everyone knowing their clout with McGreevey—correctly predicted to be the next governor. They worked to place billboards, among other places, along the Atlantic City Expressway, another of Jersey's toll roads that needs a politically appointed bureaucratic authority to administer it.

Francis L. Doyle III of Doyle Consulting Group established Philcor Media, an umbrella under which Taffet, McGreevey's campaign manager, and Levinsohn, his chief fund-raiser, developed billboards for which they needed local and state agency approval.

Just before becoming part of the McGreevey administration, Taffet and Levinsohn sold the approved billboards and billboard sites for $4 million. The *Philadelphia Inquirer* investigated and reported:[29] "Doyle is identified on public documents as the sole owner of Philcor, but his corporation received none of the billboard proceeds, sale documents show. Instead, the money was distributed to two corporations established by Taffet and Levinsohn.

"Neither of those corporations—Matthew Management Group and the Montrose Team—ever appeared on public documents seeking the government approvals."

The *Inquirer* story by Tom Turcol and Maureen Graham pointed out that Doyle's insurance business was based in Philadelphia, but he had contributed several hundred thousand dollars to Jersey Democrats and forged ties to Sen. John Lynch, the guy who used McGreevey's political ambitions to get him out of the state senate. The reporters noted Doyle's Pennsylvania company was awarded an insurance contract in Bergen County, New Jersey, after the Democrats, in a campaign engineered by McGreevey and Lynch, gained control of county government. Doyle contributed $37,000 to that effort.

The Billboard Boys maintained they had done nothing wrong, since they sold the billboard company five days before McGreevey became governor and before they became state workers. That wasn't true in Levinsohn's case. Coauthor McClure and Tim Zatzariny Jr. of the *Courier-Post* reported Levinsohn was sworn in as a deputy state attorney general in December 2001 to facilitate a smooth transition when McGreevey took the oath in January.[30] After being sworn in, Levinsohn signed documents and conducted his billboard business with NJ Transit—owner of some of the billboard sites. State employees are barred from doing business with the state. NJ Transit is the state's public transportation agency.

McGreevey's propaganda arm maintained Levinsohn had only the *title* of deputy attorney general and never worked in that capacity. But coauthor McClure showed it was wishful thinking. On January 8, 2002, a week before McGreevey became governor, Levinsohn signed a federal document in his capacity as deputy attorney general. It was a U.S. Department of Labor application for Golan Cipel, the Israeli national McGreevey named his security adviser and the governor's homosexual love interest. If Levinsohn weren't deputy attorney general, he had lied to the U.S. government—in writing.

Levinsohn maintained his innocence but resigned from the McGreevey administration, as had his pal Taffet two months earlier. Taffet had problems that went well beyond billboards. Ironically, on the day McGreevey signed a package of ethics and campaign finance reforms into law, the Securities and Exchange Commission filed a civil suit against Taffet alleging insider trading involving corporations poised for mergers or acquisitions. The SEC complaint alleged Taffet passed along the information to five unidentified people who netted $280,000, and at least one of the five passed the information on to two others who traded for profits of $1.5 million. The seven weren't named.

District Court Judge Shira Scheindlin signed an order approving the government's list of potential witnesses in its case against Taffet. They included developer and McGreevey supporter Charles Kushner, who later went to prison for interfering with a federal probe; George Norcross, the South Jersey Democrat boss based in Camden County; party boss Sen. Ray Lesniak of Union County, a longtime McGreevey pal; Assemblyman Louis Manzo of Hudson County; and then–Assembly Majority Leader Joe Roberts, a major cog in the Boss Norcross machine.

Roberts, who was a leading proponent of the ethics reform and went on to be assembly Speaker, did not attend McGreevey's ethics-bills signing. He issued a statement saying he cooperated with the SEC and there never was an indication he did anything inappropriate. Legislative financial disclosure forms indicate that Roberts earned investment income from Nielsen Media Research, one of the stocks the SEC alleges Taffet made illegal profit from. Roberts said he didn't recall why he bought the stock but the idea probably came from media reports on the stock market.

Besides Taffet, the SEC named Fiore Gallucci, of Staten Island, New York, and Ronald Manzo, of Bayonne, who is the brother of Louis Manzo, the legislator federal authorities said was not involved. Ronald Manzo pleaded guilty to insider trading, conspiracy, and perjury, and agreed to pay $1.4 million in restitution and civil fines. Gallucci also pleaded guilty to conspiracy and insider trading.[31]

Taffet never went to court. Then thirty-eight, he agreed to pay $725,000 in restitution, including fines and interest for transactions the SEC charged netted him $247,459.

Hoping to tame the Gannett State Bureau's reporting in 2002, McGreevey earlier sent Taffet to see our Gannett boss, Bob Collins. The administration was unhappy with coauthor McClure's five-month Cipel investigation, which stretched across several states and into a foreign nation. When the story ran in Gannett New Jersey newspapers it took up several pages, but there was no mention or hint of homosexuality.[32] The article was limited to Cipel's qualifications for the job.

McGreevey didn't see it that way, according to his book. "She stopped short of calling us homosexuals. But she implied not only that Golan's resume and work experience were inflated, but that they were inflated by me."[33] The story did not imply that. It said it.

The bevy of young men McGreevey surrounded himself with

was often inexperienced and inept. McGreevey kept pictures of his favorites on the refrigerator in his condo before he was elected. State police and press in the know had nicknames for all of them. One young lad who worked at the governor's mansion was known as "Cabana Boy." When a group of Gannett reporters was there for an interview, Cabana Boy made some minor error, and reporters were shocked to witness McGreevey waving the cane he used after the broken leg at him. A businessman was told if he wanted to see the governor he had to deal with a McGreevey associate known as "Towel Boy" because McGreevey reportedly met him at a gym. The businessman was surprised to find out how young Towel Boy was but even more surprised when he produced McGreevey for a dinner meeting. The businessman conveyed the story to his lawyer in amazement. In her book, Dina McGreevey labeled the young men McGreevey surrounded himself with the "Lost Boys."[34]

While the McGreeveys were going through a nasty, public divorce, McGreevey told the Associated Press that reports by his former aide, Teddy Pedersen, that he, Dina, and McGreevey had been a sexual threesome were true. Pedersen said his contact was only with Dina during the threesome events and that he was uncertain at the time whether McGreevey was gay. Dina said the claim of threesome sex was completely false.

Scared by what else we might have found—our bet is the gay connection was their top concern—Taffet was dispatched to see Collins, a tough-as-nails businessman who started as a copy boy at the *Courier-Post* and worked his way to group president, serving in numerous positions along the way, including reporter and editor. Collins certainly was not awestruck by the likes of Taffet, no matter what his title. Collins also doesn't care for politicians who try an end run around journalists doing their jobs.

Taffet asked when Gannett was going to stop running Cipel stories. Collins responded, when the public got tired of reading about it and we got tired of writing it. That should have been enough to make Taffet shut up, but he pressed on, clueless to the impression he was making. When he finally fell silent, Collins looked Taffet in the eye and asked if it were true Cipel and McGreevey were having an affair. Keep in mind this was a long time before McGreevey's "I'm gay" announcement and nothing had been in print, although speculation had been circulating for years. Taffet almost fell off his chair. We can only imagine what his debriefing was like when he returned to Trenton. The administration never tried that again with Collins.

Like Taffet and Levinsohn, most of McGreevey's hires—about 60 percent of employees brought on board in the first quarter of his administration—were former campaign workers. McClure reported they cost taxpayers $3.3 million a year in salary.[35] Some of them had six-figure salaries and only sketchy job descriptions. Many landed in Trenton because of favors due others—like Commerce Secretary William Watley, a Newark preacher McGreevey put in place, political insiders say, as payback to State Sen. Sharpe James, who at the time was Newark's mayor. When U.S. Sen. Bob Torricelli flirted with running for governor, James backed McGreevey. McGreevey owed James.

Watley, without meaningful business experience, was a disaster. He didn't speak the same language as the heads of the multinational corporations the commerce chief has to deal with. He got no respect. But his problems went beyond inexperience.

Watley was forced to resign in 2004 after it was disclosed that his church was affiliated with a Newark housing project that was going to get an $11.5 million state loan. A state audit of Watley's commission also found mismanagement, including $9 million spent without the comptroller's approval. Watley's chief of staff, Lesly Devereaux, resigned after it was revealed she had hired relatives. What they did for their salaries wasn't very clear. Devereaux was charged with theft by deception and official misconduct. Just before Devereaux's trial in June 2007, her mother and sister admitted altering public records related to their state work.[36]

But she was unrepentant. Tom Moran of the *Star-Ledger* laid out why Devereaux's reaction was so New Jersey:

> Lesly Devereaux, the latest public official hauled into court on corruption charges, conceded yesterday that prosecutors have her nailed on the key facts of the case. Yes, she threw government work to her ailing mother and her desperate sister. Yes, her secretary devoted the great bulk of her time to Devereaux's private law practice while on the public payroll. And yes, Devereaux tried to hide all this by drafting documents she now concedes were phony. But she is pleading not guilty. Her pitch to the jury yesterday boiled down to this: In the slimy pit of New Jersey politics everybody does this kind of stuff.[37]

The Jersey defense worked in part and failed in part. After a week of deliberation, a jury in Trenton told Devereaux, who sat in court with her hand on the Bible, that she was guilty on only two counts related to running her private law practice on state time. Prosecutors said it cost the state $87,000. Despite guilty pleas by her mother and sister, she was acquitted on two counts and the jury was hung on a dozen charges related to their jobs and the alleged cover-up the two admitted. Devereaux's lawyer Jack Furlong accused the state of piling on the charges. Attorney General Anne Milgram, however, described Devereaux as "brazen" and said, "A conviction is a conviction."[38]

Devereaux later pleaded guilty to falsifying documents related to the jobs for her family members. A judge sentenced her to six and a half years in jail for those charges, for running her private law practice on state time, and for welfare fraud. But the judge said that after six months, Devereaux would be considered for a program allowing her to live at home under "intensive supervision," Gannett's Michael Rispoli reported.

But Watley skated. The Division of Criminal Justice seized Watley's agency records, but no more was heard from that, as was frequently the case under Attorney General Peter Harvey. (More on Harvey in chapter 5.)

But of all the McGreevey appointments, the one he will always be remembered for is Cipel, the former Israeli sailor named homeland security adviser in the wake of 9/11, even though Cipel couldn't get the security clearance such a post would require because he was not a U.S. citizen.

At first, the official story was McGreevey met Cipel in 2000 when the governor traveled to Israel as mayor of Woodbridge, apparently the only Jersey town with a foreign policy. Cipel was the public relations guy for the city of Rishon Le Zion and must have been a whiz at it because the visiting New Jersey mayor invited him to move six thousand miles away to work on his gubernatorial campaign. In a state at that time with more than 8.4 million people, McGreevey had to go to Israel to get campaign workers.

Cipel was no stranger to the United States. He attended college in New York City and had worked there in public relations at the Israeli consulate. There are those who speculate that Cipel and McGreevey knew each other long before what was described as a chance meeting in Israel and that the whole trip was cover. That suspicion was heightened after Cipel became a daily staple in the media and, strangely, McGreevey's press people would no longer talk about how the two knew each other.

During the 2001 campaign McGreevey arranged for Cipel to get a job with the Democratic State Committee doing outreach to the Jewish community for $10,000 and arranged a second public relations job for $30,000 with developer and McGreevey contributor Charles Kushner, who later went to prison. It was obvious Cipel was special from the start. It certainly was obvious to Cipel. He entered a meeting of seasoned campaign workers and introduced himself, announced he was there to run the campaign, and asked them who they were. Veteran campaign manager Steve DiMicco walked out of the room in disgust.

Shortly after Cipel arrived, McGreevey had campaign staffers arrange for a Woodbridge apartment, not far from where McGreevey lived in a condominium. After the election, Cipel purchased a West Windsor condo about a twenty-minute jog from the governor's mansion. The governor took time from transition plans to do a walk-through of the condo.

Josh Margolin of the *Star-Ledger* said this caught seller Elaine Dietrich by surprise:[39] "According to Dietrich, she had listed the place at $189,900. Cipel saw it only once and offered $190,000, provided it was taken off the market immediately. Cipel explained 'he wanted to have a place that was in close proximity to where the governor was because he was a personal adviser on call 24 hours a day.' Before Cipel would sign the contract, Dietrich said, he wanted to make sure McGreevey saw it too." Dietrich said she thought that was bizarre.

The first thing Cipel handled as a state employee was the inaugural parade, an event no one remembers. Then McGreevey put Cipel on the state payroll at $110,000 as his security adviser. A source on McGreevey's staff said Cipel requested that specific job, and McGreevey accommodated him although a former FBI director, Louis Freeh, who was born and educated in New Jersey, volunteered to do it for no salary.

Since this was after 9/11, a horror that directly affected thousands of New Jersey residents, reporters began to ask about Cipel. McGreevey's media staff issued a biography that painted the former low-level public relations worker as an antiterrorism expert. The press office cited Cipel's military training in "preventing terrorist attacks" and lauded his tenure at the consulate, where he "oversaw terrorist-related matters." His résumé supplied by the governor's people said Cipel was "responsible for portfolios on terrorism" at the consulate in New York. Former Consul General Collette Avital, who was in charge when Cipel worked there, said the opposite was true: "He was not involved in anything relating to terrorism."

When coauthor McClure confronted McGreevey about the unsupported work history, the governor blamed the misunderstanding on "ambiguity." It couldn't have been accidental ambiguity. McClure spent months investigating Cipel and found nothing that would cause any rational person to think he was a terrorism expert. He served five years in the Israel Defense Forces with a navy patrol unit before a ten-year stint in the reserves, where his rank reached that of lieutenant. Yossi Melman, an Israeli military expert and global journalist, told McClure: "Based on his biography, he would not be considered an expert in Israel. On the contrary, he would not dare introduce himself as such. No one would take him seriously," adding that Cipel's training was routine, at best.[40]

It was not just the exaggerated qualifications in a critical area that raised suspicions. There was a concentrated effort to keep Cipel under wraps. Nothing drives a journalist harder than a public official trying to keep secrets. McGreevey's team refused requests for Cipel interviews. McGreevey spokesman Paul Aronsohn said, "The idea of having a communications office is to interlock and work with journalists while everybody else does the work of the government. He (Cipel) is busy working."

Since-retired Sen. Bill Gormley, then the cochairman of the Judiciary Committee, which oversees appointments, wanted Cipel before his committee to discuss his credentials. Until Cipel presented himself, Gormley said, he would hold up other McGreevey appointments, including mega fund-raiser Kushner's chairmanship of the Port Authority of New York and New Jersey. It was because of Kushner, not the fact a totally unqualified alien was advising on terrorism matters, that the governor felt compelled to act. McGreevey blocked Gormley by removing Cipel from security issues. The governor also rejected calls for state police to do the thorough background check on Cipel that cabinet-level officials must go through.

Undaunted by all that, McClure worked out a schedule where she visited Cipel's second floor statehouse office and approached the heavy dark wooden door, complete with state seal on frosted glass, at various times and asked to see him. She kept a log and made note of the numerous excuses given for why he was unavailable. Not only was Cipel's questionable presence costing taxpayers, he had two young male assistants and a secretary, so that when doing nothing became overwhelming they shared his load.

April 9, 11:35 A.M. Secretary has no idea where he is.

April 10, 2:35 P.M. In a meeting.

April 11, 3:05 P.M. He must have gone out for a bite.

April 12, 10:35 A.M. At a meeting.

Cipel liked the finer things, and published reports indicated he had written a book of poetry. McClure asked for it, but nothing was offered. She searched, with the help of libraries in the United States and in Israel, but no one had heard of his book. Cipel drove a Mercedes SUV, which stayed in the same spot in the statehouse parking deck. Observers saw Cipel carried to his SUV in McGreevey's trooper-driven state car late at night. During that period, a memo was issued to security personnel in the garage directing them not to discuss anything with reporters.

Gannett obtained a satellite map and found there was a large wooded area that looked negotiable between where Cipel lived and a park near the governor's mansion. We donned hiking boots and started at the park. We had no map or directions. Encountering a jogger along the way, we asked if it were possible to get to a shopping center near Cipel's place. Without hesitation, she gave directions so simple they didn't have to be written down. A short while later we were in Cipel's front yard. Did McGreevey and Cipel tread through the woods for rendezvous? Or meet somewhere in the heavily wooded middle? We don't know, but it is possible, and we found the jogging trail to prove it.

It also is likely Cipel spent a lot of time at the governor's mansion. Visitors would be surprised to see him there dressed casually. One thing for sure, McGreevey took extraordinary steps to keep his state police bodyguard out of the mansion. He even had Drumthwacket's garage remodeled at a cost of $628,925 and moved the troopers there.

The state police had used the same office off the kitchen on the main floor since the huge three-story home became the governor's official residence in the early 1980s. Before that, the previous governor's mansion had the same size room for the bodyguards. It worked for everybody but McGreevey.

The official story was that McGreevey was the first governor to live there full-time with a small child in the residence. "It was highly recommended by State Police as a security measure," said Kevin Davitt, a McGreevey spokesman, although there was no such information on the document declaring the work an emergency. Besides, how would moving the troopers farther away make it safer? Treasury records show the architect hired was not a security expert because hiring such a person would delay the project by four to eight weeks—too long for McGreevey.

Another project costing taxpayers money that Cipel was said to have his hand in was a "trade mission" to Ireland, McGreevey's ancestral stomping grounds. The governor predicted it would cost taxpayers $20,000. "He was off by $85,000. State records show the weeklong trip cost taxpayers at least $105,000 with the cell phone bill alone totaling at least $16,448," wrote Jeff Whelan of the *Star-Ledger*, who noted the McGreeveys were joined by a dozen corporate executives, state and local officials, and, of course, several of their close friends.[41] It took Whelan three months to get vouchers and receipts for the trip, and even that was after negotiations between his newspaper and the administration. State law says such paperwork should be available on demand.

Whelan pointed out that when McGreevey made his $20,000 estimate—on the day he boarded the plane—at least $36,000 had already been spent. Once he got to the Old Sod, McGreevey rode around in a Mercedes, stayed in fancy hotels, and held a family reunion that cost taxpayers almost $3,200. The state purchased coach fare on Continental Airlines for $800, but, Whelan reported, almost all the state people got moved to first class, where a ticket would have cost $4,900.

"Earlier in the month," Whelan wrote, "McGreevey enacted an overhaul of the corporate tax that included a provision that capped the amount Continental will have to pay in corporate taxes at $2.5 million." A registered lobbyist for Continental was on the plane with the entourage.

New Jersey was having its customary financial problems, and McGreevey's partying was causing his poll numbers to plummet. He apologized and said the state Democratic Party would pay for all but the cost of his security detail and his reunion dinner, which he would take care of himself.

It didn't get him off the political hook. Senator Diane Allen, a Republican, said, "The governor said this was a trade mission, and it was—he traded our hard-earned tax dollars for a good time."

Nor was it the only time contributions to the state Democratic Party were used to buy McGreevey out of an embarrassing situation. He couldn't stay away from state helicopters. A Gannett New Jersey investigation showed he took helicopter trips 272 times during his first ten months in office. Laura Kaessinger, who worked in our Trenton bureau in her first year out of college, compared the trips to his official schedule and determined fourteen of the chopper rides, which cost $1,200 an hour, had nothing to do with government, including a trip to a lawmaker's wedding.[42] McGreevey refused to divulge the nature of other private journeys he took. The Democrats stepped forward to pay for the fourteen trips at a cost of $18,200 and weren't apologetic about helping the leader of the "party of the people" keep his itineraries secret.

There was one other planned trip Cipel had his hand in, this one to Israel—perhaps for the duo to relive old times—but it never happened. After the tumult over Ireland, the Israeli adventure was canceled. The official reason came after Gannett New Jersey published U.S. State Department warnings. It was then that the governer's office determined the Middle East was too dangerous. Why wouldn't an antiterrorism expert who grew up there have known that without reading us?

McGreevey tried creating a new profile for Cipel. He sought to make the public believe that he had been misunderstood, that Cipel wasn't really supposed to be in charge of homeland security. He might have gotten by with blaming it on sloppy reporting by news media had coauthor McClure not found a February 8, 2002, letter from William G. Dressel Jr., executive director of the New Jersey League of Municipalities, to his membership about coordination of antiterrorism efforts with federal and state governments. It identified Cipel as the governor's special counsel for homeland security.

McClure also found that the National Conference of State Legislatures listed Cipel as the homeland security contact for New Jersey on January 14, 2002, and identified Cipel as "special counsel to the governor for homeland security." More damaging, she found immigration papers signed by McGreevey Chief Counsel Levinsohn detailing Cipel's security duties.

Amid the growing chorus of questions from news media, Cipel

departed the McGreevey administration, but one of his two aides continued with the state. Eliot Mizrachi went to the Board of Public Utilities and got a raise from $45,000 to $51,450. BPU Board Chairwoman Jeanne Fox is the wife of Steve DiMicco, who was a key consultant to McGreevey's campaign and later to Jon Corzine's and Sen. Robert Menendez's.

Cipel became a vice president of the MWW Group, a public relations and lobbying firm that has strong Trenton connections. He didn't last long. A high-ranking MWW executive told McClure that Cipel did not think he had to show up for work. His next job was across the street from McGreevey's statehouse office with State Street Partners, a position that Rahway Mayor Jim Kennedy, a partner in the firm, arranged. Kennedy was best man for at least one of McGreevey's weddings. Cipel's job at SSP was liaison to the Jewish community, which is what he was during the gubernatorial campaign.

Having him back in Trenton made a lot of McGreevey people nervous. He didn't last long there, either. Next, he worked for Shelly Zeiger, who said he met Cipel when he was working on that ill-fated trip to Israel. Cipel was hired to expand Zeiger Enterprises's business to include Israeli imports, but Zeiger told coauthor McClure that Cipel returned from the Middle East with supplies that did not complement the business. "I don't think his heart was in it," Zeiger said, adding they parted by "mutual understanding." Cipel moved to a New York apartment at Columbus Circle, where he was out of sight and out of mind. (Don't worry—he'll be back in a few pages.)

McGreevey's fund-raisers got him in as much trouble as his bad hires. Multimillionaire developer Charles Kushner, a big-time political campaign contributor who helped fund McGreevey's political career, was the star of one of those bizarre episodes they say can only happen in New Jersey—involving sex, lies, videotape, and family backstabbing. Alert: Once again we aren't making any of this up.

U.S. Attorney Chris Christie was investigating tax filings and campaign contributions by Kushner's companies. In an attempt to convince witnesses, including his own family members, not to cooperate, Kushner hired a prostitute to engage in videotaped sex with his brother-in-law, William Schulder, then sent the tape to his sister, Esther Schulder, just before a family party. Both Schulders were cooperating with authorities.

Kushner was charged with witness tampering, obstruction of justice, and promoting prostitution. Each carries a penalty of $250,000 and between five and ten years in prison. Kushner could have gotten twenty years. Under a plea agreement, however, he was sentenced to two years at Federal Prison Camp at Maxwell Air Force Base in Montgomery, Alabama.

Kushner had given McGreevey more than $1.5 million in campaign contributions, and his troubles first began when McGreevey named him to the Port Authority of New York and New Jersey, a plum spot for a real-estate developer since it controls hundreds of millions of dollars in development contracts. That appointment brought Kushner to the attention of the New Jersey Senate Judiciary Committee, whose cochairman Republican Bill Gormley called Kushner in to answer questions about potential conflicts. Kushner, much like Golan Cipel, resigned from the authority rather than make the trip to Trenton.

Another McGreevey fund-raiser was Rajesh "Roger" Chugh (pronounced *chew*), a onetime political gofer, New York cabbie, and failed travel agent. He got into the McGreevey circle the old-fashioned way—by raising an estimated $1 million for the candidate.

In return, McGreevey first got him a $10,000-a-month consultant job with the state Democrats, then, after the election, and despite a budget crisis, created an $85,000-a-year post in the secretary of state's office that Chugh boasted made him assistant secretary of state and the third most powerful guy in New Jersey government. Chugh liked himself a lot. But he got it all wrong. The job was assistant commissioner. Chugh first came under widespread scrutiny when a reporter surfing the Internet ran across his self-made Web site, a cross between a dating service and an exaggerated résumé. The prose was wrapped around photos, one of the more memorable showing him in a pool next to a poodle on a raft.

Two *Bergen Record* reporters, Jeff Pillets and Clint Riley, did an exhaustive investigation of Chugh, but what they found was hardly funny. They reported evidence that Chugh attempted to extract campaign contributions from business owners who had been cited for code violations or were seeking zoning variances while McGreevey was mayor of Woodbridge. One woman said Chugh told her he could "take care" of her problem for a $3,000 contribution.[43]

After the Pillets and Riley investigation got underway, the governor said Chugh resigned "to pursue other opportunities." Two months later, the FBI presented the Democratic State Committee with a subpoena for documents related to Chugh's work on behalf of McGreevey. He hasn't been heard from on the political scene since.

Federal subpoenas to Trenton also sought information on another Democratic fund-raiser, David D'Amiano, an old friend of McGreevey's. According to McGreevey, he met D'Amiano—a Carteret waste recycling operator who produced more than $100,000 for McGreevey's campaigns—at a high school party, then became reacquainted with him twenty years later when McGreevey was mayor of Woodbridge. "Casual friends" is how McGreevey described their relationship. McGreevey said in his book that D'Amiano "used to set me up with women."[44]

When McGreevey got to the statehouse, there were numerous

occasions on which D'Amiano lobbied for help with various issues, suggested appointments for state jobs, or requested aid in dealing with state agencies. The one that grabbed headlines was the case of Mark Halper, who asked D'Amiano's assistance in dealing with the governments of Piscataway Township and Middlesex County, which wanted to take Halper's Cornell Dairy Farm via eminent domain for a park. Halper balked at offers of $3.2 million from the state and $4.3 million from the county, both intended to prevent commercial development of the property. That was thought to be much less than fair market value for seventy-five acres in New Jersey, where land is disappearing at a rapid clip.

D'Amiano worked out an arrangement with Halper whereby the farmer would donate money to the Democrats in exchange for assurances that elected officials would get him a better deal. To let Halper know the officials were aware of the plan, they would mention the code word "Machiavelli" in conversations—under the circumstances an apt choice, since the Italian philosopher was a master of political intrigue and deception. Even juicer was the origin—it was suggested to Halper, who was working undercover with the feds, by U.S. Attorney Christie.

Those conversations were caught on tape after Halper went to the feds complaining of extortion and for eighteen months wore a wire for the FBI. On February 18, 2003, D'Amiano introduced the governor to Halper at a fund-raiser at the East Brunswick Hilton. During the conversation with Halper, McGreevey said to an aide, identified by sources as Amy Mansue, that Halper should read Machiavelli's *The Prince* to learn how to deal with farm negotiations.

Later, when Halper's scheme became public, McGreevey maintained that his utterances were merely a coincidence—that he was alluding to Halper's reading habits, apparently thinking farmers routinely keep sixteenth-century Italian literature right next to the seed catalogue.

McGreevey said that D'Amiano's repeated use of the word before introducing the farmer "planted it on my tongue." McGreevey wrote in his book, "I honestly thought I'd said it of my own volition," and noted, "It's a word I've used before and since, many, many times—after all, this is New Jersey, as close to Machiavelli's cutthroat Venetian principality as any place on earth."[45] Machiavelli was from Florence, but we move on.

In the end, D'Amiano was charged in a forty-seven-page indictment with eleven counts of shaking down Halper for $40,000 in cash and contributions.[46] McGreevey was not mentioned by name, but as "State Official 1" he was referred to eighty-three times. No one but D'Amiano was indicted. He pleaded guilty to two counts of mail fraud and was sentenced to twenty-four months in prison.[47] An appeals court later upheld a $17.9 million award to the Halper family for their farm, Ken Serrano of the *Home News Tribune* reported.

McGreevey was unscathed. Or was he? Before it all came down on his longtime acquaintance D'Amiano, prosecutor Christie's FBI agents visited the governor at Drumthwacket and played the taped conversations.

That visit and other brewing scandals are more likely than his sexual orientation to be the reasons McGreevey stepped down a few months later, with his "gay American" label, intended to paint him as a victim of prejudice and blackmail not the head of one of the most scandal-ridden administrations in generations.

McGreevey's problems came to a head at his party's national convention.

The Democratic Party held its 2004 convention in Boston to nominate John Kerry for president. We and our Gannett colleagues were happy for a change of scenery even though the people we covered in Boston were the same ones we covered in New Jersey, which for us is what going to national conventions is about.

On the first day, a Washington-based acquaintance of coauthor Ingle took him aside and said, "I think there is something you need to know. The word is out among the Kerry people to keep their distance from McGreevey. Something is going down."

That evening Ingle told McClure he was relieving her of convention coverage duties while she tracked down what that something was. When you've been a reporter as long as McClure, you develop a sixth sense about whether there is fire to go with the smoke. That alarm went off quickly in Boston. When she took aside longtime sources, they were unusually nervous about talking to her where they would be seen. For days McClure got to visit parts of the old city that other convention-goers missed as she met sources in out-of-the-way places and over coffee and clam chowder in dinky little restaurants.

The picture that emerged was that party insiders were thinking the corruption-plagued governor was an embarrassment and didn't have much of a chance for a second term. While McClure was interviewing discreetly from behind tall monuments and by boats on the bay, her blond hair tucked under a baseball cap, something peculiar was happening at the headquarters hotel, the historic Parker House, every morning when the New Jersey delegation met for breakfast.

Then-Senator Corzine was taking every opportunity to publicly praise McGreevey, saying things like, "I'm proud you're my governor, Jim." This was way overblown and too frequent and totally out of step with what McClure was picking up undercover. What are the chances, we asked ourselves, that Corzine, who was in charge of raising money for Democratic U.S. Senate candidates, is the one guy in the party who doesn't know what's going on? Not likely, we concluded. The more probable scenario is he knows and sees himself as the heir apparent when McGreevey takes the fall.

McGreevey hosted the Jersey delegation at a big bash in a tall building with a beautiful view of Boston and the bay beyond. His party turned out to be full of surprises. For one thing, the special guests were Gov. Thomas Vilsack of Iowa and his wife, Christie. Mrs. Vilsack had been in the news for something she said about New Jerseyans a few years earlier that had only recently come to light in the Garden State. She wrote in a local newspaper in Iowa she would rather learn Polish than try to speak like people from New Jersey. "The only way I can speak like residents of New Jersey and eastern Pennsylvania is to let my jaw drop an inch and talk with my lips in an 'O' like a fish."

Ingle spotted George Norcross, chief Democratic fund-raiser of Camden County and one of the top three political bosses in the state. Although Ingle had taken on the county machine in print on numerous occasions, he and Norcross got along reasonably well. More important, Norcross wasn't likely to let Ingle think something was going on he didn't know about.

Ingle waded through the throngs of backslappers and past the stuffed potato bar to where Norcross was sitting with his daughter and asked him who was going to be the Democrats' gubernatorial candidate in 2005. Norcross had several options. He could have said, "Jim McGreevey," or he could have said, "I don't know," but either would indicate he was in the dark, and he seldom was on party matters. Beyond that, despite their differences, he was a straight shooter with Ingle. So he was evasive, saying, "All I know is what I read in your column." Making another run at it, as the two walked swiftly across the crowded room, Ingle asked, "Will Jim McGreevey be the Democrats' choice in '05?" Again, Norcross said, "All I know is what I read in your column."

Ingle understood Norcross well enough to recognize a signal. He returned to McClure and told her, "What you hear is true. McGreevey is out." He meant that as in out of a job, not out of the closet sexually, although in retrospect his choice of words was indeed prophetic.

The big Sunday story for Gannett papers from Boston that week wasn't about John Kerry. It was that numerous sources, who didn't want to be publicly identified, were saying McGreevey was in deep trouble.[48] That brought a strange response from McGreevey's press people. Usually when they didn't like a story, they came by and yelled at us. But this time Micah Rasmussen (a press aide who McGreevey during a legislative correspondence club speech jokingly compared to "Baghdad Bob," the Iraqi Minister of Misinformation) wrote a letter to the CEO of Gannett, telling him, in effect, he felt compelled to report McClure had violated the company's ethics policy on unnamed sources. It was a bush-league move, one that could have been avoided had Rasmussen done his homework and known what he was talking about. Here was a flack for the most corrupt administration in recent Jersey history complaining about the ethics of a media company that has a written ethics policy, one that is taken seriously and adhered to.

Similarly, in his book, McGreevey singled out Gannett and reporter McClure as a cause of his troubles. It meant we did our jobs, and we wear it like a badge of honor.

After Boston, Ingle left for California, as he does every August because he and an extraordinary number of nephews and nieces have August birthdays. In 2004 the trip had to be made before the Republicans gathered in New York. August 12 was the travel day. Ingle's plane landed at LAX in the late morning, and he headed for the rental car pickup, remembering he'd promised to keep his cell phone on in case Gannett State Bureau news editor Michael Symons had any questions, although the time between the national conventions was expected to be quiet news-wise, as it usually is.

The cell phone rang about the same time Ingle stepped on the shuttle van. "Bob, it's Mike. I think there's something you need to know. They're saying McGreevey is calling a news conference to say he is resigning because he is gay and has had an affair with another man." Still a little groggy from an early morning five-and-a-half-hour flight, Ingle responded: "Mike, that sounds like something I would make up as a joke. You better recheck the source on that." Symons said emphatically there was no doubt about it.

Glancing at his watch, Ingle realized he couldn't be on the East Coast before late that night. "What can I do to help, Mike?" Symons told Ingle he could talk to all the TV networks that kept calling, apparently having found Ingle's McGreevey columns on the Web. And so he did. CNN and MSNBC's *Hardball with Chris Matthews* wanted him at the same time. CNN called first but would only do TV, while MSNBC would handle it by phone as a last resort. Los Angeles traffic wouldn't permit time to get to CNN studios, so Ingle parked in a no-parking zone—that was a ninety-dollar ticket—and ran into a guitar shop on Sunset Boulevard, telling a startled young clerk, "I know this sounds crazy, but I need to borrow your phone to be on network TV in thirty seconds." Luckily, she was a journalism major. Ingle's nephew Nick Gomez took notes and answered the continually ringing cell. It went on like that until after midnight. When things settled down, Nick, then nineteen, who had been silent throughout, had only one question, "Uncle Bob, are you and the governor still friends?"

The next day in L.A. was no less hectic for Ingle. Two nephews, a niece, and a sister had to go ahead with the day's plans without Uncle Bob, who still was in demand from radio across the country and network TV. Chris Matthews wanted him back, and so did CNN and Fox and even E! Trouble is, Ingle went to California expecting a fun time with the kids. He packed shorts and T-shirts and Teva sandals. Sensing his desperation, Monie Hamilton, a friend since college, told her boss she had to take the day off and took command of Ingle's itinerary. That included a trip to Macy's at Burbank to buy a dress shirt and tie—all he needed since those TV guys only show you from the chest up. She snapped a shot of him as he looked to the real world, which Ingle sent along with his expense account for the new duds. Upon receiving that, Bob Collins, Ingle's boss, remarked, "Well, at least you didn't stick me for socks."

MSNBC's Matthews was fascinated by reports Golan was a poet. It gave Ingle a chance to set the record straight before a national TV audience for *Hardball:*

Matthews: "Well, I also am taken with the word 'poet.' I mean, a poet would be an odd person to name as your homeland security chief, given the fact he had no training in terror fighting or terrorism at all. He simply was an Israeli who had caught this guy's eye . . . I mean, this guy was taken with this person, to say the least. And this . . ."

Ingle: "Well, let me go back to the beginning there."

Matthews: "Yes."

Ingle: "Sandy McClure, who is one of our investigative reporters, did the majority of the work on this story. And as far as the poet thing goes, there was a rumor going around that the fellow had written a book of poetry. We can't find it. If it ever happened, we can't find the publisher. We can't find the poetry. So I'm not sure where that came from and if, in fact, that ever actually happened."

CNN's interviewer questioned whether the New Jersey press corps had been doing its job.

"So from what I've been able to learn, he had no experience," she said. "You mentioned he was an Israeli citizen. He couldn't even get clearance to find out the kind of things he needed to get this job. Weren't you guys sniffing around? Didn't this seem suspicious at the time?"

"Of course we were," replied Ingle. "That's why we spent three months investigating it. Sandy McClure did a great job. After she did her job, he resigned."

That second day, Ingle finally got to see the big event when the news shows replayed the press conference. Right away there was a major giggle. A while back, McGreevey had replaced the traditional wooden podium for gubernatorial press conferences with a clear acrylic one because someone thought it made him look taller. He glared at any reporter who tried to put a tape machine up there. When the "I am a gay American" press conference opens, you can clearly see McClure put her recorder on the podium and McGreevey pick it up and hand it back to her. Without hesitation, McClure returns it to where she had it.

How typical of McGreevey. Here he was making the big speech that would end his political career, embarrass his family and friends, and cause chaos to the people who worked for him, but his main concern was that McClure's tape recorder would ruin the aesthetics.

Even in this situation, during this soul-searching made-for-TV moment, there was room for one more lie before McGreevey left the spotlight in disgrace: He said he was tendering his resignation November 15 to provide for a smooth transition. Actually, it was about making sure the office went to Senate President Dick Codey. If McGreevey had resigned before September 3, there would have been a special election to fill his unexpired term, and considering what a mess he created for Democrats, there was a chance voters could have chosen a Republican as their governor, although a sizable number of Democrats wanted the rich and popular Senator Corzine to run in a special election. Remember, Corzine in Boston seemed to be setting himself up for that. By McGreevey saying he would resign August 12, but not actually doing it until November 15, there would be no special election where the voters had their say. Press flack Rasmussen defended McGreevey's decision to deny voters their right to choose their leader. The decision "was in the best interest of the state," he said. "Politics is the last thing on our minds." Baghdad Bob couldn't have said it any better.

The unexpired fourteen months of McGreevey's term went to Codey, a career politician who had been around Trenton for thirty years but was little known outside his own area of North Jersey. A likable chap with a quick wit, an eternally rumpled look, and an undertaker's license, Codey has a natural knack for knowing what to do and say for every occasion. At his first news conference as governor, the wooden podium was back, and Codey wouldn't start until he offered McClure the chance to put her recorder on it. As she did, other media people passed theirs on to McClure for placement alongside Gannett's. The Codey era was under way.

The day after McGreevey's final gubernatorial press conference confirming what McClure wrote two weeks earlier—that McGreevey was in deep trouble—press flack Rasmussen got a letter from Gannett saying it had looked into McClure's investigative stories and found she had violated no company policy.

When Codey took over, he kept many McGreevey appointees. Rasmussen wasn't one of them. He and his boss, McGreevey communications director Kathy Ellis, joined a gas utility.

Codey didn't mount a primary challenge to Corzine, the former Wall Street businessman who said he turned to government to make a difference. After a brief stint in the U.S. Senate, Corzine decided to run for New Jersey governor, a more powerful position. Even before that decision was made, he pulled some stupid stunts while campaigning for U.S. Senate in 2000.

Editorial writers had a field day when it was reported Corzine made not just one but two ethnic jokes about Italian Americans. The *New York Daily News* labeled its brief article "How Not to Run for Public Office" and said, "Jon Corzine, the Wall Street moneybags seeking the Democratic nomination for the U.S. Senate in

New Jersey, came under fire for ethnic slurs against Italians. In the first alleged incident, during a political gathering at an Italian restaurant in Newark, Corzine was introduced to a lawyer named David Stein. 'He's not Italian, is he?' Corzine reportedly said. 'Oh, I guess he's your Jewish lawyer who is here to get the rest of you out of jail.' Later, Corzine was introduced to an Italian-American contractor. 'Oh, you make cement shoes,' Corzine quipped, according to a witness. A spokesman for the candidate denied the first remark and apologized for the second."[49]

Corzine also was caught lying during the 2000 Senate campaign, something pols in New Jersey seem to think they can do and no one will notice. When a group of black ministers endorsed him, they were offended with press questions about how much the wealthy Corzine had donated to their churches. Corzine watched while one stepped forward and said Corzine gave only what he put into the collection plate. That blew up when records showed his foundation had given $25,000 to an influential black church. Corzine's explanation was out of the Bill Clinton playbook: "My foundation is different from Jon Corzine." he explained. The foundation was controlled by him and his wife.[50]

By the time Corzine ran for governor, his wife was long gone and he was a bachelor whose dating decisions were as bad as his ethnic jokes. He was divorced from his wife of thirty-three years, Joanne, in 2003. Just as he was about to be elected governor, Joanne went public in the *New York Times*, accusing him of making deals with political bosses and predicting he would "probably let New Jersey down" the way he had let his family down.[51]

Affair rumors always surface during major political campaigns in New Jersey, with each side desperate to get the allegations into print. Rumors swirled that as a U.S. Senator Corzine had an affair with one of his aides.[52] Next it was rumored Corzine's married opponent, Doug Forrester, had an affair with a former Miss New Jersey who worked on his failed U.S. Senate bid in 2002. Both candidates denied the published rumors, while *New York Daily News* columnist Ben Widdicombe wrote that New Jersey politics makes *The Sopranos* look like *7th Heaven,* the long-running TV show about a Protestant minister's family.[53]

Since then Corzine has kept up the tradition of ill-advised actions. During the 2005 gubernatorial campaign it became known Corzine had dated Carla Katz, head of Communications Workers of America Local 1034. The CWA is the largest state government union, representing more than 36,000, or 48 percent, of state workers. When Katz gave Corzine her union's endorsement, she recalled how they met at a union function. Corzine wouldn't comment about Katz, except to say they, too, were no longer together. Later, as governor, he would say their financial arrangement was not ongoing. Financial arrangement?

During the campaign, it was learned Corzine loaned Katz $470,000 for a home, then forgave the loan a week after he announced his candidacy for governor. Katz bought a pastoral Hunterdon County house from her former husband for $361,850, which made veteran reporter Tom Baldwin of the Gannett State Bureau wonder what happened to the other $108,150.[54] Katz refused to say. Corzine said he thought the money went to repair the two-hundred-year-old house.

Were that the case, Baldwin reasoned, there would be building permits. A check revealed there weren't any. But Katz had received permission from the state Department of Environmental Protection to exempt her land from the Highlands Water Protection and Planning Act, a state law that severely limits development in the region. Despite those limits, she got permission to add a driveway, dig a swimming pool, and put on an addition. Katz's union represents 2,379 of DEP's 3,450 employees.

In 2007, Deborah Howlett of the *Star-Ledger* reported that Katz, who makes slightly more than $100,000 a year, purchased for $1.1 million a luxury condominium in the same Hoboken building where Corzine lives.[55] The purchase of the Hudson County condo Katz had rented for two years came at the same time the Corzine administration and her union were in contract negotiations, continuing to fuel conflict-of-interest questions. The condo with a view of Manhattan was purchased through a newly formed corporation with Katz as the sole corporate officer. There was no mortgage on the property. The Mercer County lawyer listed as the registered agent for Katz's company, Barry Szaferman, handles "complex matrimonial litigation," according to a Web biography. Szaferman wouldn't confirm Katz was a client. But another member of his firm, David Beckett, was brought in by Corzine to head the state Office of Employee Relations and was a state negotiator with unions, including Katz's. Katz made Corzine look like a tough negotiator by opposing a new contract many state workers saw as generous.

But on the ethics side, things looked even more dire for New Jersey's chief executive when Gannett's Baldwin revealed that only one other condominium buyer (a three-man group of executives with the company owning the building) got a better purchase price than Katz in the exclusive building where Corzine continued to rent.[56]

With questions hanging in the air about whether Corzine and Katz communicated on the labor contract, Corzine asked a two-man ethics panel, set up just for governors, to review his e-mails and other communications related to the labor contract. That might have helped him, except he said he had no intention of sharing them with New Jersey's citizens.

Katz said she wanted to stay in Hoboken to be close to Seton Hall University, where she attended law school on a full scholarship. With reports that foundations controlled by Corzine gave more than $1 million to Seton Hall and the Newark Archdiocese, the

Archbishop of Newark, who also is chairman of the board at Seton Hall, called for an investigation. The school investigated itself and reported back to the archbishop the scholarship was "completely legitimate" and thus the case was closed. *Star-Ledger* columnist Tom Moran reported Corzine admitted writing her a recommendation for the grant-in-aid.[57]

Only in the Soprano State would a student need a full scholarship for law school, then purchase a $1.1 million condo to cut the commute on class days.

When the condo purchase came to light, Corzine fessed up—as the *New York Post* put it—to giving Katz and her children substantial gifts beyond the $470,000 home loan.[58] He raised the possibility that he paid for her two kids' Pennsylvania private school education—$44,000 a year combined—but he didn't seem sure.

Even with the condo purchase, Katz continued with the 3,200-square-foot addition to her Hunterdon County home, which the *Star-Ledger* reported now included a spa and septic system.[59] She used the same Pennsylvania contractor that a Corzine pal, disgraced former U.S. senator Bob Torricelli, had used for renovations on his Hunterdon County home. All this while she was renting a four-bedroom home nearby. Incidentally, the work on union leader Katz's place was done by nonunion labor.[60]

Corzine took an upper-crust attitude of "let them eat cake" when reporters pressed him for answers on why his former squeeze and current state labor union official had millions to play with and why a matrimonial lawyer was involved. He slapped a privacy label on the subject and called his relationship with Katz, who was taking up permanent residence in his building, simply cordial. He told Howlett of the *Star-Ledger,* "She's around Trenton regularly so it's not like I never see her, but this is not an ongoing, active relationship. It's no different than my relationship with (state AFL-CIO leader) Charlie Wowkanech." Funny, Katz, with her long, curly dark hair, appeared quite different from the sometimes gruff Wowkanech, an institution in the hallways of the statehouse.

A *New York Times* story in May 2007 made national news when sources close to the settlement said Corzine paid Katz more than $6 million when they broke up.[61] And Corzine was still dogged by the secret e-mails Katz sent him during the state's negotiations with the labor unions. Katz chose to clear things up during an interview with Cindy Adams of the *New York Post*. Katz said she wasn't holding anything over Corzine's head. The money was given after he proposed marriage and then reneged. As for why, Cindy Adams could merely speculate. She described Katz as a knockout with a shelf life: "Bare legs, low top, long hair, four-inch stilettos, diamond chain."[62]

More eyebrows were raised in Trenton and more money was taken from taxpayers' pockets when in June 2007 Corzine caved on something Katz wanted during union contract negotiations. After saying that future state government retirees would have to start paying part of their health benefits, Corzine backtracked and, in New Jersey style, gave the retirees a free ride.[63]

Katz wasn't the only woman to cause embarrassment in Corzine's life. Karen Golding worked on Corzine's 2000 Senate campaign and wound up as a lobbyist for Prudential Financial. One night during a sit-down dinner with state senate Democrats, Corzine, then governor, got what was described as a hysterical call from Golding, who was in jail and in need of $5,000 bond money. The governor dispatched an underling with the cash right away.[64]

Turns out the reason Golding was in the pokey was that after a stalking investigation, she was accused of breaking into the unlocked car of her ex-boyfriend Assemblyman Joe Cryan—the guy Corzine had just named to head the Democratic State Committee. The governor said he didn't know his friend was the alleged stalkee, and he expected to be repaid the $5,000. Later, he said the loan was written off.

In another odd twist, lawmaker Cryan ended up having to repay Prudential Financial $1,394, for golf tickets and gifts—including dinners he received from Prudential lobbyist Golding while the stalking investigation was going on, Gannett reported. The freebies from a lobbyist to a lawmaker violated ethics rules, which even in New Jersey limited gifts for lawmakers to no more than $250. Cryan's two pricey dinners with Golding totaled $466. Cryan's explanation for the dinners, as told to Gannett's Gregory J. Volpe, was that when he was sipping the soup, it was not yet confirmed that she was the one who would be arrested in the wake of unwanted e-mails and phone calls.[65] The embarrassment from that started a movement in the legislature to stop gifts altogether.

Golding avoided a criminal trial by entering a two-year pretrial intervention program in Union County. But after only ten months she came crying to the court, saying the requirements were keeping her from her full-time job as a New Jersey lobbyist. Golding presented the court with letters from psychiatrists saying she was mentally stable and argued that she had met "most" of the court's requirements—including paying fines, sixty hours of community service, drug screening, reporting to probation, and psychological counseling. "I have suffered a tremendous financial hardship due to this matter," she told the court.[66]

While Golding was trying to get out from under the court restrictions, four members of Cryan's family filed a harassment complaint against her after police traced six hundred calls to Golding's cell phone. They wanted a new stalking investigation.[67] Golding later pleaded guilty to stalking Cryan's girlfriend. The penalty? Golding's pretrial intervention program was extended to May 2009, the *Star-Ledger* reported. She agreed not to contact Cryan or his family. The initial charge of breaking into his car was dismissed.

Not for the first, or last, time did observers see a link to a certain TV drama. Republican State Committee Chairman Tom Wilson said of the Golding-Corzine incident, "The whole thing seems more appropriate for an episode of 'The Sopranos' than it does for a chapter in New Jersey history."[68]

But Corzine managed to write another chapter of state history that added big-time to the stupid things governors do—and it almost cost him his life.

In 2007, Corzine shattered his femur, eleven ribs, sternum, and collarbone in a high-impact auto accident that occurred while he was not wearing a seat belt and his driver, a state trooper, was going 91 mph. The emergency lights were flashing, but it was hardly an emergency: He was en route to a meeting with the Rutgers women's basketball team and radio host Don Imus, who had just been fired for calling team members, many of whom were black, "nappy-headed hos."

State police almost immediately admitted Corzine wasn't wearing a seat belt, but they danced around the speed issue, saying it was not a factor, until information from the "black box" on board the SUV revealed it was traveling 91 mph in a 65 mph zone just five seconds before the crash.

While New Jersey residents felt sympathy for the injured Corzine, his chief of staff, Tom Shea, summed up what people thought about the lack of a seat belt and Corzine barreling down the highway with lights a-blaring. Approaching Corzine's bedside for the first time after the accident, Shea used a favored and familiar term with new meaning: "Hey, schmuck."[69]

Just to prove that governors can't stop themselves from doing stupid things, after eighteen days in the hospital, a tearful Corzine apologized for his stupidity and then headed to Drumthwacket in a van clocked at fifteen miles over the speed limit.[70]

Corzine declared he was lucky to be alive. Four months later, he complained he would be fighting one issue to his grave—and it wasn't seat belts. It was Carla Katz.

Corzine denied and then admitted to the *Star-Ledger* that he gave Katz's brother-in-law, Rocco Riccio, $10,000 after Riccio was forced from his state job. The newspaper said the gift contradicted Corzine's claims he had severed financial ties to his old girlfriend. Corzine said, not so, that the money had nothing to do with Carla and was intended to help Riccio. As for $5,000 of the payments being in $1,000 money orders, a Corzine spokesman said, "Politics is a contact sport in New Jersey," and then added that those involved were not eager to give out a check with Corzine's account number on it. Sounds like they were trying to hide it.

Imagine this happening in some other state. New Jersey governors must think their constituents are stupid too.

Corzine ran into Florio-style trouble with New Jersey's taxpayers when he proposed increasing tolls by nearly 800 percent by 2022 to pay off some of the state's debt and to fund road repairs. The fun began when Corzine explained in his State of the State address that pigs would fly over the statehouse before spending cuts or taxes would fix the state's financial woes. And so that's what happened. Reminiscent of the 1990 antitax protests, more than seven hundred rallied at the statehouse while scores of pink pig balloons rose in the sky above the Capitol's gold dome, Gannett's Tom Baldwin reported. The event was sponsored by New Jersey 101.5 FM, the radio station where the outspoken Jersey Guys—Ray Rossi, Casey Bartholomew, and coauthor Ingle—needle the governor and his minions. A sign in the crowd had this to say to Corzine: "Duh—Cut Spending, Governor Financial Genius."

Balloons and Carla Katz aside, Corzine showed real Soprano State style when he stood by his deputy chief of staff Javier Inclán even after he testified during a corruption trial that he twice handed a New Jersey mayor envelopes of what Inclán said he believed were thousands of dollars of cash campaign contributions from a bar owner, *The New York Times* reported. Inclán also said the contributions were not reported on campaign reports, something required by state law. Inclán was never charged, and Guttenberg Mayor David Delle Donna was acquitted on mail fraud charges related to those payments. But as the result of that trial, Delle Donna and his wife, Anna, were convicted of accepting bribes from that bar owner, Luisa Medrano. U.S. Attorney Chris Christie said Medrano got a break on liquor license violations and the Della Donnas got cash for cosmetic surgery and gambling in Atlantic City and a Yorkshire terrier with canine insurance. Now I know you think we are making this up. But just remember, this is New Jersey. So you aren't surprised that Corzine praised Inclán for his testimony. The governor did not ask for, but accepted, Inclán's resignation.

3

Like Days of Yore Minus the Shining Knights

Since the turn of the twentieth century, New Jersey has been ruled by bosses who carve up the state like medieval fiefdoms. The bosses fall into two categories: the ones elected at the ballot box, and the ones scarcely known to the public even though they pull the strings that influence every part of Garden State living, especially the level of taxes and how that money is spent.

Bosses decide who gets the best spots on the election ballot— the first column on the left is prime—and help ensure victories by providing anointed candidates with more campaign money than their competition can raise. The unelected bosses are insulated from the financial disclosure that elected officials have to make each year. That means an unelected party boss can have conflicts not readily apparent. "There's no way to hold that person accountable," political scientist Ingrid Reed of Rutgers University told Gannett. "It's like a privately held company, yet they have a tremendous amount of political influence."

Gannett New Jersey newspapers did a series on the boss system in October 2004, one with revelations that caught even lifelong residents by surprise. In it, Paul D'Ambrosio, investigations editor of the *Asbury Park Press*, wrote:[1] "This is how it works: A candidate anointed by a boss is then blessed with an almost bottomless pit of campaign cash. Candidates who displease a boss are denied the campaign money needed to buy expensive media ads or mail out glossy fliers.

"The boss system has grown to such proportions in New Jersey that politics has become less about public issues and more about rewarding the bosses' campaign contributors—and even the bosses—with public contracts, say many government officials and political observers.

"This souped-up version of 19th-century politics has left New Jersey as the last state that relies heavily on party bosses to control elections, redistricting, patronage jobs and much of state, county and local government."

The bosses have one thing in common—they expect their asses to be kissed by the weak-kneed sycophants they support for office. It is a bastardization of our democratic system of government in which people making decisions are supposed to be accountable to voters. Voters aren't as important in a boss/machine system. That results in an oligarchy, the rule of a few, in which an individual vote is less important to a candidate than the favors of a boss.

U.S. Rep. Rob Andrews, who came out of the South Jersey Democrat machine run by boss George E. Norcross III, is a critic of the system that launched his political career. Andrews is independent of the machine now, largely due to his popularity with constituents. He is ever mindful, however, that he will need bosses if he seeks higher office, such as governor or U.S. senator.

Out of forty New Jersey legislative districts, Andrews said, maybe only five are competitive. Otherwise, if there is competition, it is usually a revolt where an old boss is replaced by a new boss. "One kind of feeds on the other," Andrews told editor D'Ambrosio. "If you control the elected offices in the area, people want to give you money because they need the influence. You not only can raise more money per donor, but more donors want to give to you because you have something you can do for them. You are in power. And the people challenging you do not have that power."

New Jersey has twenty-one counties but less than a dozen powerful bosses, who influence candidates from the smallest town to the governor's office. Out of that number there are several whose tentacles have reached beyond their home bases to manipulate government activity across the state.

Ironically, the bosses' power was increased because of a 1993 campaign finance reform law that allowed noncandidates—like party bosses—to raise seventeen times more cash from a single donor than those running for office. Before the change, candidates could raise an unlimited amount from an individual or a corporation. After the change, candidates were limited to a maximum of $2,200 per person or business. In 2005 that went to $2,600. But county party chairmen can raise up to $37,000 per contributor. The party can transfer any amount to local candidates. Because of what's called "wheeling," the money can be transferred—or wheeled—from one part of the state to another.

Some say the "reform" that made party bosses even more powerful was an unintended consequence. More likely, it was exactly what the bosses and their puppets had in mind to increase boss stranglehold on government. The boss system is fueled by New Jersey's legal pay-to-play arrangement in which campaign contributors get no-bid contracts and other government work. In most states, that's called bribery. New Jersey's U.S. Attorney, Chris Christie, who has brought down more than a hundred political crooks, labels corruption a "hidden tax."

The granddaddy of Jersey bosses was Frank "I Am the Law" Hague, who ruled in Jersey City, across the harbor from Manhattan, from 1917 to 1947. He was known for doing whatever it took to get his way, and the joke was the governor had on his desk a direct line to Hague. Like his modern-day counterparts, he got his strength from patronage, corruption, and public jobs doled out to supporters. Various prosecutors took him on, but Hague always skated.

In 1946, Hague backed the late William V. Musto for the state assembly, where he served nineteen years, followed by seventeen years in the state senate. Among the people Musto mentored were Donald Scarinci, a lawyer and Democratic leader who served as his aide for more than three years, and U.S. Sen. Robert Menendez, who broke with him after a federal grand jury indicted Musto for racketeering, extortion, and fraud. Menendez testified against Musto, who was convicted and sentenced to seven years in prison in 1982.

When Menendez ran against Tom Kean Jr. for the U.S. Senate in 2006, the Musto situation was spun as a young Menendez doing the right thing. Not everyone agreed. Deborah Howlett of the *Star-Ledger* interviewed Libero Marotta, who said he had known Menendez since he was a high school senior: "I've read some of (Menendez's) comments about being a reformer, and it turns my stomach . . . he's always been a Bill Musto guy."[2] The *New York Times* quoted Menendez opponent Bob Haney as saying Menendez worked his way through the machine and then took it over.[3] And Tom Moran, columnist for the *Star-Ledger*, wrote, "Menendez is the boss in Hudson County, which is ground zero for the state's corruption problem."[4]

Two months before the 2006 general election, the U.S. attorney's office launched an investigation into a rental deal between Menendez and a nonprofit organization. As landlord for the nonprofit, Menendez collected more than $300,000 in rent, while as a member of the U.S. House of Representatives, he helped the agency paying the rent get federal grants. Employees of the agency, the North Hudson Community Action Corporation, contributed $33,450 to Menendez's campaigns.[5] The lease stated the agency's ability to pay rent was dependent on the agency getting certain federal or state funding.[6]

Menendez said he had verbal permission from Mark Davis of the House Ethics Committee in 1994 before entering into the lease.[7] A Capitol Hill publication said Davis didn't work there then. And Davis couldn't be questioned when the agreement became public during the Menendez/Kean Senate campaign because he died the year before. Menendez's spokesman said it must have been someone else who gave the approval.[8]

Menendez suffered another blow to his campaign when a tape-recorded conversation between Scarinci—who ran Hudson County for Menendez—and a Dr. Oscar Sandoval was made public.[9] The secretly recorded conversation appears to have Scarinci threatening Sandoval's $1 million contract with the county if he doesn't do Menendez a favor by hiring a certain Dr. Vicente Ruiz.[10]

"The law of the jungle" would apply if the favor wasn't done, Scarinci said on the tape-recorded conversation. Sandoval took that to mean if he wanted protection for his contract, he would do Scarinci's bidding on the hire. Scarinci, a major fund-raiser for Menendez and treasurer for his House campaigns, was publicly taken to the woodshed by the Menendez 2006 organization which said because of Scarinci's lapse of judgment he would no longer play a role in the campaign.

Scarinci said none of his dealings with Sandoval was authorized by Menendez, who had managed to come away unscathed by a previous Scarinci scandal—Scarinci's involvement in the early release of mobster Angelo Prisco. (See chapter 8.) This time Menendez would have a harder time dodging the boss image.

"The only reason I stuck my nose in this Ruiz thing is because Menendez asked me," Scarinci is heard saying on the tape. He tells Sandoval, "My point of view, it makes sense for you because it gives you protection." Sandoval said a lawsuit filed against him by Hudson County to recover money lost to vendors who allegedly paid bribes was really retaliation for his helping federal investigators in their successful case against former county executive Robert Janiszewski.

"They know that I was the person working voluntarily for the FBI and the prosecutor's office on my own," Sandoval told Gannett's Gregory J. Volpe.[11] "This was more of a retaliation for having done that and to show the rest of the people of the machinery what happens when you go against the family."

After the Scarinci tape became public, the Menendez campaign had an odd comment about Sandoval, saying the Hudson County Democrat was pulled "out of the sewer of New Jersey politics." It was strange in that Menendez is the boss of Hudson politics, which would make him the boss of the sewer.

Volpe also reported that while a member of the House of Representatives Menendez worked to ease the prison transfer of Nicholas Parlavecchio, a racketeer, convicted on cocaine charges, who was eventually sent to the same federal prison as his son, jailed for similar crimes.[12] Menendez made this plea for the racketeer reunion: "I would greatly appreciate it if you would review this matter and advise my Jersey City office if there is a possibility of having Mr. Parlavecchio [the elder] transferred to a facility closer to his family."

Just a month later the son, Antonino, was approved for transfer to the Fort Dix Federal Correctional Institution, where Nicholas was later transferred. The son, also known as Antonio, was the brunt of cartoons after he and his wife, Maria, were caught in a scheme to smuggle his sperm out of federal prison. Described in news accounts of the crime as a reputed New York mob associate, Antonio teamed with John Edward Alite, identified by the *St. Petersburg Times* as the "central figure in a Tampa Bay area offshoot of the Gambino crime family," to get sperm collection kits in and the sperm out.[13] The Web site InTheseTimes.com showed prison guards and dogs chasing prison-garbed sperm down a tunnel and dubbed the crime the "Great Sperm Escape" aimed at "breeding the next generation" of presumably New Jersey gangsters.[14] Antonio got an extra six months in jail for the caper.[15]

Menendez spokesman Matt Miller said Menendez, who had no records of the request for the Parlavecchio letter, had no relationship with the Parlavecchios and there was nothing unusual about a family asking for a prison transfer. But those familiar with the federal system said requests from congressmen have dramatic and quick effects, and Menendez could ill afford the connection to "family" requests from those in the rackets.

In another salvo a week before the November 2006 election, the *New York Times* detailed how Menendez secured $30 million in federal money for waterfront development in Bayonne within sight of the Statue of Liberty and how his friends and political supporters reaped the benefits.[16]

"His work provided the seed money for a plan to produce movie studios and shops, marinas and waterfront parks, and 6,600 homes," reporters David Kocieniewski and Ray Rivera wrote. "The project has also produced considerable work for some of his chief political supporters. The first major contract to develop the site went to a company that hired a Menendez friend and political confidant, Donald Scarinci, to lobby for it. That developer later took on Mr. Menendez's former campaign treasurer, Carl Goldberg, as partner. Bonds for a portion of the project were underwritten by Dennis Enright, a top campaign contributor, while Kay LiCausi, a former Menendez Congressional aide and major fund-raiser, received lucrative work lobbying for the project."

The *Times* also did an in-depth look at the relationship between Menendez and successful lobbyist and former Menendez aide LiCausi, something Trenton observers just whispered about.

"The tale of her swift success . . . is complicated by the widespread belief among elected officials and political consultants in Hudson County and former members of Mr. Menendez's staff that she and the congressman had a romantic relationship," wrote *Times* reporter Jeffrey Gettleman.[17] "Both Ms. LiCausi, who is 33 and single, and Mr. Menendez, 51 and recently divorced, refused to address any aspect of their nonprofessional lives."

LiCausi left Menendez's staff in 2002, and he admitted helping her get more than $200,000 in lobbying work for campaign committees he controlled or could influence.

As the final kick in the butt during the 2006 campaign, Menendez was targeted by a *Sopranos*-style cable TV spot funded by Bob Perry, the Texas tycoon and GOP contributor who financed the "Swift Boat" ads against Democratic presidential candidate John Kerry.[18] The thirty-second TV ad shows a mobster in a black leather jacket talking on his cell phone in an alley. "We got a problem . . . our boy down in Washington, Bob Menendez, he's caught in this federal investigation . . . right . . . feds start looking into these fixed contracts, bada-bing, we're in it but deep."

Despite all the bad publicity—which maybe in New Jersey's

warped political scene helped rather than hurt—Menendez easily defeated Thomas Kean Jr., a state senator and son of the popular former governor, for the U.S. Senate seat, as Democrats seized control of Congress in the wake of public anger at President George W. Bush over the Iraq war. In a year when "Republican" and "reformer" couldn't be said in the same breath, Kean lacked even the hope of having enough charisma to come off as a reformer.

A little farther south, John Lynch was known as the all-powerful boss of Middlesex County, in the middle part of the state. Lynch spent twelve years as mayor of New Brunswick and twenty as a state senator, which included his being majority and minority leader and senate president. His rise to power started unusually early since his father was a longtime state senator who also rose to be senate president. His father founded the law firm Lynch Martin, which made millions from public contracts. Right after McGreevey became governor, the state Department of Environmental Protection went all the way to Louisiana to hire a law firm to seek damages from corporate polluters. The Louisiana firm then teamed with the Lynch firm. The firms can get up to 25 percent in commissions for any recovery, which could run into the millions.

When *Home News Tribune* columnist Rick Malwitz asked Lynch if his role as a party boss enriched his law firm, Lynch ironically responded, "Quite the contrary. My role as mayor and as state senator has cost the firm money."[19]

Lynch was a longtime backer of Woodbridge Mayor McGreevey, for various reasons, and in the end, making McGreevey governor was to be Lynch's crowning achievement. But things started falling apart after the newly elected chief executive took over the statehouse and surrounded himself with the young, inexperienced staff we've already met. Not ready for prime time, they were a lot more impressed by the wealth of developer Charles Kushner, whom

Lynch opposed, than by Lynch's years of Jersey political experience. Lynch described the tenure of the McGreevey administration as "the worst 34 months of my political life." That was before
both Kushner and Lynch went to prison on federal charges.

McGreevey was the creation of the bosses, especially Lynch,
more than any other recent chief executive. When the governor
announced on August 12, 2004, that he was quitting, he became
the target of a kind of boss tug-of-war. Lynch and Norcross reportedly told McGreevey if he would go by September 3—so there
could be a special election to replace him—they could provide a
soft economic landing. The plan, wrote *Asbury Park Press* investigations editor D'Ambrosio, was to recruit U.S. Sen. Jon Corzine to
run in a special election, which he would win. Corzine would then
replace himself with Congressman Menendez.

But Sen. Ray Lesniak—another boss, McGreevey ally, and enemy of Lynch and Norcross—persuaded the governor to stay on
until November 15, too late for a special election. Also not supporting a special election was Senate President Dick Codey, who
was aligned with Lesniak and didn't like Norcross or Lynch but
had another motive as well: Without a special election, Codey
would serve out the remaining fourteen months of McGreevey's
term.

In 2005, Corzine—even though he was denied a special
election—spread enough money around with the county bosses to
lock up the Democratic Party's nomination for governor and went
on to an easy election. After taking office, he appointed Menendez
to replace him in the U.S. Senate. The plan happened as Norcross
and Lynch had envisioned, albeit almost two years after originally
planned.

Five years earlier, in 2000, Lynch had started a political action
committee, the ironically named New Directions Through Responsible Leadership, to, as he described it, bring new blood into

the Democratic Party and make Democrats strong where Republicans traditionally have ruled the roost. Over the next six years, the PAC expanded Lynch's influence by distributing $1.3 million to candidates, including those far from Lynch's Middlesex County. A close examination showed the PAC money often went to candidates and committees where Lynch's business partner, developer Jack Morris of Piscataway, was seeking local approval for projects. Morris also contributed at least $72,000 to the PAC over the same six years.[20]

Lynch said it was only a coincidence Morris had projects where the PAC doled out money. Ingrid Reed, director of the New Jersey Project at the Eagleton Institute of Politics at Rutgers University, told the *Star-Ledger,* "Anyone can say it's a coincidence. But if so, why is there [campaign] support in places . . . when developments occurred?"[21]

Federal agents, who don't believe in coincidences, raided Lynch's office in Tinton Falls in Monmouth County. It turned out the PAC paid more than $165,000 in consultation fees to a business run by the mayor of a town where Morris wanted to build a development. The mayor, Richard Pucci of Monroe, also worked as a political consultant for Lynch's PAC.[22]

Bill Bowman of the *Asbury Park Press* noted Pucci's Professional Management Consultants was run out of Mayor Pucci's home and was paid $4,000 a month by the PAC.[23] In addition to the $25,000 a year he received for being mayor, Pucci earned about $135,000 a year as executive director of the Middlesex County Improvement Authority and $12,000 a year as Monroe's police commissioner. "As mayor," Bowman wrote, "Pucci sits on the township planning board—which would eventually rule on Morris' project, should an application be filed—and Pucci created a task force charged with evaluating Morris' and several other development projects."

Lynch responded to the media coverage by withdrawing "entirely, permanently and irrevocably" from "a wide range of public organizations, whether political or philanthropic in nature." He said, however, being the magnanimous soul he was, he would remain available to elected government officials to discuss public policy issues. Those doing business with Lynch and his wife, Deborah—Democratic fund-raiser and sister of an admitted mobster—say he remained in the boss business. The criminal record of the brother-in-law, Louis Auricchio, and Auricchio's role, pulling the trigger, in the murder of mob capo John DiGilio are believed to be what kept Lynch from running for governor.[24] Lynch, who suffered from back problems and a bout with prostate cancer, apparently did not intend to end up in prison or retreat from socializing. The *New York Times* reported in January 2006 that he and Deborah were building an estate with a room large enough to seat one hundred in Lawrenceville near the governor's mansion.[25]

Lynch, the living symbol of the rot and stink that is New Jersey politics, said he had been besmirched in media reports that called him derogatory titles like "boss," "power broker," and "warlord." He blamed former U.S. senator Bob Torricelli and the "failed McGreevey administration," the very one Lynch devoted so much of his time and energy into putting in place. Torricelli became an enemy because, among other things, he mounted a brief challenge to McGreevey's second run for governor. Lynch suggested it was Torricelli who prompted the U.S. attorney's office to investigate Lynch.

But it was Lynch who brought on his own downfall, in typical Jersey fashion. Like most of his ilk, he was greedy. On September 15, 2006, Lynch pleaded guilty to mail fraud and tax evasion involving kickbacks to get approval for a Middlesex County sand company's pet project to mine state parkland. He also admitted failing to declare $150,000 in extra income for 1999. His business partner, John Westlake, pleaded guilty to one count of tax evasion in connection with the same land deal.[26] "Today an era of corruption and influence peddling has been put to an end," said U.S. Attorney Christie. But he tempered that later. "You get rid of one set of corrupt bosses in New Jersey and another seems to come in and replace them. In the end, it's up to the public and the leaders in our state to determine whether they're going to change the culture or not."

Observed Republican Assemblyman Alex DeCroce, "Another day, another public corruption scandal in New Jersey. Sometimes it seems that there is an endless assembly line churning out corrupt officials in this state."

Ross Baker, a Rutgers University political science professor, told the *Home News Tribune*, "The world of New Jersey politics is a very intimate one. It is a compact club. When someone comes to dominate a county or a region, like a John Lynch or George Norcross, he becomes an outsize figure. John's fall is big news."[27]

The week after Lynch pleaded guilty, McGreevey's book came out, adding insult to the injured boss who had helped propel McGreevey to the governor's seat.[28] McGreevey said Lynch had operated a "peculiar form of checkbook government" with his consulting company helping developers win government approval for their projects. Of developers, McGreevey said, "As a result of their financial clout, developers were able to pull strings at every level of government—they literally owned many of the local politicians, including many bosses."

When McGreevey was the most powerful governor in the nation, he said, he had been beholden to the state's warlords, of which Lynch was the most powerful. "Lynch and the other bosses had been a political compromise that I'd accepted in order to advance my career," McGreevey wrote. "I had my people strike backroom deals I kept myself in the dark about or forced from my mind if I learned too much."

One covert operation McGreevey probably would rather not have known about was Lynch's connection to State Police Lt. Vincent Bellaran. Kathy Barrett Carter and Josh Margolin of the *Star-Ledger* laid it out:[29] "A former lieutenant in the New Jersey State Police says that for three years he was involved in a covert operation that used confidential State Police records to discredit the Whitman administration and boost the candidacy of Gov. James E. McGreevey. Vincent Bellaran, the former lieutenant, said he was recruited by Lt. Col Cajetan 'Tommy' DeFeo, but the operation was orchestrated for much of the time by McGreevey's mentor, former state Sen. John Lynch.

"Bellaran said he and DeFeo dug up dirt on the State Police between 1999 and early 2002. Internal State Police information was passed to Lynch for use in legislative hearings on racial profiling; internal documents also became the basis of a newspaper story about the son of a former aide to Gov. Christie Whitman and were used to embarrass a State Police lieutenant colonel who was a Whitman favorite."

Lynch told the *Star-Ledger* he got information from state troopers for the hearings on racial profiling but denied any conspiracy against Whitman or for McGreevey.

In another story related to the covert operation, Carter and Margolin later reported that a longtime supporter of McGreevey, Robert D'Anton, a Lavallette developer, said he supplied cell phones and paid bills for the covert operation but did not know what the funding or phones were used for. McGreevey appointed D'Anton chairman of the New Jersey Lottery Commission.[30]

Lynch's sentencing was like a family reunion scene with public officials of various ilk (ten former or current lawmakers), family, businessmen, friends, and clergy sending letters to the judge asking for leniency and telling of Lynch's charitable deeds. His lawyer was Jack Arseneault, who almost was appointed attorney general by McGreevey and represented Linden Mayor John Gregorio during a grand jury that was dismissed without indictments. Arseneault also had represented Albert Cernadas, president of the International Longshoremen's Newark local, who was described by the grand jury that indicted him as an associate of the Genovese crime family. After Cernandas pleaded guilty to wire and mail fraud conspiracy, Arseneault presented the judge with 292 letters asking for leniency.[31] And it worked. Cernandas, who made news by inviting McGreevey to a five-night stay in Puerto Rico on the union's tab, was sentenced to only two years probation. That's probably what Arseneault thought he could accomplish with the 172 letters that went to the federal judge sentencing Lynch.

But this time, with the eyes of the state watching the arrest of the most powerful political figure in recent memory, U.S. District Judge Stanley Chesler sentenced Lynch to three years and three months in federal prison. The sixty-eight-year-old political boss, infamous for his temper, was cowed in the courtroom. "One of New Jersey's most powerful political figures learned today that no one is above the law," U.S. Attorney Christie said. "There has got to be a point in time when public officials in this state get the picture."

And if they don't, Christie had another solution for New Jersey's electorate: "You have to elect better people and hold them accountable for the promises they make to you. Do not wait for days like today, years after crimes are committed, for prosecutors to do it."

Westlake, Lynch's business partner, who had heart problems, was fined $30,000 and sentenced to three months in a prison hospital and seven months of home confinement for not declaring $350,000 on his income taxes.[32] The money was paid by the developer as part of the influence-peddling scheme.

One of the lawmakers who asked Judge Chesler to go easy on Lynch, according to the *Star-Ledger,* was the longtime assemblyman from Lynch's home county, Peter Barnes.[33] Corzine nominated Barnes to be chairman of the state parole board, where insiders long sensed Lynch had informal, quiet influence. Barnes, seventy-eight, was an FBI agent on Lynch's turf before Lynch took over New Brunswick. Two years before Lynch's arrest, Barnes sang Lynch's praises in a Gannett New Jersey story and said Lynch had been the "catalyst" for needed change in the city.[34] But what grew with the city was Lynch's power base of patronage and, in the end, corruption that landed him in jail. Barnes promised to end political influence at the parole board and, as reported by Gannett's Michael Rispoli, said he would contact the state attorney general if the governor's office tried to use political influence on paroles.[35]

Of all the Jersey bosses, the best known is the one who eschews publicity and never held elective office, South Jersey's George E. Norcross III, whose operation is run out of Cherry Hill in Camden County. He didn't invent machine politics, but he raised it to a fine art form. Candidates he supports generally are too weak to stand on their own, and people wanting government contracts know they have to buy expensive tickets to political events to support the Democrats. South Jersey suffers from an inferiority complex and maintains, not without good reason, that the populous North Jersey counties like Essex and Hudson traditionally get all the goodies.

Norcross also is known as a political bully. Ellen Karcher, a Democrat in Monmouth County, said Norcross called her during her state senatorial campaign and told her to drop out of the race or he would spend a million bucks to defeat her. She didn't, and neither did he. Karcher won. Karcher told the *Asbury Park Press*'s Jason Method she also ran afoul of Democrat Lynch when she ran against Republican State Sen. John Bennett in 2003 without talking to Lynch first. "I wasn't going to wait my turn at the deli counter to ask this guy if I'm going to run. Where did it say I had to go to him first?"[36]

Norcross's lasting contribution to Jersey political lore are secret audio recordings, known as the Palmyra tapes, that gave an inside view of what Jersey boss politics is like and embarrassed some of Norcross's puppets. The tapes were made after a Palmyra politician, John Gural, went to authorities with charges that his employer, JCA Associates of Moorestown, threatened to fire him unless he voted against the rehiring of Palmyra solicitor Ted Rosenberg, a political enemy of Norcross. Gural wore a wire for then–Attorney General John Farmer Jr., a Republican. When nothing came of the probe, Gural filed a civil suit and reach a settlement with JCA. But that wasn't enough, Gural and Rosenberg filed a federal racketeering suit against Norcross. While that suit was eventually dismissed, it led to the release of some damning recorded conversations.[37]

Two attorneys general later, Governor McGreevey's man, Peter Harvey, fought public release of the tapes. Harvey lost in court; the *Courier-Post* secured the tapes and shared excerpts with its readers.[38] (More on Harvey in chapter 5.)

The recording captured Norcross telling Gural, "I want you to fire that fuck. You need to get this fuck Rosenberg for me and teach this jerk-off a lesson. He has to be punished. . . . Rosenberg is history and he is done and anything I can do to crush his ass, I wanna do because I just think he's just done, an evil fuck."

Later, Norcross explained how he handled a member of the New Jersey legislature. "I sat him down and said . . . 'Don't fuck with me on this one . . . if you ever do that and I catch you one more time doing it, you're gonna get your fucking balls cut off.' He got the message."

On another part of the tape Norcross was bragging about his successes while complaining about the hard work. One of the politicians who owes his career to Norcross is Assemblyman Joe Roberts, who became majority leader, then Speaker.

Norcross explained: "You know Joe Roberts got his position, we got to redistricting . . . and you know we quote we won and get all that shit. You know what I have to do [to] run McGreevey's campaign day to day, plus this company, plus whatever else I'm doing and you know I'm nuts, I'm gonna have a heart attack.

"All I want to see is a South Jersey strong Democratic Party. It's not always going to look great, but I'll tell you this: After the fight we had last year, no one will ever, ever again uh, not include or look down or double cross South Jersey. Never again will that happen. Because they know we put up the gun and we pulled the trigger and we blew their brains out. They know it. We're just like Hudson County and Essex County now."

Hudson and Essex are known for bosses as well as the extraordinary amount of money that government in the Democratic strongholds costs. Machine politics, with all the contracts that have to be handed out, and the hangers-on who have to be added to the payroll, drive up the bill.

Local government in New Jersey costs an average of $3,000 per person. Newark, in Essex, costs $5,197 per person. *Star-Ledger* columnist Paul Mulshine figured out bringing the cost of government in Newark to the state average would save $511 million annually; in Hudson's Jersey City it would save $218 million annually, and in Boss Norcross's Camden it would mean $202 million in savings to taxpayers.[39]

Another part of the recorded Norcross conversation had to do with Assemblyman Louis Greenwald, a lawyer known for dressing well but for not being the sharpest knife in the drawer. Despite that, thanks to Norcross and the man Norcross made Speaker, Joe Roberts, Greenwald was named chairman of the assembly's budget committee, a powerful post he didn't seem qualified for.

Gural told Norcross about a rumor Greenwald was going to work for Remington & Vernick, an engineering firm. Norcross confirmed it and said competition forced the engineering company to "make Lou an offer he couldn't turn down."

"And his job is more like marketing?"

"Oh, what else would it be?" replied Norcross. "Yeah. I'm sure he will do some legal work for him, but it's gonna be a joke."

"And he's gonna stay as the assemblyman?"

"Oh sure. He doesn't like practicing law."

"He doesn't?"

"No, he never did."

That set tongues in motion. His colleagues called Greenwald "the Suit" because of his fancy clothes. After the Norcross conversation became public, one of his fellow assembly members quipped, "Now, I guess we call him the 'Empty Suit.'" Making unflattering comments about a colleague, as Norcross did on the tape, thereafter was referred to as "being green-walled."

Greenwald's new job with Remington & Vernick led to an ethics complaint filed by Mark Otto, a Republican who challenged Greenwald in a 2003 assembly race. Otto asked the Joint Committee on Ethical Standards to investigate whether Greenwald's job with the engineering firm—which had a vested interest in legislation affecting the company—created a conflict for Greenwald.

The complaint also dealt with a segment of the recordings in which Norcross is heard describing, in Greenwald's presence, a meeting in which Norcross told Voorhees Mayor Harry Platt which engineering firm the town was to hire.

"This is evident of the system of pay-to-play that runs rampant through New Jersey politics where big campaign contributors are rewarded with public contracts," Otto said. "I call upon the committee to make a thorough investigation."

The committee voted 10–1 to dismiss the complaint. Later, the committee, a statehouse joke, would decline to investigate Greenwald's colleague, Sen. Wayne Bryant, on grounds he was being investigated by both federal and state authorities, but U.S. Attorney Christie said not to stop on his account. (More on Bryant in chapter 4.)

What did Greenwald, who had been exposed to embarrassment by the guy who pulls his strings, have to say about the tape? It was the media's fault. The media blew it out of proportion. "For people that hear or read the tapes, it is not an accurate characterization of the leadership of elected officials," said he. That's why they call Greenwald "the Empty Suit."

Next, Gural charged that the tapes were edited by the attorney general's office before they were made public. Coauthor Ingle dealt with it in his May 22, 2005, column:[40]

As revealing as the secretly recorded Boss George E. Norcross III conversations are, Palmyra Mayor John Gural says something important is missing. He thinks Attorney General Peter "See No Evil" Harvey edited one of the tapes made public recently.

Gural, who wore a wire for a former attorney general, said Norcross, Camden County Democrat grand poobah and power broker extraordinaire, made a reference to then-acting Gov. Donald DiFrancesco, a Republican considering a run for a full term. In court papers, Gural stated:

"At one point in the conversation, Norcross said that he

had been appointed co-chairman of the McGreevey campaign, but it didn't really matter because if Donald DiFrancesco was governor, he would make even more money."

That led Gural to submit a declaration to Superior Court Judge John Sweeney maintaining, "This conversation was deleted. . . ."

DiFrancesco didn't run, but he wound up on the board of Commerce Bank. Norcross runs the insurance arm of the bank and became a board member the same day as DiFrancesco. Gural said in his filing that DiFrancesco's law firm does work for Commerce.

Elsewhere in the 330 hours recorded, Norcross bragged that politicians like then-Senator Corzine had to go to Norcross—not because they liked him but because they had no choice. He also said a way of getting rid of troublemakers was to get them appointed to judgeships. Norcross wanted a political foe, John Harrington, out of his way. "Make him a fucking judge," Norcross said. "Harrington disappears; Harrington becomes a judge, whatever the case. We move on."

For the record, Harrington became a judge.

"It shows that political influence isn't always exposed and transparent, that there are people behind the scenes pulling strings— sometimes they're political contributors, sometimes they're political figures with favors to call in," said Bill Allison of the nonpartisan Center for Public Integrity in Washington, D.C., not referring to any particular appointment.

The next controversy dealt with another tape, this time video. In July 2001, Norcross and his attorney, Michael Critchley, met Anthony Zarrillo, a high-ranking official of the attorney general's office, and urged him to drop an investigation with implications for

Norcross. Unbeknownst to Norcross, the forty-five-minute meeting was captured via a hidden camera as well as on audiotape. "I'm not a thief. I'm not a crook. I can sleep at night," Norcross said. "The only thing I have to worry about is a prosecutor or investigator who has an evil agenda." He didn't define evil, and more than one observer noted the irony in the staunch Democrat quoting Republican Richard Nixon. Norcross also told prosecutor Zarrillo it was all a Machiavellian scheme—as we've seen, a favorite phrase of New Jersey politicians.

Gural characterized the meeting as Norcross using his political influence and contacts in an attempt to kill an investigation. In his conversation with Zarrillo, Norcross engages in name-dropping: "By the way, Jon Corzine is a very good friend of mine." At another point Norcross refers to the "McGreevey campaign, where I spend two days a week on a regular basis, running the campaign."

William Tambussi, lawyer for the Camden County Democrats, said Norcross was not at the meeting for himself but to ask for fairness for Louis Gallagher II, Democratic chairman in neighboring Burlington County. In the conversations secretly recorded by Gural, Gallagher is heard suggesting Gural receive "some monetary benefit," via contracts for his engineering firm, for firing Rosenberg as solicitor.

Judge John Sweeney wanted the video. But Guy Emmons, a supervising investigator in the Electronics Surveillance Unit of the Division of Criminal Justice, certified to the judge that "to the best of my knowledge the . . . conversation was not video recorded." Deputy Attorney General Lisa Sarnoff Gochman told Gural, "Any claim of the existence of videotape of this meeting is simply in error."[41]

Sweeney wasn't buying it. He told the attorney general's office to look again. The second time around, the state's chief law enforcement agency admitted, contrary to what it had been main-taining, the meeting was videotaped. Gural was right.

Where was the tape? Tossed into a recycling box where it just disappeared.

The Office of Government Integrity, a misnamed division of the attorney general's office, investigated the missing tape and pro-duced a thirty-nine-page report, which was kept from the public, supposedly because it contained confidential information.

Then the feds got interested, but to no avail. After the missing video saga, U.S. Attorney Christie announced that his office was looking into Mayor Gural's complaints. Several months later, Christie said he would not prosecute anyone in connection with the case. A blistering letter from Christie offered a seven-point critique of the state's handling of the case and included allegations of missed opportunities, faulty plea bargains, and a refusal to let federal officials into the case until the state wanted to prevent pub-lic release of the tapes.

"He was left with a case that was intentionally sandbagged," Gural said. "Chris Christie put in writing what I've been saying for five years. The AG's office is both corrupt and inept."[42]

While important cases slipped through the cracks, Attorney General Peter "See No Evil" Harvey, a nickname coauthor Ingle gave him, chose to put his office's resources into going after Block-buster for the late fees the video rental company charged.

In some states Harvey would have been summoned before the Senate Judiciary Committee to explain such incompetence. But no such call occurred. The chairman of the committee was Sen. John Adler, who—like Assembly Budget Chairman Greenwald, Senate Budget Chairman Bryant and Assembly Speaker Roberts—is a product of the Norcross machine and owes his political life to what is jokingly called La Cosa Norcross.

Whatever it's called, Mark Lohbauer maintains the machine

has a long memory and is unforgiving. He was a top-level planner at the Schools Construction Corporation, the state agency in charge of building schools in poor areas. Lohbauer said he lost his job when the Democrats took over the statehouse because he had exercised his right as a citizen to run against the Norcross machine eleven years earlier as a GOP candidate for county office.[43]

Jim Walsh of the *Courier-Post* reported Lohbauer was summoned to the office of Alfred T. McNeill, the agency's CEO, and told he was unemployed. "I like you. I want to keep you," Lohbauer remembered McNeill saying. "But they [Gov. McGreevey's office] told me George Norcross wants you gone—and I don't even know who he is."[44]

McNeill wouldn't talk to reporter Walsh, and McGreevey's spokesman, Micah Rasmussen, said the governor's office does not make personnel decisions at the Schools Construction Corporation. Balderdash! The whole outfit appeared to be a patronage pit that wasted more than $8 billion with little to show for it thanks to being laden down with political appointees whose main focus was filling the pockets of the politically connected.

The extent to which Norcross and his allies will go in pursuit of a goal is demonstrated in the multiphased drive to take over the Fourth District state senate seat, which is only partly in Camden County. The first step was getting the incumbent, Republican John Matheussen, named executive director of the bistate, patronage-rich Delaware River Port Authority (DRPA). The post paid $195,000 a year, way more than the senator's $49,000 annual salary, but more importantly a nice figure for filling the pot at the end of every Jersey pol's rainbow, the overly rich state retirement plan with health care for life. New Jersey's pension is based on the highest-paying three working years.

Matheussen became the first DRPA employee to be allowed to remain in New Jersey's pension system. Since the 1930s, employees of the DRPA, which gets its money from tolls paid to cross the Delaware River into Pennsylvania, have drawn their pensions from Pennsylvania. The difference the special arrangement made? As a state senator, Matheussen would have qualified for a pension of $12,000 a year. With the DRPA salary, he qualified for $60,000 after just three years.

Assemblyman George Geist, also a Republican, was appointed Matheussen's replacement in the senate. A move to get Geist out of the way and appointed to the Superior Court—Norcross's solution for troublemakers, remember—fell through when the Camden County Bar Association, apparently one of the few bodies in the county Norcross didn't control, failed to endorse him.[45]

So the Norcross crowd did it the hard way. Norcross and his machine raised $4.4 million to win the seat for Democrat Fred Madden, a former state police officer, by only sixty-three votes. They spent $4.4 million for a job that pays $49,000. Why? In addition to stroking ego, New Jersey has an unwritten, unofficial tradition so old nobody knows where it came from called "senatorial courtesy." Using it, any senator can block any appointment in his county for any reason, or no reason at all. They all know it's wrong, but no one wants to give it up. Since Norcross controls the senators from his area, it gives him enormous say in who gets judgeships and other important and high-paying jobs.

The DRPA wasn't Democrat Norcross's first choice for Matheussen. When McGreevey became governor, Norcross worked to get Matheussen a $137,000 job as state transportation commissioner. He was offered the post but rejected it. Next, his name was briefly floated as a candidate for—what else?—the state supreme court.

With Norcross, the political game is a family affair. His father, George Norcross Jr., who died in 1998, was president of the Southern New Jersey AFL-CIO Central Labor Council and was a Cooper

Hospital trustee. Coauthor Ingle noted, "I've met people who hate George but loved his dad." The father's union job is now held by Donald Norcross, George's brother. George III was a Cooper trustee who went on to be the board's chairman. He has done well by the hospital in helping it to get grants and to raise money—by selling tickets to events to people who hope to do business with the Camden institution. Another brother, Philip, works for a law firm that gets a good share of government business.

Thanks to the union connection, Democrats in South Jersey are far better now at turning out the vote on Election Day and packing the crowds at demonstrations and rallies. It looks good on TV. A reporter from the Gannett State Bureau in Trenton covered such a demonstration once and asked a participant what was going on. "I don't know anything about this," the big burly guy said. "I'm here because the union sent me."

Norcross was a college freshman dropout who started an insurance brokerage company in 1979 that sold a lot of policies to public agencies and towns, often the ones controlled by Democrats. In 1996, Commerce Bank purchased the company, and with the financial institution's backing it has grown continuously. Government deposits increased ninefold after Norcross joined the bank. From 1981 to 2003, Commerce's government funds went from 7 percent to 21 percent of deposits. The industry average is less than 5 percent. The bank also purchased an insurance company owned by Ocean County GOP Chairman Joseph Buckelew.

Norcross has been good for the bank, and the bank has been good to Norcross, paying him a salary second only to that of bank chairman and founder Vernon W. Hill II, a marketing genius who shook up the banking world with seven-day-a-week operation and consumer-oriented practices. The bank has used TV personality Kelly Ripa—Regis Philbin's sidekick on *Live with Regis and Kelly*—in its ads. Ripa's father, Joe, is an elected Camden County official who, like all of them, got there with the backing of the Norcross machine. Before that he worked with Donald Norcross in labor. Kelly Ripa also has done ads for Camden's Cooper Hospital. The machine is a close-knit family and takes care of its own.

Over the years several politicians have been named to Commerce's boards. They include Democrat John Lynch, former GOP governor Donald DiFrancesco, and Dale Florio, Republican boss in Somerset County, whose lobbying firm works for the bank.

The bank has been good to Norcross in other ways. In 2002, it approved a $32.5 million line of credit for Norcross, his brother Philip, Assemblyman Roberts, and others to buy a majority share in U.S. Vision, Inc. Roberts and Philip Norcross later sold their interests in the mall-based vision service.

Before selling his 15 percent interest, an irate Roberts defended his decision to introduce legislation allowing optometrists to perform corrective eye surgery in New Jersey. Questioned by Gannett reporters, he said his motive was more affordable eye care, not profit for U.S. Vision, which leased equipment to optometrists at its mall sites. He turned the bill's sponsorship over to another Democrat and said optometrists who were subcontractors at U.S. Vision locations had no intention of doing the pricey surgery.

Commerce Bank, along with its founder, Hill, and Norcross, came under increased federal scrutiny, culminating in Hill's resignation from the bank in June 2007, raising questions about the effect on Norcross's power. First, the bank shut down its political action committee, ending its generous donations to politicians. In the five years prior to the shutdown, the influential committee had given $1.6 million to New Jersey political campaigns.[46] Next, two Commerce officials in Philadelphia were nailed by the feds along with the city treasurer who was convicted of steering bond deals to the bank in exchange for loans and gifts.[47] But what preceded Hill's departure was regulators' concern about the bank's payments to companies whose partners included his wife and other relatives. His wife, Shirley, was paid $9.2 million in 2006 for her design and management work at the bank.[48] When Hill departed, the bank promised federal regulators that there would be no more Jersey style all-in-the family deals. In October 2007, Canada's TD Bank Financial Group said it would buy Commerce Bank for $8.5 billion and agreed to negotiate the sale of its insurance division to Norcross.

It often was speculated that Republican boss Glenn Paulsen of Burlington County had an agreement with Norcross that they wouldn't seriously challenge each other's candidates in their respective counties. Alan Guenther of the *Courier-Post* wrote that the GOP-controlled Burlington County Bridge Commission gave lucrative no-bid contracts to Commerce Insurance Services.[49] "And Phoenix Strategies, a consulting firm headed by Norcross' close ally, Dennis Culnan, received a $120,000 contract from the bridge commission to do marketing research. Culnan is frequently involved with campaigns supported by Norcross. Paulsen's firm, Capehart Scathard, has done well in Democratic Camden County." Data from Thompson Financial, a bond tracking firm, indicated that from 1999 through the first half of 2003, Paulsen's firm did $490 million in government bond issues, and 75 percent of it came from Camden County, the Burlington bridge agency, and the state. Paulsen denies there is a "nonaggression pact" between him and Norcross.

Norcross usually does not give interviews or talk to the media. One exception has been coauthor Ingle, who in print has been one of boss Norcross's biggest critics. But their personal relationship is not so negative. Ingle explains: "Over the years George has been helpful to me on background. He knows a lot. He's plugged in. He knows and respects I have a job to do. I detest the political machines of any stripe because they subvert representative democracy and make government cost more than it needs to. George didn't invent the Jersey political system; he's just good at playing it because it is lubricated by contributions. George is good at raising money. George works long days; he values teamwork and loyalty, although there can be a dark side to it. But, hell, I work long days and value teamwork and loyalty, too. That was first pointed out to me by George himself over dinner. 'We have a lot in common,' he said."

There also is a mob-boss-like generosity to Norcross, who arranged with the national gift firm Harry & David to send a monthly fruit basket to Ingle as a Christmas present. Gannett ethics rules prohibit accepting anything of value, and repeated efforts to stop the baskets were unsuccessful. Finally, Ingle's boss suggested he tell the company everything would be returned—and to drive the point home say it publicly in his column. Ingle did. Norcross was unhappy and called the columnist. When Mrs. Norcross went to the gym, he said, others there teased her about the column.

In sometime opposition to the Norcross gang is Union County's Sen. Ray Lesniak, who convinced McGreevey not to quit in time to hold a special election, as Lynch and Norcross had wanted. Lesniak said of the struggle with the duo, "It was an eye-opener to me and demonstrated that we (party bosses) have way too much power."[50]

That's right, he said "we." Lesniak, known for an oversized ego, confessed, "When you talk about the bosses, I'm one of them. I can't deny it." Union County is in the north just below Essex and Hudson counties.

Lesniak maintained he wanted McGreevey to stay on until November 15 to take care of personal affairs. But by siding with Senate President Codey, who without a special election could walk into the governor's office unchallenged, Lesniak managed to keep himself on top of the political totem. "The guy who's come out on top is Ray Lesniak," Elizabeth Mayor J. Christian Bollwage told reporter Kathleen Hopkins, then of the *Home News Tribune*.

Lesniak also managed to keep himself in the spotlight by being a kind of window on McGreevey's world as the former governor left public life and ran from the reporters he used to court night and day when he thought he had a political future. Lesniak and McGreevey had been pals for twenty-five years, and yet Lesniak says he didn't know McGreevey was gay. "I heard the same rumors as everyone and dismissed them as gossip." His role, Lesniak said, was political adviser. "I was the go-to guy whenever he got into trouble politically. It was either me or Sen. Lynch."

Republican Frank Lehr, a former Union County official, told reporter Hopkins, "If he (Lesniak) has somebody he wants to get a job, he gets it. . . . I don't think there's any question that he is the boss of Union County." Dina Matos McGreevey first encountered Lesniak when she was twenty-two and newly appointed to the planning board of Elizabeth, the Union County seat. "If you wanted to secure a state or government contract or run for office, he was the one whose blessing you'd have to get," she said in her autobiography.[51]

The *Record* of Bergen County, in its 1990 series "The Politics of Greed: How New Jersey Lawmakers Parlay Political Power into Personal Gain," devoted an entire day to Lesniak.[52]

"Lesniak, D-Union, chairman of the powerful Senate Labor, Industry and Professions Committee, has greatly expanded his law practice by taking on as clients the state's two largest banks, a second-mortgage company and insurers," the *Record* said. "Those businesses had vested interests in the legislation Lesniak was shepherding through his committee."

Research by the *Record* showed that in the five years after he assumed the powerful chairmanship, Lesniak's law firm grew from a three-person operation in a converted home to a twenty-five-lawyer firm in a modern stone and glass office building. "In 1987, while the Democrat pushed legislation that relaxed state regulation of second-mortgage companies, his firm handled scores of closings for The Money Store, a second-mortgage lender that was a major proponent of the legislation. And Midlantic Banks Inc. and First Fidelity Bancorporation, the state's two largest banks, became clients of Lesniak's law firm around the time in 1986 that he sponsored and pushed through the Senate two bills that those banks could have benefited from greatly."

Lesniak, responding to the *Record*, said the firm grew because it was good at what it did.

But hey, it's New Jersey, and Lesniak wasn't breaking any ethics rules because the state allowed lawmakers to push for legislation that benefited them professionally—as long as others in their profession benefited, too.

Lesniak claims his law firm has not done legal work "in his district" for twenty-five years. That didn't mean he passed up government work. The *Home News Tribune's* Hopkins wrote that a search of records from various local governments found that several lawyers in Lesniak's firm drew annual salaries from government entities outside Union County in 2003 ranging from $1,500 to $58,063. "Some of those lawyers submitted additional legal bills to the governments they worked for . . . ranging from $9,005 to $11,202," Hopkins said. "One attorney in the firm was not paid a salary for representing North Bergen last year but submitted bills for $215,687."

Lesniak's firm earned $4,466,494 from Woodbridge as its legal counsel while McGreevey was mayor, from 1992 to 2001. Soon after McGreevey left the governor's office, he joined Lesniak's law firm, whose clients included partners in a $1.3 billion, state-sponsored 5-million-square-foot sports and entertainment project called Xanadu in the Meadowlands of North Jersey. The Mills Corporation of Virginia and Mack-Cali Realty of Cranford, New Jersey, were chosen for the project by the McGreevey administration about a month before McGreevey left office. Former state employees are barred from doing business with the state for a year, but not governors specifically. Governor Codey asked his counsel to review the law to clarify the role of former governors, and that night McGreevey resigned from Lesniak's firm.

It was Lesniak who helped cement McGreevey's support in 2000 when Senator Torricelli briefly challenged McGreevey with his announcement of Democratic primary aspirations for governor. According to the McGreevey book, Lesniak gained key support from Newark Mayor and State Sen. Sharpe James with a brief, private talk.[53]

"Ray and I got down to business, pushing Sharpe every way we knew how," McGreevey wrote. "We tried policy, we tried loyalty, but none of it seemed to be working. Finally, Ray asked Sharpe to step outside for a walk, just the two of them. I don't know what went on out there, but when they returned to the table, Sharpe was ready to give me backing in the primary."

A few months later, Lesniak told McGreevey only that "I made Sharpe a commitment that he never called me on."

There are second and third tiers of New Jersey bosses, including a colorful has-been, former Senator Bill Gormley of Atlantic County, where GOP bosses are a tradition. McGreevey outlined in his book how Gormley played both political parties to his advantage. "He made an art of creating crises to secure whatever goal he had in mind, or to accrue a debt he could call in later. . . . It was just business."[54] Gormley resigned February 15, 2007, and his long reign of influence ended.

Other lesser bosses are Bergen Democratic Chairman Joe Ferriero, who teamed with Lynch and Norcross to bring Democratic control to that northern county across the Hudson River from

Manhattan; Essex County Democrat Stephen Adubato Sr., who is reported to have a picture of Machiavelli in his office; already mentioned Republican Dale Florio of Somerset County; and George Gilmore, the Ocean County GOP chief who operates behind the scenes.

In September 2008, Christie indicted the most prominent of the lesser party bosses, Ferriero, and the Bergen County Democratic Organization's former lawyer, Dennis Oury. The indictment accused the two of conspiring to defraud the borough of Bergenfield. According to the feds, the two quietly formed Governmental Grants Consulting, a company created to help Bergen County municipalities garner grant money. Bergenfield hired Governmental Grants Consulting without knowing that the borough's own lawyer, Oury, was involved in the company, the feds said. After Ferriero wrote a letter to the state on behalf of Bergenfield, the borough received $1.4 million in state and federal grant money, and Ferriero's company got a $128,625 fee. Ferriero's lawyer, Joseph Hayden Jr., told the Associated Press that the feds turned a valuable public service into a criminal charge.

4

All Aboard the Gravy Train

Sometimes people joke that New Jersey's sky-high taxes are almost justified by pointing to the legislature—a collection of misfits, self-serving loons, and boss-created puppets—and asking, "Where else could you have so much entertainment in one place?"

Lawmakers have managed to create a kind of paradise on earth for themselves where part-time work delivers big perks while they're on the payroll and yields even bigger payouts when they retire, since taxpayers foot the bill for overly generous pensions and health care for life for them and their dependents.

People of conscience, morals, and ethics would feel a tinge of embarrassment about this, but the Jersey pols have long since moved past that. They created an oligarchy (rule by the few) that morphed into a kleptocracy—a corrupt government in which funds are used to sustain private wealth and keep officials in power. The masses are taken advantage of to make life easier for those relative few who have the gall to actually call themselves "public servants."

Thanks to carefully drawn districts, there isn't much competition for offices. Voters, too, are a part of the problem, because they apparently think their guy is the good one but everyone else's is a crook.

Senator Sharpe James spent most of his working life on the public payroll. It's arguable whether his years as mayor of Newark (1986–2006) or as a member of the state senate (1999–2008) did much good for the public, but those years have been good for James. While he held both posts, state and city salaries totaled about $250,000 a year, which allowed him to purchase numerous real estate holdings and to tool around in a Rolls-Royce on land and a fifty-four-foot yacht at sea. The latter, purchased in 2004 for $360,000, turned out to be an oceangoing lemon. In a lawsuit filed to get his money back, he claimed that when he took it out for its maiden voyage in 2005, the port engine overheated and burst into flames somewhere in the vicinity of the Statue of Liberty. James, whose city is known for crime and poverty, complained he had lost the whole yachting season.

His father died before he was born, and his mother was a short-order cook who came to Newark from Florida and emphasized the value of owning property. She made an impression. In November 2004, a four-story building was sold for $2.6 million to a corporation whose sole officer was James, who was negotiating plans to invest $210 million of Newark's money to build a hockey arena just five blocks away.

"It was far from Mr. James' only land acquisition," David Kocieniewski wrote in 2006 for *the New York Times*.[1] "During the past 15 years, Mr. James, his wife and their three children have bought and sold 18 properties in Newark, on the Jersey Shore and in South Carolina, selling them for $1.4 million more than the purchase price, records show."

Reporter Kocieniewski found that the acquisitions followed a pattern: Many were financed by Crown Bank, whose president has done extensive business with the city, and several properties were in areas where the James administration was investing public redevelopment money. "And on at least three occasions, Mr. James used campaign funds to rent buildings he owned."

In his thirty-six years on Newark's council and in the mayor's office, the James administration was investigated numerous times, but he wasn't indicted until July 2007. Generally, when James (who is African American) is challenged by media or others in public office, his response is racial in nature, as if anyone questioning him must be a racist. He is a blowhard and a bully and unashamedly uses the race card when it benefits him. And he got by with it until there was a serious challenge to his tenure in the form of Cory Booker, a one-term councilman who earned bachelor and master's degrees from Stanford University, a Yale University law degree, and was a Rhodes Scholar at Oxford, England. He's a young man who seems to care a great deal more about helping Newark than helping himself. Most think his future is bright although the execution-style murders of three Newark college students have put his city and the New Jersey court system under scrutiny.

James was known for outrageous behavior. His housing authority was ordered to return $6.9 million in federal money intended for police and health services but instead used for James's pet project, the arena wags call "the Pork Palace." He also bought fancy garbage trucks with homeland security funds.

But with only months left in his city tenure, he tried a stunt that was overboard even by his standards. James made a play to get $80 million in aid from the Port Authority of New York and New Jersey, which would be placed with two nonprofit groups that would be controlled by James—not in his capacity as Newark mayor, a term that was ending, but by James personally. The James plan quickly passed in Newark without a public hearing. Then James, who was vice chairman of the state senate budget committee, and eight of the nine Newark councilmen came to Trenton for what he thought would be a closed-door private session with Gov. Jon Corzine, who had been in office less than four months. James probably thought he and his council sidekicks would show Corzine who really runs the state.

Instead, that session turned out to be an indicator of how smart the Corzine people can be, on occasion. The Gannett State Bureau and other Trenton-based media were notified at the last minute that a public meeting was taking place in the governor's office, which it technically was since a majority of Newark's council was there and doing business. When the press showed up en masse, James complained mightily, apparently realizing he had been outsmarted. Department of Community Affairs Commissioner Susan Bass Levin, also in the meeting, listened politely, then responded that Corzine promised a transparent administration.

After the meeting, James got back on his high horse. "There are going to be times when municipalities and DCA meet and then should come out and hold a joint press conference." Levin repeated that Corzine wanted open discussion of policy issues.

Having the press there was but the first sign the times might be changing. Corzine ordered a halt to James's piggish plan for the $80 million. That brought the predictable tossing in of the race card. Councilman Ras Baraka said, "You're looking at it from a racially and economically privileged position. I don't have that privilege. I live in Newark where kids are getting shot in the streets and parents are coming to me saying, 'My child needs a job.'"

Council President Donald Bradley made a veiled threat of civil disobedience if Corzine didn't give in. "I was part of the civil rights movement," he said. The Rev. Reginald Jackson, head of the Black Ministers Council and a leader in the fight against real racism, was appalled by such expressions. He told columnist Tom Moran of the

Star-Ledger, who took them all to task, "Whenever something comes up now, the easy way out is to blame it on racism."[2]

After James left the mayor's office July 1, 2006, he ran up against another man determined to change the way Jersey pols do business—U.S. Attorney Chris Christie, who sent the FBI out armed with subpoenas for James's travel records. This came after the *Star-Ledger* reported city taxpayers paid thousands of dollars for James to go to exotic locations, including a trip to Brazil during his final week in office. The Newark paper disclosed James accumulated charges of more than $200,000 on two credit cards—one assigned to the city, the other assigned to the police department—over fifty-four months, with about $125,000 of that related to travel. During his final three months in office, when he knew his time as mayor was ending, he spent almost $50,000 on travel and entertainment, including jaunts to Puerto Rico, Martha's Vineyard, Detroit, and Brazil.[3]

Furthermore, the paper's Ian T. Shearn said, unlike other city employees, his travel requests didn't have to be preapproved. He came and went as he pleased, and often his expenses were reimbursed without an explanatory voucher.

James defended himself with—what else?—race, saying the 2006 trip he took to Rio was a follow-up to a 2004 trip during which he lectured on "affirmative action, sanitation, housing and poor people." Looking at downtrodden Newark, why would anyone think James has solutions to those problems? Columnist Mike Kelly of the *Record* responded, "This is classic James-speak. When he meets an ethical pothole, he digs a moral trench."[4] James said he had to take two bodyguards because "Brazil is a hot spot for crime."

Brazilian officials told reporters James called them asking if he could come down for a one-hour meeting. That sixty-minute session meant five days in luxury hotels with meals at high-priced upscale restaurants, a trip that cost more than $6,500, charged to the police credit card. The *Star-Ledger* reported that the federal probe expanded to include a "travel companion" for the married James.[5]

While taxpayers finally got rid of James as mayor, they certainly didn't get him off their backs.[6] He gets an annual city pension of $124,654. He is one of only two public officials in a special pension system set up by Newark. In 1981, then-Assemblyman Dick Codey sponsored a law that allowed cities with populations of more than 400,000 to set up a separate account for elected officials. That population figure applied only to Newark, where the population today is about 280,000. Nonelected employees had their pensions capped at $12,000. But elected officials receive two-thirds of their salary when they retire. The *Star-Ledger* reported that the city council approved a measure giving James $25,000 extra to be used for annual expenses. That amount was added to his salary, so his pension is based not on $161,981 in salary but on $186,981, with the expenses added in. That $25,000 boosted his pension by $18,562 a year.

James went on to head the Urban Issues Institute at Essex County College, which comes with an annual paycheck of $150,000—all while earning $49,000 a year as a senate member. As if that weren't enough, James accumulated $988,000 in the county college's alternative benefits plan because he worked there before he was mayor and—this is Jersey, remember—officially was placed on leave of absence for twenty years while the investment in the benefits plan grew. James lasted only a year after returning to the post at Essex County College. With the feds investigating him, the college said he would have been a "distraction" had he stayed. But retirement from the college post meant James could begin tapping into the fat pension that grew to nearly a million dollars while he was on leave.[7]

Newark, the state's biggest city, which sits in the shadows of

Manhattan's skyscrapers, has a third of its citizens below the poverty line and depends on taxpayers elsewhere in New Jersey for its school system and other basic services. They must be so proud when their globetrotting former mayor drives by in his Rolls en route to the marina.

On Thursday July 12, 2007, one day before Friday the 13th, things changed for James. He found himself in federal court wearing a navy suit, handcuffs, and leg shackles. The charge was fraud. The accusation: spending the city's money on himself. U.S. Attorney Christie said that while James was supposed to be protecting Newark's residents, "All he protected was his own wallet."

James was charged with making hundreds of credit card charges between 2001 and 2006 for luxury travel, dining and sporting events. Jonathan Tamari reported for Gannett: "He allegedly paid for luxury hotel suites, rented a Jaguar convertible and booked himself a cruise. The indictment alleges James crafted bogus reasons to justify travel expenses for himself and his companions, such as going to a beachfront Dominican resort to see whether the tropical gardens there should be replicated near Penn Station." Tamika Riley, described by the feds as a companion of James, was charged with fraud and tax evasion. James was accused of helping Riley buy nine city parcels for $46,000. The parcels were then sold for $665,000. After deliberating for six days, a jury convicted James and Riley on all charges related to the land scheme. After that significant conviction, the U.S. attorney decided to dismiss the charges filed against James for using city credit cards for travel and lavish personal expenses. Federal Judge William Martini sentenced James to twenty-seven months in prison and Riley to fifteen months. Christie wasn't happy with what he considered a light sentence and vowed to appeal. But Martini—much to prosecutors' dismay—questioned their talk of a history of corruption.

At a time when James was billing the city for meals and even movie tickets, newly appointed Attorney General Anne Milgram noted 36 percent of Newark's residents were living in poverty.[8]

If James has any competition as a poster child for using public office for personal gain, it is Wayne Bryant, who lives at the other end of the state, in Camden County just across the Delaware River from Philadelphia. Bryant served in the assembly, then moved on to the senate, where he became chair of the budget committee. The *Courier-Post*, especially investigative reporter Alan Guenther, has chronicled Bryant's feasts at the public trough.[9] In a two-year period from 2003 to 2005, Bryant collected $167,000 annually from taxpayer-supported positions. "Bryant, his wife, his son, two brothers and a sister-in-law earned a total of $685,000 in annual salaries while holding 10 jobs financed by the public," Guenther wrote.

That doesn't include the millions in fees Bryant and his law firm have been paid by public agencies. As a result of a federal audit, in 1996 the Camden Housing Authority was asked to repay $1.58 million in "unsubstantiated costs" to the federal government, including $733,391 in legal fees to Bryant's firm. In an April 2005 interview, Assemblywoman Nilsa Cruz-Perez of Camden said the Bryant law firm's $270,000 contract to represent Camden in eminent domain matters against residents was a conflict of interest for Bryant, whose district includes the city. Bryant later said Cruz-Perez, who like Bryant was backed by the Boss George Norcross machine, told him that the comments were misinterpreted.[10]

Camden not only is one of the poorest cities in America, it is one of the most dangerous. South Jersey's machine-dominated lawmakers go to Trenton and come up with schemes to pump more money in, supposedly to change Camden's misery. Camden never gets any better, but the politicians and their cronies always make out well. Bryant himself authored legislation that designated $175 million to rebuild the once prosperous town, which was home to poet Walt Whitman and the site where RCA scientists invented television. Senator Martha Bark, a Republican from neighboring Burlington County, said she agreed to cosponsor the bill because she believed Bryant to be "a man of courage" whose word could be trusted. Bark herself came under scrutiny by an ethics panel and the state attorney general for public jobs she held without a lot to show for what she did for the money.[11]

(Bark is a perfect example of how female politicians in New Jersey keep up with their male counterparts. She not only threw her support to Bryant on the Camden bill but appeared to get rewarded for another vote with the Democrats. One day after Bark gave Democrats the deciding vote they needed on a 2007 tax relief plan, a legislative ethics panel, controlled by the Democrats, announced the dismissal of a complaint alleging she was a no-show at her jobs with the Burlington County Bridge Commission and the Burlington County Institute of Technology. The complaint was filed by the chairman of the Burlington County Democrats, but ethics panel members voted by mail to clear Bark because the two-year statute of limitations had run its course while the panel members pulled a no-show themselves. Bark, who had opposed the Democratic tax plan, said her change of mind had nothing to do with the dismissal of her ethics complaint. "I wouldn't even think of doing that," she told Gannett's Gregory J. Volpe.[12] She decided not to seek reelection that year. The county's GOP leadership passed over Assemblyman Fran Bodine as its nominee to succeed Bark, in part saying he objected to a lobbyist gift ban because it would cut out golf green fees paid by lobbyists. So Bodine, a Republican for thirty years, quickly transformed into a Democrat and announced his intention to run to succeed Bark.)

The final version of the legislation to rebuild Camden included $1 million for CAMcare, which provides health services for poor people in Camden. Bryant's brother Mark is president of the not-for-profit agency, which depends on government financing. Mark Bryant gets paid more than $165,000 a year by CAMcare, and both he and his brother the senator declined to discuss how money for CAMcare got into the legislation.

Another Bryant brother, Isaac, is an assistant education commissioner for the state. Bryant's sister-in-law works for Camden County. Another brother is the mayor of Lawnside.

Reporter Guenther found that of the $175 million in aid, about $20 million was deposited in area banks, including three that got deposits because they had Camden branches. Another institution, Equity Bank, also got $5 million even though none of its eighteen branches were in Camden. Guenther noted that Senator Bryant was a paid member of Equity's board of directors.

One year just before New Jersey's budget was finalized, Bryant helped obtain a $1 million grant for New Jersey Network, the state's public TV operation. That money was in addition to what NJN normally gets and followed by six months the hiring of Bryant's son, since deceased, as a TV producer who was paid $36,000 annually.

Adding to Bryant's own wallet, the Camden Redevelopment Agency approved a contract that could provide up to $270,000 in fees to Bryant's law firm. That same agreement could award up to an additional $108,000 to two other firms, including Parker McCay, which employs Philip Norcross, brother of political boss George Norcross. Philip Norcross served as bond counsel for Camden and the redevelopment agency. Arijit De, executive director of the redevelopment agency, said the agency pays no attention to political connections but seeks to employ professionals with knowledge of Camden.

While serving in the legislature for more than two decades, Bryant also did legal work for the Gloucester County Board of Social Services, Atlantic City, Cherry Hill, and Lawnside. But somehow he still found time to serve in two positions given him by state universities, one at Rutgers–Camden and the other at the University of Medicine and Dentistry based in Newark.

Bryant was paid $30,000 a year to lecture at Rutgers-Camden, but he gave only two of twenty lectures he was supposed to in 2005. The school's provost, Roger Dennis, was subpoenaed to tell authorities what he knew. Dennis said the job was about bringing diversity to the campus. Dennis also nominated Bryant for the Rutgers Hall of Distinguished Alumni. Arthur Z. Kamin, former Rutgers board of trustees chairman, said Bryant should be removed from the hall because he didn't deserve it in the first place.[13]

But it was the UMDNJ post that proved to be one job too many. As part of U.S. Attorney Christie's look at the UMDNJ's corrupt operation, detailed in chapter 1, a federal monitor found that the $38,220-a-year job the school gave Bryant did not exist before Bryant had it, In addition, during the three years Bryant was on the payroll, 2003–2006, state funding for the university's School of Osteopathic Medicine increased to $12.8 million, up from a total of $8.4 million for the three years prior to Bryant's tenure. Bryant, as chairman of the senate's budget committee, was in a position to influence his employer's funding.

It wasn't clear what, if anything, Bryant did for the pay except to lobby for more money for the school. Wags said he actually was paid to lobby himself as chairman of the budget committee. People interviewed by the monitor said he sometimes showed up once a week and read newspapers. When Christie launched his investigation, Bryant tendered his resignation from UMDNJ.

"Senator Bryant is no longer employed by the university," Anna Farneski, the school's spokeswoman, said. "The people who hired him are no longer employed by the university. The kinds of actions described in the monitor's report would not be tolerated now, and will not be tolerated in the future." That wasn't entirely true. R. Michael Gallagher, dean of the osteopathic school, was the one who told his staff to create a position for Bryant, according to the monitor's report. Gallagher resigned his post as dean, but six months later he was being paid $128,695 a year as a clinical professor.

Corzine suggested Bryant step down as chairman of the budget committee, a job he had held since January 2002, but senate Democrats closed ranks behind their colleague, with Senate President Codey saying he wanted the process to go forward with Bryant keeping his position. Media referred to it as a circling of the wagons to protect "their homey." Codey's reputation was morphing from one of the good guys to just another longtime pol protecting the status quo.

Despite backing from his Democratic buddies, Bryant lost the Gloucester County Board of Social Services job as of January 2007, and U. S. Attorney Christie subpoenaed records in Cherry Hill, where Bryant's law firm did city work.

Over in the assembly, there was support from Lou "the Empty Suit" Greenwald, a fellow Norcross machine pol. In his defense of Bryant, Greenwald uttered the kind of statement that has made him a statehouse joke: "In meetings I've had with him, Wayne has been as critical of UMDNJ and some of the abuses there as anyone else."

The monitor's report also said Bryant pressured UMDNJ to pay $20,000 to sponsor a designated driver program at the Tweeter Center, an entertainment venue in Camden where Jodi Nash, wife of Camden County elected official Jeffrey Nash, worked on marketing. Jeffrey Nash, a thin-skinned whiner whose lackluster political career is yet another creation of the Boss Norcross machine, also serves as vice chairman of the bistate Delaware River Port Authority, where Bryant's wife, Cheryl Spicer, was hired for a $153,000-a-year management position, a job that had been eliminated previously as unnecessary.

Bryant brought home the bacon to his district, so he tended to sail through elections. But he raised the ire of his Lawnside neighbors, who noticed that as Bryant's law firm was evicting opponents of a redevelopment project, the senator was building an elegant home on land he purchased from Ernest Edwards, who wanted Lawnside to award him a contract to build apartments and condominiums at the redevelopment site. In addition to being a resident of Lawnside, where his brother Mark was mayor, Bryant was borough attorney, and his son, until his death, was on the town's planning board. The senator was in a position to help Edwards, who spent six years in prison for stealing public money. Reporter Guenther checked the cost of the land for Bryant's new home and raised questions about whether the price was too cheap.[14]

But questions about Bryant were nothing new. For more than a decade, he had been a controversial figure. In 1992, Bryant, an African American, got a lot of attention for a segment on CBS's *60 Minutes* during which he said that government should stop rewarding women for having babies if those women couldn't support themselves. Bryant has a problem with traditional welfare but sees no problem with political welfare—lawmakers using their office to feather their nests or build their nests and those of their allies and families.

Bryant also was investigated that year as part of a probe by Attorney General Robert Del Tufo into state office leases for prominent Democratic landlords. All Bryant got was a reprimand by the legislative ethics committee, known for protecting rather than punishing the state's lawmakers. A source inside the attorney general's office told coauthor McClure, who broke the story on Bryant's sweetheart lease, that from the start the attorney general had no intention of bringing indictments in the case.[15]

Despite a legislative ethics code prohibiting a lawmaker from leasing space to the state, Bryant's law firm landed a lease worth

$2.6 million over five years, with Bryant entitled to 16.6 percent of the profits. Bryant said everything was on the up-and-up because a month earlier he had put the Cherry Hill office building into a trust fund—a fund whose profits went right into a Bryant bank account. At a time when office space was going empty and offices in Cherry Hill were leasing for $12 to $18 a foot, the state lease was for $18.25 a foot.[16]

"To fill Bryant's new four-story building, about 80 human services workers will be transferred from two office buildings 25 minutes away in Hammonton—where the state pays $10 to $15 a square foot for office space," McClure wrote for the *Trentonian*. "Hammonton workers say Bryant's building not only will be more expensive but will be farther from the clients and institutions they serve in an eight-county area stretching from Ocean County to Cape May and Camden counties."

But it wasn't until fourteen years later that Bryant began to feel the heat for his behavior. On September 25, 2006, Bryant notified Codey by letter, "After thoughtful discussion with you during the week, I request that I temporarily step down from the Budget and Appropriations process and that an interim chairperson be appointed." It was signed "Yours in Humanity."

Next in line to head the committee was Sharpe James, but since he, too, was under investigation by federal and state authorities, the post went to Sen. Bernard F. Kenny Jr., the senate majority leader.

In the wake of the federal probe, Bryant had already lost his two university jobs and the county social services contract, but that didn't stop him from telling the state he was ready to start collecting pensions for those posts in 2007, an amount that, counting his senate service, could exceed $82,000 a year. Then in early 2007 came the announcement that Bryant would not seek reelection to the senate and was even leaving his law firm, which had garnered

$270,000 in legal contracts from the state takeover of Camden. Bryant provided U.S. Attorney Christie with what he needed for an indictment: the job at UMDNJ and an application for a pension for his government-funded jobs.

Christie charged Bryant with trading the job at UMDNJ for his aid in getting state money for the university—and with patching together public no-show jobs to boost his state pension. The indictment said Bryant did little or no meaningful work at UMDNJ, Rutgers University, and the Gloucester County job, but the three jobs tripled his state pension. When the indictment was announced, Christie said those who would label Bryant a good lawmaker had become numb to the corruption that was business as usual in New Jersey.

"Today one of New Jersey's most powerful politicians is now charged with having put his personal financial greed ahead of the good of the people of the state of New Jersey," he said. ". . . All to feed his own insatiable desire for more public money to put in his own pocket."[17]

In June 2008, a federal judge denied a motion to dismiss the Bryant indictment, keeping the UMDNJ allegations that Bryant traded an official act for a benefit, but striking the charge that his job at Rutgers involved little or no work, Newhouse News Service reported. The judge said there was no standard by which to judge the work.

Christie and the FBI speared another big fish in early 2008 when retired state senator Joe Coniglio was indicted on extortion charges. Much like Bryant, Coniglio, a plumber, was charged with trading a consulting contract with the Hackensack University Medical Center for using his influence as a senator to get funding for the hospital.

James and Bryant are senators of the Democratic stripe, but the practice of using the public trust to enrich yourself in New Jersey knows no party.

John Bennett III is a Republican who was serving in the senate at the same time he was full-time Marlboro Township attorney. During the period from 1992 to 2002, Bennett individually was paid $1.5 million in salary from eight government entities, and his law firms billed $5.2 million more.[18] In Marlboro alone he was paid $116,754 a year as a full-time township employee, yet his firm billed Marlboro $160 an hour for other legal work. His contract with Marlboro allowed him to bill for special projects.[19] Moreover, Bennett was attorney for three other government entities—the borough of Little Silver, Hopewell Township, and the Keansburg Board of Education. In 2002, according to the *Asbury Park Press*, Bennett personally drew government-related paychecks totaling $220,359. Over a ten-year period his take from public jobs was enough to entitle Bennett to a state pension of more than $100,000 a year at age sixty.

Stringing together many publicly financed jobs to hike your pension is called tacking. In 1998, the State Commission of Investigation criticized the practice: "This tacking, which the law permits, can result in huge public pensions for services that were actually performed in the course of private professional practice."[20] But the practice continued.

Bennett and Marlboro Mayor Matthew Scannapieco formed a mutual benefit society of two. Scannapieco was sworn in as mayor in 1992; he then nominated Bennett for township attorney. Bennett returned the favor by recommending Scannapieco to Gov. Christie Whitman for a commissioner's job on the state Victims of Crime Compensation Board, an agency that is supposed to help people who have hardships because they're crime victims. In any other state that might be a volunteer post or at least a low-paid one, but in Jersey it paid $107,000 a year until the fiscal '08 budget made the board voluntary.[21] While in that job, Scannapieco pleaded guilty to tax evasion and accepting $245,000 in bribes while mayor.[22] (Need we remind you that we're not making any of this up?)

Bennett not only helped himself but used his political influence to help family members. His wife, Margaret, worked as a health care consultant for the state. His mother and his mother-in-law were on his legislative payroll.[23]

For a brief time, Bennett was elevated to governor. Until New Jersey elects a lieutenant governor in 2009, when the governor is out of state, resigns, or is unable to do the job, the president of the senate is acting governor. The senate president is elected by the body's members, so the dominant party decides who gets the post.

When Governor Whitman left early to join the Bush administration, Senate President Donald DiFrancesco became governor. But being governor was based on his being senate president, and his term in the senate ended a week short of when McGreevey came to power. For that week, the new senate president would have to serve as governor. The problem was, there were two. A twenty-twenty split in the Senate between the GOP and Democrats meant each party elected its own senate president.

For seven days, Codey and Bennett took turns being governor in three-and-a-half-day stints. Both tried to see how many social events they could have at the governor's mansion during their reign. Each printed stationery with his name on it and used personalized ceremonial pens to sign bills into law. It was one of those only-in-New-Jersey moments the rest of the country loves to read about.

During the final hours of Bennett's "term," he issued a pardon to an old friend, business associate, and former campaign contributor, Hugh G. Gallagher, who was convicted of carrying a concealed weapon, bookmaking, and possession of stolen goods in the early 1960s.[24] More egregious, Bennett signed into law a bill that would provide $15 million in state money to buy 750 unspoiled acres of a Superfund site in Dover. That same day Bennett signed a contract with Dover to act as the town's bond counsel, a deal that would be worth thousands of dollars.[25]

Bennett declined comment, but political scientist David Rebovich of Rider University told the *Asbury Park Press* it looked like Bennett "used this very small window as governor to reap huge benefits. It looks very bad, especially in this particular situation."

When McGreevey took over as governor, he blocked use of the $15 million and set a priority for the 2003 midterm election of helping Democrats get a majority in the state senate. They picked up two seats. One came because Ellen Karcher defeated Bennett, who was weakened by the *Asbury Park Press*'s investigative reports. Codey was again elected senate president, but this time he had it all to himself.

Sometimes the legislative gravy train is a milk run, a short ride. Such was the case for Evelyn Williams. Wally Edge, pen name for a columnist on the Web site PoliticsNJ.com, told her story, which was brief, like her tenure.[26]

The online columnist noted that by skipping a legislative session, she missed half of the sessions during her shortened tenure. "She sponsored no legislation, used her only speech on the assembly floor to thank a former legislator removed from office following a criminal conviction, and was arrested for shoplifting just seven days after taking office."

Two days later, Williams was fired from her Essex County Corrections job after those in charge learned she was collecting state retirement checks while working.

Wally Edge calculated Williams earned about $4,083, before tax deductions, for her day in the legislature, $4,023 more than police said she tried to save by putting a cheaper price tag on a sheet and comforter at Valley Fair.

Essex County Democrats had selected Williams to replace Assemblyman Donald Tucker, who died. But she resigned from the post after she was fired from her county job.[27]

Sometimes the legislative gravy train helps a sweetheart. "Only days after veteran Burlington County Assemblywoman Barbara Ka-lik lost her bid for re-election on Nov. 5, she gave all the money she had left for running her legislative office—$10,681—to the man she plans to marry," McClure wrote for the *Trentonian.*[28]

With no rules for the annual $70,000 dole Kalik received to run her district assembly office, the night she lost she called the two women who worked for her and told them they no longer had jobs. The check for Alexander "Bud" Slakie, who proposed to Kalik on the floor of the assembly one month and was put on her payroll the next, was the last of payments totaling $37,000. Kalik said she hired him because he was "probably the best person in the district for the job." In Trenton, you get rewarded for such shenanigans. Florio ap-pointed Kalik to a post on the state parole board.

Sometimes the legislative gravy train delivers real gravy. Thanks to a relationship between then-Senate President John Russo and a restaurateur, members of the legislature didn't have to go out to dine like kings on the taxpayers. Coauthor McClure, covering the statehouse during the Florio era, wanted to know why the hallway of the legislative annex smelled fishy on session days. Her nose led her to a story about how the state's taxpayers shelled out $124,000 over a three-year period to purchase three hundred lunches each day the legislature was in session to feed eighty members of the assem-bly and forty members of the senate. What about the additional 180 meals? A spokesman for the assembly's majority office said it was for "constituency groups," which basically meant lobbyists.[29]

McClure found that the primary beneficiary of the fine dining was the financially troubled Top o' the Mast restaurant in Ocean County. Senator Russo helped not only owner Joseph "Ben" Nitti but also friend and former senator William Hiering Sr., whose fam-ily was the restaurant's landlord. Russo and Hiering were on the board of a bank that loaned Nitti and his business more than $1 million that had not been repaid.

The restaurant was fifty-seven miles from Trenton. At first the food was trucked to just outside the capital and reheated at a local restaurant. Later, insulated trucks brought the eats directly from Ocean County. When the deal started in 1986, each catered lunchtime cost $585 for the senate and $1,665 for the assembly.

Not only did Russo arrange for legislators and lobbyists to eat well on the taxpayers, but for a ten-month period overburdened Jersey taxpayers forked over $1,085 per month to lease two luxury cars for the senator.[30] He got a new car but kept the older one. Both came from an Ocean County dealership owned by a political contributor, as did three other luxury Lincoln Town Cars used by Democratic assembly leaders: Speaker Joe Doria, Speaker Pro Tem Willie Brown, and Majority Leader Wayne Bryant. Bryant ordered his in red. When McClure wanted to know why, he fled into the legislature's men's room only to emerge and tell her "not today" when it came to questions about his flamboyant style at taxpayer's expense.

While the assembly leaders rode around in luxury on the taxpayers, Florio was asking for sacrifices. But not from the assembly, which helped itself to a 58 percent budget increase, even as it raised taxes and cut funds to state agencies.[31] Legislators created a stash of cash by routinely budgeting more money than they needed then carrying over the predictable surplus in a budgetary sleight-of-hand. The result: from 1980 to 1989, the Legislature's private kitty grew from $385,397 to $4.8 million. They used part of it to give themselves $10,000 pay hikes.[32]

Some of the slush fund went to pay for $528,000 in junkets to such far-flung spots as the Virgin Islands, Hawaii, Alaska, and Reno, the *Trentonian* reported.[33]

One lawmaker explained to McClure that the taxpayer-funded trips were "mostly junkets. Most of them didn't attend most of the meetings. They lay by the pool. They go sightseeing. They eat. They do what you do on vacation."

Russo went to national conferences for lieutenant governors—even though New Jersey had none. He said that was because as senate president he filled in for the governor. Asked how the trips helped him do that, he said, "It's hard to put your finger on." But when asked whether the trips should continue, he said, "Absolutely."

Under Speaker Doria, assembly members were issued gold badges and leather carrying cases.[34] The gold badges—crafted by a friend of Doria—were the final straw. They became a symbol of what New Jersey residents saw as a government at the hog's trough. When Jim Gearhart talked about it on his 101.5 FM morning show, stories were accompanied by pig sounds.

Doria repaid the money to the state for the badges. He called it a "misunderstanding."

But there is no misunderstanding when it comes to taxes in New Jersey. Taxpayers still pay through the nose while arrogant lawmakers ride the gravy train of high pensions and dual salaries.

5

"See No Evil" Law Enforcement
and Court Jesters

The cornerstone of any democracy is its police and court system, pledged to serve and protect all citizens and to dispense justice evenhandedly. If you've read this far, you might suspect we do things a little different in Jersey, and you'd be right.

Democrat Gov. Jim McGreevey's first attorney general was a Republican, David Samson, a man of impressive credentials. Samson's chief assistant and head of the Criminal Justice Section was Peter C. Harvey, whose past work as an assistant U.S. attorney, a special assistant state attorney general, and a legal analyst for a New York TV program was less impressive. Harvey was born in New York but grew up in Tuskegee, Alabama. About Harvey, Ingle was told by a long-trusted source, "The deal is Samson is in for one year, then he leaves and Harvey will look like he has enough experience for the job. Watch this one."

The son of a Baptist minister, Harvey speaks with a lilt and cadence reminiscent of sermons in the rural Deep South tradition.

Just as Ingle's source predicted, Samson left after about a year and Harvey moved up to acting attorney general. During his confirmation hearing Harvey pledged to be a corruption watchdog: "Stay tuned. Watch the record we amass."[1] Unfortunately for him, we had been watching Harvey closely for some time. He was a disaster and added to the negative image of McGreevey's administration.

The attorney general is the top law enforcement person in New Jersey, with a staff, at that time, of about 813 lawyers and 803 investigators and a budget of $929 million. The AG also oversees the state police. It's a constitutional office, meaning once the AG is confirmed by the senate, it takes resignation or impeachment to get him out.

Harvey's law enforcement calls were controversial from the start. As first assistant attorney general, Harvey issued an order forbidding anyone in the state police outside the control of State Police Sgt. Matthew Wilson from putting information from an investigation of the Newark Police Department in writing.[2] That's a tad odd given how much paperwork a police investigation generates—it's the bane of cops everywhere.

To run the New Jersey State Police—a nationally respected, well-disciplined paramilitary outfit organized in 1921 by H. Norman Schwarzkopf, father of the famed general "Stormin' Norman" from the First Gulf War—McGreevey chose Joseph Santiago, a former Newark police officer. Santiago was the first Hispanic in the job, but he resigned his state police superintendency after seven months, following a number of embarrassing incidents, including reports about his prior personal bankruptcy and a disorderly conduct conviction.

Wendy Ruderman, reporting for the *Record*, said Santiago raised thousands of dollars from businesses and community leaders through an unlicensed foundation run out of a Newark gas station.[3] She continued: "It is not the first time Santiago has run an unlicensed operation. Santiago admitted to running an 'off-the-books' security firm in the late 1980s that failed to pay state and federal taxes. He filed for bankruptcy protection in 1994 because he couldn't pay the more than $30,000 in taxes he owed the IRS. He eventually paid his state taxes through a 1996 amnesty program."

State police officers said Harvey literally refused to accept damaging reports on Santiago or take them to the senate judiciary committee for his confirmation hearing. Retired State Police Maj. Frank Simonetta, a former commander of the Investigations Section, told coauthor McClure he tried to hand the Santiago reports to Samson and Harvey.[4] "When I told them what I had, they didn't want to see the reports. The attorney general turned to Harvey and said, 'Pete, you handle it.' And he (Samson) walked out of the room. And Mr. Harvey—it was like a hot brick in his hands—did not want to see it, would not even look at it."

An ongoing lawsuit by three state troopers alleges that Harvey failed to heed a trooper's request to share with the senate judiciary committee allegations in those reports about Santiago, who was their boss, including charges that Santiago was friendly with mob figures who loaned him money. The troopers' suit also alleges Harvey wanted an investigator who received the allegations about Santiago to delete a written suggestion that they be shared with the Judiciary Committee.[5]

"When you think of the implications of this, that the head of the State Police was allegedly associating with organized crime and the State Police thought it was important enough to tell the Judiciary Committee, and that was withheld from us, I am talking about a real significant gap in our ability to perform," Sen. Robert Martin, a member of that committee, told reporter McClure.[6] The assertions, which came from confidential police informants, alleged that Santiago, then serving as Newark police

director, was overly friendly with mob figures, was tied to the protection of illegal gambling establishments and a no-show security
scheme, and had used Newark police officers to build his Morris
County home.[7]

A separate attorney general's office investigation was started
into whether Santiago improperly inspected the investigatory files
on his past after he became superintendent, a violation of law. It
concluded he did.[8] Plus his office furniture was special ordered
with eight invoices totaling $105,980 and avoided state Treasury
scrutiny of purchases exceeding $20,000.[9] The furniture order was
cancelled and troopers involved disciplined, but Santiago saw no
discipline. By the time the investigative report was issued, he had
departed state government.

While state police's top cop, Santiago defended himself by saying
he was the victim of rogue state troopers who resented he was an outsider making changes. (The troopers' image had been damaged by
the issue of racial profiling on the highways.) The growing publicity
about Santiago was hurting McGreevey's public image. According to
published reports, the governor's advisers met at Drumthwacket to
plan Santiago's ouster; among them were Attorney General Samson,
our old friends Middlesex County boss Sen. John Lynch and Camden County boss George Norcross, and top aides. Dina McGreevey
said her husband knew of Santiago's problems long before he was
forced to resign. "Santiago had stepped down in October 2002, after
months of charges against him, including the allegation that he had
friends in organized crime, an allegation Jim had known about from
the beginning," she said in her autobiography.[10] (Santiago went on
to become Trenton's city police director and was replaced temporarily by retired State Police Lt. Col. Fred Madden, who later saw Boss
Norcross's machine elect him to the state Senate.)

Instead of supporting the state police, investigators told Mc-
Clure, Harvey—when it came to investigating Santiago—put an

unprecedented burden on the information gathered about Santiago by demanding the identities of the informants and wanting those supplying the confidential tips to take lie detector tests. Internal investigative reports indicated state police informants feared for their safety if their identity were to become known.[11] Harvey's action irked many of the veteran prosecutors in his office, some of whom said privately that they feared cases touching on influential Democrats were undermined after Harvey took over.

Senator Martin also raised questions about Harvey's handling of the case investigating the land deal for a trash-transfer station in Linden involving politically connected Mayor John Gregorio, who later paid a $2,000 civil ethics penalty while maintaining he did nothing wrong.

The state's trash-transfer investigation ended when Harvey became first assistant attorney general and rejected plans by prosecutors to seek indictments. Gregorio and his son-in-law Dominick Pucillo, both Democrats, were targets of that probe, sources told the Gannett State Bureau. When Harvey was an equity partner (meaning he shared in the firm's profits) at the Morristown law firm of Riker, Danzig, Scherer, Hyland & Perretti, the firm represented solid-waste disposal companies run by Pucillo in negotiations with the state over a number of solid waste violations, sources told McClure.[12]

Harvey had no comment, but his former boss, David Samson, who was attorney general before Harvey, separated himself from the trash-transfer matter because as a private lawyer he represented a witness in the case.

Michael Lyman, a national criminal and civil litigation expert from Columbia, Missouri, said Harvey would have been wise to do the same. "This may not be a direct, but it is certainly an implied, conflict of interest."

Questions also were raised about Harvey's handling of a probe into a South Jersey engineering firm—JCA Associates—that touched on South Jersey power broker George Norcross. Norcross never was charged with anything, although as we saw in a previous chapter, tapes made by a man wearing a wire in connection with the case turned into a major embarrassment for several well-known and politically connected people. Harvey opposed release of the tapes but was overruled by a judge.

In the JCA matter, a local Democratic campaign treasurer, Daniel Wilson, was found guilty of concealing JCA's campaign contributions, and a JCA employee, William Hampton, pleaded guilty to stealing nearly $360,000 from the company. Three JCA executives, Mark Neisser, Henry Chudzinski and William Vukoder, who admitted to hiding more than $100,000 in campaign contributions to the West Deptford campaign committee, were granted probation that ended when fines were paid.[13]

Less than a year later, Superior Court Judge John A. Almeida, citing a conflict of interest on Harvey's part, tossed the guilty pleas of the three JCA executives. His rebuke: "The public is entitled to the confidence that its criminal justice system is free from bias and free from conflicts. . . . That confidence is lacking in the situation before me." Lawyer Ken Marino, Harvey's close friend, represented the company—which was not charged in the case—around the time he was representing Harvey for his own ethics violations over free ringside passes for Atlantic City boxing matches. Harvey's chief of staff, Mariellen Dugan, also was a former employee of Marino. The guilty pleas were later allowed.[14]

Harvey's meddling in New Jersey boxing got him into more ethical trouble. When he was first assistant AG, Harvey announced he was taking control of the State Athletic Control Board, known as the boxing commission.[15] He told boxing commissioner Larry Hazzard Sr., a nationally respected professional, to report to Gerard Gormley Jr., whose credentials consisted of being the older brother of Republican State Sen. Bill Gormley, whose support was needed to get Harvey's controversial nomination cleared by the senate judiciary committee and the full senate. Gerard Gormley made $10,000 a year as chairman of the part-time athletic board, but two of younger brother Bill's senate colleagues led an effort to make the job full-time and pay him $66,000 annually. It was short-lived. Under pressure for reform and after Gerard was booted out, the legislature took the full-time salary away from the post. Hazzard and his staff were doing all the work anyway. Gerard's only task was handing out boxing credentials to buddies. Later, brother Bill expressed relief Gerard got off as light as he did.

Gerard had to resign and pay a $14,000 fine for giving out free Atlantic City ringside boxing passes to the politically connected, which included Harvey's wife and friends.[16] Harvey was fined $1,500, the first time an attorney general was fined by the state ethics commission in its then-thirty-one-year history.[17]

Harvey said his only interest was in bringing Atlantic City boxing to the level of that in Las Vegas, an odd goal for an attorney general. What he didn't mention was that before he came to government he was a lawyer for Cedric Kushner (no relation to Charles, the fund-raiser who set his brother-in-law up with a prostitute on video and later went to prison), a boxing promoter who testified in a federal case that he had made payments to the International Boxing Federation.[18] The state Division of Gaming Enforcement said it constituted commercial bribery, and New Jersey Attorney General John Farmer Jr. asked that Kushner, Harvey's client, be disqualified from doing business in Atlantic City. However, four months after McGreevey came to office, Harvey's client was requalified.

Another investigation by coauthor McClure that the Web site BoxingScene.com called "a bombshell of a story that blows the whistle on behind-the-scenes dealings to bring big name fights to

Atlantic City, New Jersey," revealed sources said Harvey held private talks with McGreevey's chief of staff, Gary Taffet, and Taffet's brother Mark, who was senior vice president of HBO Sports.[19]

In sworn testimony as part of an Executive Commission on Ethical Standards probe, a witness testified Gerard Gormley said a meeting of the boxing commission was canceled because boxing was being arranged at the highest levels of New Jersey government.[20]

Gary Taffet's spokesman denied he spoke with Harvey or the others about HBO boxing. Harvey's spokesman did not: "The only thing we can say is there was a number of meetings with people."

Longtime boxing regulators in New Jersey and Nevada said they do not get involved in industry negotiations. "It is quite obvious there is a conflict of interest, or at least the appearance of a conflict," New Jersey's Hazzard said. Marc Ratner of the Nevada boxing commission echoed that sentiment. Gerard Gormley declined comment.

Hazzard wrote McGreevey asking for help because Gerard Gormley and Harvey continued to try to take over the boxing agency and "ingratiate themselves to the industry promoters, as if there is not a commissioner in charge," according to a letter obtained by McClure. McGreevey's office, unaware McClure had the letter in hand, claimed it had no records of any such communication. In late 2007, Attorney General Anne Milgram fired Hazzard after he wrote a letter to the governor complaining about boxer safety issues. Milgram told Gannett it was just about a change in leadership, but Hazzard filed a whistle-blower lawsuit charging retaliation.

Harvey's bumbling started long before he tried to take over boxing. His first bonehead move was to subpoena State Senator Martin, a Republican, after the senator revealed he had information on the case of Angelo Prisco, a mobster who got an early parole from prison.[21] (More on this in chapter 8.) Curiously, the subpoena came after Martin cast the lone "no" vote when Harvey's confirmation was before the senate judiciary committee. "I was personally alarmed and disturbed by the actions of the acting attorney general yesterday, actions which I believe were based on retaliation and intimidation," Martin, a law professor, told McClure. Lawmakers are immune from such subpoenas for what they say in their official capacity. But the subpoena was in keeping with Harvey's other request that confidential police informants go on record and take lie detector tests.

As we've seen, politicians in New Jersey can take care of their own. After the Martin subpoena, Martin wrote to the co-presidents of the senate, Democrat Dick Codey and Republican John Bennett. Codey said the subpoena was wrong but didn't merit holding up Harvey's confirmation.

Later, Harvey appointed Codey's brother as acting prosecutor of Cape May County, despite the fact that the brother, Robert, lived at the other end of the state in Essex County.[22] That move boosted Robert Codey's salary and pension.

Incredibly, in his fog of arrogance, Harvey apparently thought incoming Gov. Jon Corzine was going to keep him on as attorney general. Finally, someone from the Corzine camp made it clear he and his embarrassing baggage were history. On his way out, Harvey mailed law firms and others throughout the state a slick fifty-six-page report touting what he thought were his accomplishments, officially called the 2003–2004 annual report.[23] It bears six pictures of Harvey, five of them on the first five pages, including three on the opening page, and tells how he turned heads in Trenton and demanded respect, although it doesn't claim he actually got any. Page 20 has a large photo of him with actor William Baldwin, hip-hop comedian Russell Simmons, and the Rev. Run (Joseph Lloyd

Simmons), formerly "Run" of hip-hop recording act Run-DMC.
Using federal funds, Harvey's office organized hip-hop events to
encourage attendees to vote, although many of them appeared too
young to register. In 2007, after Harvey was gone, the state got the
bad news that some of the money had to be returned. The federal
government wanted back the $64,000 Harvey spent to transport
and feed students at the hip-hop summits. The federal Help America Vote Act was intended to improve voting, not feed and enter-
tain teenagers.[24] But there was worse news on Harvey's tenure as
attorney general in May 2007 when U.S. Attorney Chris Christie
told a Gannett New Jersey editorial board that he "got burned"
when he agreed to let Harvey handle the case of mobster Prisco.
Harvey investigated for two years and then closed the case.[25]

Corzine was smart enough to send Harvey on his way, but he
used New Jersey–style bad judgment in naming Harvey's successor,
Zulima Farber, a black Cuban émigré lawyer who had been around
Jersey politics for some time. She was briefly considered for the
New Jersey Supreme Court by McGreevey but was rejected because
of past problems with the law.

In a letter to the editor published in the *Asbury Park Press* on
February 8, 2006, Charles Cressy of Ocean Township said of
Corzine's Farber appointment, "I propose a new state motto: We
don't condone corruption, we insist upon it." Here is how coauthor Ingle summarized Farber's situation in his "Politics Patrol"
column July 9, 2006:[26]

Controversial since she arrived in Trenton with at least a
dozen speeding tickets and at least three driver's license suspensions on her record, Farber even logged bench warrants
for failure to appear in traffic court. Former Gov. Jim Mc-
Greevey, not known for great appointments, refused to
name her to the state Supreme Court.

She angered homeowners by maintaining people have no right to defend their possessions with deadly force—but burglars were pleased. Next, she said she didn't think convicted crooked politicians should be mandated by law to go to jail or give up their pensions.

She's also holding up an audit of the Board of Public Utilities that reportedly talks about a $100 million bank account outside the state's purview, and reportedly she was a counsel to one of the outfits that received a grant from the secret account.

But the stunt that left Corzine looking like a fool for naming her the chief law enforcement official happened on Memorial Day weekend at a "Click It or Ticket" road stop, the kind of feel-good program Farber prefers to catching crooked pols.

Her live-in boyfriend, Hamlet Goore, a lawyer who has been reprimanded twice by the Office of Attorney Ethics, was stopped, and the cop found his driver's license suspended and his car's registration expired. That's when Goore informed the cop he was the attorney general's boyfriend.

Farber was 13 miles away, but it didn't take long for the state trooper driving the state car Farber rides around in to get to her beau. The mayor of the Bergen County town where it happened also showed up. Presto! Those tickets were discarded.

The attorney general later explained there were sensitive documents in that unregistered car driven by the guy with a suspended license who didn't have his seat belt fastened. What the hell were sensitive state documents doing there?

The county prosecutor launched an investigation, and then it occurred to someone that prosecutors ultimately report to—tah-dah!—the attorney general. In administrations past that potential conflict might not have mattered. But Corzine's chief counsel is a guy named Stu Rabner, a straight-arrow type who came from the office of U.S. Attorney Chris Christie. Rabner says there must be a special prosecutor. They chose a good candidate, a former judge.

Sen. Gerald Cardinale has written Senate Judiciary Committee Chairman John Adler asking for a hearing on Farber. Adler will rise to the occasion and put Farber under oath. If even half of what's been reported is true, Farber should resign, be fired for cause, or impeached, because, as Shakespeare wrote: "Something is rotten in the state of Denmark."

That's from the other *Hamlet*.

To straighten out his problem, Goore didn't go to his local Motor Vehicle Commission office in North Bergen. Instead he drove twenty miles to Elizabeth.[27] There, he stood in line with others, including Angel Estrada, the MVC manager and an elected county official, a freeholder, who had been alerted by the attorney general that her boyfriend Goore was coming to see him. Why? Because, she said, she and Estrada had been friends for thirty years. But there certainly was no favoritism involved.

Farber and Goore, who is divorced, had lived together since at least 1997, and he held the Bible when she was sworn in as attorney general.[28] His son, Darius, was a spokesman for then–U.S. Senator Corzine, who in 2007 as governor named Goore's former wife, Joyce, to the State Council on the Arts. Everybody knows everybody in Jersey. But that didn't save Farber's job. The special prosecutor found Farber broke even New Jersey's lax ethics rules. She resigned, and Rabner replaced her. But that wasn't the end of Farber's involvement in New Jersey government. She landed a job as special counsel to the public schools in Elizabeth, where she had used connections to get her boyfriend special service at the Department of Motor Vehicles.

The New Jersey legal system is headed, of course, by the New Jersey Supreme Court, mostly composed of lawyers with political connections but little prior judicial experience. In New Jersey the court effectively makes its own laws and orders them carried out, thus acting as all three arms of government. Seemingly few justices have read the state constitution, and if they did, they didn't understand it. The result is seven unelected, largely unknown political appointees controlling housing and education and all manner of other elements of daily life. They have managed to restore "taxation without representation" in one of the original thirteen states more than two hundred years after the Boston Tea Party. Their meddling and acquiescence by the governor and state legislature are the major reasons the Garden State has the highest property taxes in the nation.

In most states and at the federal level, supreme court justices are chosen for their demonstrated ability to handle legal cases in appellate and lower courts. That can happen in New Jersey, but seldom does.

The first female chief justice was Deborah Poritz, a Republican named by Gov. Christie Whitman in 1996. A former college English teacher, Poritz began her legal career as a summer law clerk. She served in several positions in the state attorney general's office, then left state work for private law practice until Republicans returned to power in 1994 and Whitman named her attorney general. When Whitman nominated her to the high court, it marked the first time Poritz sat on a bench that wasn't in a park. She had her hand in some outrageous rulings that especially irked the conservative and fiscally moderate lawmakers, but Gov. Jim McGreevey renominated her, and the senate went along—even Minority Leader Leonard Lance, who had constantly criticized the court for overstepping its bounds. "Debbie is an old friend," he said when asked to justify his vote. Cronyism trumps principle.

When Poritz went to the New Jersey Supreme Court, she was replaced as state attorney general by Peter Verniero, who had been Whitman's chief counsel and chief of staff and, before she was governor, her private attorney. After a stint as attorney general, he followed Poritz to the state supreme court. Even though the biggest state lawyers' group said he was not fit for New Jersey's top court, Verniero was one of the more arrogant people to serve in a high state office, especially considering he started his career driving Tom Kean around during his 1981 gubernatorial campaign.

Under a pact established in 1969, the governor submits names of candidates to the state bar association's Judicial and Prosecutorial Appointments Committee. The lawyers' group deemed Verniero "not qualified."[29] After the bar did that to her guy, Whitman excluded it from reviewing her supreme court nominees, the gubernatorial equivalent of taking her football and going home. McGreevey reinstated the bar review in 2002.

Supreme court justices serve for seven years, and almost always are renominated by the governor. If the senate approves the nomination a second time, justices have tenure until they're seventy. Verniero was forty-five when he announced he was leaving at the end of August 2004 to return to private practice. Word was McGreevey had no intention of renominating him, and since Verniero was so unpopular it didn't matter much to anyone but him.

Jaynee LaVecchia went to the state supreme court from being commissioner of banking and insurance. Prior to that she was in the attorney general's office and served as an administrative law judge for the Office of Administrative Law (a low-level court). She was involved in a highly controversial merger of a health plan that resulted in the disappearance of some $300 million. Consumer advocates were outraged. An editorial in the *Courier-Post* outlined the outrageous circumstances:[30]

> The water in Trenton must have something in it that prevents public trough-swillers from admitting mistakes.
>
> Take the testimony before a state Senate committee by three Whitman administration members on what went wrong with the merger of HIP Health Plan of New Jersey and a Virginia-based company.
>
> It was a disaster. HIP is bankrupt. . . . People had to find new medical care. Doctors and hospitals were not paid. Up to $300 million is missing.
>
> But the Whitman trio—Banking and Insurance Commissioner Jaynee LaVecchia, Senior Services Commissioner Christine Grant and acting Attorney General Paul Zoubek— might as well be the three blind mice. Or those monkeys that see, hear and speak no evil.
>
> LaVecchia approved the sweetheart deal negotiated in secret as an "asset" sale rather than a "complete" sale, which it was. That meant the new owner didn't have to be classified as a health maintenance organization (HMO) subject to state regulations about maintaining financial reserves. Then, LaVecchia left the Attorney General's Office to be insurance commissioner just in time to oversee the liquidation of HIP, so she dealt with it on both ends.
>
> PHP Health Plan started its drive to take over HIP by hiring Dale Florio, a lobbyist who happens to be the Somerset County Republican chairman and a friend of Gov. Whitman. Former Attorney General Peter Verniero relied on a consultant hired by HIP to determine HIP's market value. The consultant's fee was based on finding a buyer for HIP.

If so many people hadn't been harmed, this would have been hilarious, Government by The Three Stooges. But millions are missing and people were hurt.

A consumers' coalition, New Jersey Citizen Action, asked for a temporary restraining order to block the merger until an independent probe could be conducted, contending Banking and Insurance Commissioner LaVecchia's investigation was flawed because two years earlier she was chief of the division in the attorney general's office that approved the merger over the objections and warnings from staff.

The coalition wanted three questions answered:

1. Why was the nonprofit HIP not required to transfer its HMO license to the for-profit PHP, a failure that left the now bankrupt company unregulated?
2. Why was a $73 million deal arranged so PHP could get HIP in an asset sale rather than a complete sale, which it was?
3. What happened to the $300 million PHP collected from HIP customers?

Good questions all, but they were never answered. In an incredible act of covering its butt in the tradition of "let them eat cake," the Whitman administration filed court papers opposing the independent probe. Superior Court Judge Jack Latimer denied the bid for a temporary restraining order, saying he had to see proof the public actually lost some charity money.[31]

The judge lectured the state, too. He chided the attorney general's office for saying the public had no legal standing in the case.

A *Courier-Post* editorial summed it up: "We hope the consumer coalition gets back soon with the level of legal proof the judge needs so this sweetheart deal allowed by Verniero and LaVecchia can get the close scrutiny it deserves. It stinks to high heaven."[32]

There was speculation the federal government was going to look into the HIP merger. State Insurance Department spokeswoman Winnie Comfort refused to comment on reports her agency had been subpoenaed, typical of the Whitman administration's disregard for the people's right to know. That was 1999, and there has been no word since on what happened to the $300 million. Despite having their hands in this mess, LaVecchia and Verniero went on to sit on the state supreme court. Comfort became the court's spokeswoman. In 2006, Gov. Jon Corzine nominated LaVecchia for tenure on the court, and the state senate supported her. She was not questioned about the missing $300 million during her confirmation hearing. When asked why later, committee chairman John Adler said the missing $300 million was old business. Only in Jersey.

Roberto Rivera-Soto spent two years as an assistant U.S. attorney, but most of his career was spent working for casino companies. In 2004, he became the first Hispanic on the court, nominated by McGreevey, who had backed away from a promise to appoint Zulima Farber, whom we met earlier as attorney general. McGreevey dropped Cuban American Farber after black legislators objected because they wanted the seat to go to an African American. (And it did with the appointment of John E. Wallace Jr.) But publicly, McGreevey said his about-face was because, thanks to the news media, it became known Farber had thirteen traffic violations, three license suspensions, and four bench warrants for failure to appear in court. How could a state background check miss that?

One day after McGreevey nominated Rivera-Soto, his own traffic woes came to light. It was revealed Rivera-Soto had eight speeding tickets between 1984 and 1994 and had his driver's license suspended for failing to pay a fine. A McGreevey spokesperson, in the finest tradition of Baghdad Bob double-talk spin, said this was different because Rivera-Soto never had a warrant for failure to appear.[33]

In 2007, Rivera-Soto faced a formal complaint from the state supreme court's disciplinary committee, which accused him of using his position to influence a court decision on a school dispute involving his son. Rivera-Soto called the cops and filed a criminal complaint against a captain of the Haddonfield High School football team after his son's mouth was injured at football practice during a head-to-head collision with the captain. The school said it was an accident. Rivera-Soto's son said it was intentional. The judge was accused of reminding those handling the case just who he was. The dispute between the boys was settled. But Rivera-Soto, who said he was profoundly sorry, was in hot water with even New Jersey's ethics watchdogs for the courts.[34] The disciplinary committee ruled that Rivera-Soto misused his judicial office and recommended censure. The final decision was left to Rivera-Soto's colleagues on the court, who agreed.[35]

Do all these interlocking connections matter? They matter plenty. One of the big reasons New Jersey is hell on property owners can be traced to a series of eleven supreme court rulings going back for decades. The Education Law Center of Newark filed suit maintaining the state had failed its constitutional requirement to provide a "thorough and efficient system" of education in thirty-one mostly urban districts with low property tax bases. The goal was to give the thirty-one "Abbott districts" (the case was captioned *Abbott vs. Burke*) supplemental state aid to make their per-pupil spending equal to that in rich districts. There was no requirement that the students have to perform as well, though. The result was that more than 50 percent of the state's education budget went to 25 percent of the state's students in 31 out of 615 school districts. Many of the Abbotts exceed per-pupil spending of rich areas. Camden, for instance, had a per-pupil expenditure of $15,600 when the statewide average was $12,160. Other Abbotts were higher.

The 585 non-Abbott districts rely heavily on property tax, a major reason why New Jersey's is the highest in the nation.

Under the court's rules, the Abbott districts file budgets to be reviewed and approved by the state. In fiscal 2006 they totaled $4.5 billion. For the next year, they wanted another $500 million to make it an even $5 billion. Camden alone asked for $78 million in new aid, an increase of more than 100 percent. Corzine, in his first year as governor, asked the court for a one-year freeze. As the state's case was argued, the governor sat in the front row where the justices could see him. They might have been thinking about coming up for renomination or who would be elevated to chief justice when Poritz stepped down in less than a year. Or maybe the logic of not pouring more and more money down a rat hole finally was clear to them. Whatever, the court agreed.

A freeze didn't fit well with many of the districts, which sent forth people to play the race card. "The day is coming when Jon Corzine will learn he cannot count on the support of people in our community when he no longer supports our children," said James Harris, president of the state NAACP. Others said it takes time for the Abbott decisions to show results, ignoring it already had been thirty years.

The biggest problem with the Abbott schools is that there is so little to show for the billions that have been dumped there over three decades—more than $30 billion in the past ten years. This is more than $20,000 per student per year, and the only improvement documented was a one-time slight hike at the fourth-grade level, with Camden leading the way. This was much ballyhooed, even though there was reason to believe the improvement was fiction.

Joseph Carruth was still new to being principal at Brimm Medical Arts High when, he says, he was called to Camden's district office in January 2005. There, he said, Assistant Superintendent Luis Pagan gave him detailed instructions on how to cheat on the state's standardized test scores.[36]

Carruth faced a moral dilemma. He didn't have tenure, and he had a baby daughter with a serious medical condition; he needed the medical insurance. Putting his career on the line, he went to state education officials with his story.

The state board of education launched an investigation of Carruth's allegations as well as a probe of test scores at Camden elementary schools. An analysis by the *Philadelphia Inquirer* found several elementary schools' scores to be unusually high. At Brimm, the newspaper found more than 91 percent were reported proficient in eleventh grade math, a twenty-one-point gain.

Pagan, reached at his home in a posh Burlington County suburb far from the misery and poverty of Camden, told the *Inquirer* he never had such a conversation with Carruth. Superintendent Annette Knox declined comment. Carruth was fired, and he filed legal notice of intent to bring a suit against the school board, accusing it of negligence and failing to supervise central administrators who "threatened to coerce (Carruth) to join a test-fixing plot" and then wrote negative evaluations of him when he refused, the *Courier-Post* reported.

Incredibly, it got worse in a case ugly even by Camden standards. Carruth was told in a May 15, 2005, letter that he would have health insurance until September 1, 2006.[37] But the family got a call July 28 saying that was a mistake: The insurance would end August 1, and a medical equipment company would send a representative to their home to get the feeding pump used to sustain their daughter, Brianna.

"I'm curious as to if this was done on purpose or if this was an actual mistake," Mrs. Carruth told Sarah Greenblatt of the *Courier-Post*. "I feel very cynical and scared." With good reason. When she called in June asking about continuing the family's insurance under the federal COBRA program, she was told to call back in August. Following a barrage of negative publicity, the district said it would pay $2,000 for the feeding equipment and formula for another month but not pay the $1,100 monthly insurance bill, which would have included the equipment and formula. If Camden school administrators had honored the original September 1 date, it would have saved taxpayers $900.

The district, known more for corruption than educating kids, sent a message about what happens to people who don't play along. Monica Yant Kinney, columnist for the *Philadelphia Inquirer*, kept up with Carruth from the beginning. She wrote:[38]

When Carruth tells me he is desperate for a $500 weekly unemployment check that won't cover his mortgage and is reluctantly spending money from Brianna's college fund to keep her alive, he sounds like a man defeated.

Every time we've talked since this cheating scandal broke in March, I've asked Carruth whether he regretted his decision.

This week, for the first time, he said he had come close.

"I've gone from making six figures to needing to take charity," Carruth marveled. "I'm looking in the mirror, thinking, 'If you can't take care of your daughter, was it worth it?'"

But Kinney concluded that Carruth could not have kept quiet about the request to cheat any more than he could have cheated.

Superintendent Knox, meanwhile, ran into problems of her

own. Although she was paid $185,483 annually for a district that was on life support, she gave herself $17,690 in performance bonuses that the school board did not approve. Even so, her contract was renewed. The Corzine administration wanted her out, and Knox was willing to go for a $600,000 severance payment. She settled for $200,000 as an investigation of her continued. Unlike Carruth, she got a year's health insurance thrown in.[39]

The district had no money for Carruth, but Knox's executive secretary, Helen L. Hammond, was paid overtime for forty-six hours over eleven days when she was off for various reasons, a *Philadelphia Inquirer* analysis of the 2005–6 school year showed. She even put in for overtime during a two-day period when she was hospitalized.[40] Carruth filed a formal whistle-blower lawsuit in June 2007.

Scandal after scandal has rocked the Camden school system. Local taxes pay for only 2 percent of its operation. That means suburban taxpayers are supporting two school systems—their own and the ones in urban areas. Thanks to the New Jersey Supreme Court, the people footing most of Camden's bills live elsewhere, which means they can't even vote to remove the school board that allowed Carruth to be fired and Knox to get her contract renewed, then to be paid $200,000 to walk away even though she was under investigation. It's Taxation Without Representation, twenty-first-century style.

On the other end of the state, Newark asked New Jersey taxpayers to finance its schools and a lot of the city's expenses to the tune of $750 million a year while the city earmarked $250 million for a hockey arena.

An analysis of Newark's school system in 2006 by 101.5 FM radio newsman Kevin McArdle found 327 teachers and administrators being paid more than $100,000 a year for a total of $38.3 million. Putting that in perspective, the median teacher salary in the state was $57,707.[41]

McArdle also found that Charles Epps, the superintendent of Jersey City schools, also an Abbott district, took himself and others on a trip to London in 2004 at state expense. The trip included $400 spent on chauffeured limousines and one meal where $160 was paid for two ribs of beef and $25 for two bowls of asparagus soup. Epps also is a member of the state legislature, a double-dipper, which makes one wonder how he could serve the needs of both posts simultaneously. He announced in early 2007 he would not seek reelection to the assembly.

Epps told McArdle the purpose of the trip to Great Britain was to learn best practices and leadership design for the future of public education. The trip was approved by the state-appointed district superintendent.

It also bears noting that another Abbott district is Hoboken, Frank Sinatra's hometown, where houses and condos begin at many hundreds of thousands of dollars, but taxpayers from elsewhere support the school system. Hoboken already was providing full-day preschool for children of Wall Street parents when it decided to place a new $25 million high school on the backs of taxpayers statewide. Paul Mulshine, *Star-Ledger* columnist, expressed his contempt.[42] Mulshine said officials planned the new school although the current facility is relatively new and has an indoor swimming pool. Hoboken resident Jon Corzine won't be contributing a cent through property taxes, the columnist noted.

As a renter, multimillionaire Corzine was exempt from school taxes, and the luxury building in which Corzine was considering purchasing a condo was being constructed under a tax abatement program that exempted it from school taxes. Hard for the rich governor to sympathize when his wallet is exempt.

Why did governors and lawmakers let the supreme court get by with the Abbott district fiasco for three decades? It served their needs and the needs of their cronies in the districts where billions of dollars flow. Very little of it gets to the classroom, but that's of little consequence when it makes your allies wealthy. It was convenient to sympathize with voters while saying, in effect, "The court made us do it."

Columnist Mulshine suggested Corzine write the Supremes a letter like this:[43]

"Dear members of an Equal, not Superior, Coordinate Branch of Government:

"I have reviewed my copy of the state Constitution and seem to have missed the section which permits you to dictate spending on anything. Should you, in the future, see fit to opine on the subject, I will happily consider your views, as I do those of every other constituent. However, as, in my view, you lack the authority to compel the state to spend a single nickel, should you purport to order us to do so, I will politely but firmly decline."

Beyond ordering billions in taxpayer money dumped down rat holes despite lack of evidence that anything positive is being accomplished by it, the state supreme court demonstrates other wacky reasoning and thinking that defies logic. And does it stay out of politics? Fuggeddaboutit!

Let's look at the 2002 U.S. Senate race. Bob Torricelli, badly bruised by scandal, dropped out of his reelection campaign: Polls showed Torricelli—"Torch," as he is known because of his incendiary style—was not going to win. Some say he was down in private polls by as much as twenty points—quite a shock for a guy who always thought he was the smartest guy in the room. The senate ethics committee "severely admonished" Torricelli for not paying market value for a CD player and a TV from Korean-American businessman David Chang, who pleaded guilty to illegally funneling more than $53,000 to Torricelli's 1996 campaign.[44] Prosecutors found evidence that Torricelli helped Chang's business while accepting cash, Italian suits, and an $8,100 watch, the *New York Times* reported.[45]

Chang Hwan Choi, a Korean tailor, told reporters in 1997 that he was taken by Chang to the home of a man called "John" to take measurements. Choi made ten suits for "John" over the next two years, which were charged to Chang's credit card. When asked whether "John" was Torricelli, the tailor said he couldn't recall the guy's face but knew he was a size 40 regular with a fondness for pinstripes and French cuffs.

Torricelli dropped out of his reelection race thirty-five days before Election Day. According to New Jersey election law, a candidate who drops out less than fifty-one days before the election cannot be replaced on the ballot.

Ignoring the law, the court ruled unanimously that the Democratic Party could substitute Frank Lautenberg, who spent eighteen years in the U.S. Senate before retiring in 2000. Some, such as the military living overseas, already had voted by absentee ballot. The court said new ballots could be printed and sent to them at an expected cost of $800,000, with the Democrats footing the bill.

"Today, the people of New Jersey lost," said Douglas Forrester, the Republican who was leading the race against Torricelli. "The Torricelli-Lautenberg machine's disregard for the rule of law, fair elections and the people of New Jersey will, once again, make our great state the butt of national jokes."[46]

It certainly was a disadvantage for Forrester, whose campaign was geared toward taking on Torricelli's ethical lapses. The U.S. Supreme Court declined to interfere in the New Jersey court's decision. Editorial writers and think-tank occupants called it a perversion of law. One of them was Robert A. Levy, senior fellow in constitutional studies at the Cato Institute, who wrote:[47]

The New Jersey Supreme Court, disregarding utterly the rule of law, has chosen to circumvent the state legislature and interpret a provision of New Jersey law to mean the opposite of what the law expressly says. Nothing could be clearer than the procedures duly enacted by New Jersey's lawmakers "in the event of a vacancy, howsoever caused, among candidates nominated at primaries." Those procedures apply only when the "vacancy shall occur not later than the 51st day before the general election." Ignoring that crystalline text, the seven Supreme Court justices declared, in effect, "We will write the law as we prefer it to be, no matter what the voters of New Jersey, through their elected representatives, have decided."

Levy had particularly harsh criticism for the court's statement that the relevant state law "does not preclude the possibility of a vacancy occurring within fifty-one days of the general election."

"That astonishing statement," Levy wrote, "if carried to its logical conclusion, would establish this legal standard: All government actions that are not expressly precluded are permitted. Of course, such a standard turns the law on its head and arrogates powers to the judiciary that are quintessentially legislative.

"Basically, the state Supreme Court, by its interpretation of state law, has disenfranchised New Jersey voters, who elected the state's legislators."

It also set a precedent that if a party's candidate is in deep trouble some time before Election Day, another candidate can be switched at the last minute for any reason. Such is the arrogance of the New Jersey Supreme Court, which didn't even bother to pretend it was interpreting the law rather than writing a new one.

Lautenberg beat Forrester, 1,138,193 to 928,439. When Lautenberg first ran, in 1982, his Republican opponent was Rep. Millicent Fenwick, who was immortalized in the comic strip "Doonesbury" as Lacey Davenport. Using code words, Lautenberg questioned her fitness due to her age. She was seventy-two. When the Democrats put Lautenberg on the ballot in 2002, he was seventy-eight. He has said he would run again in 2008. But at eighty-three, his age was questioned.

Another controversial interpretation of the state constitution became known as the Mount Laurel doctrine. It held that municipalities must use their zoning to provide an opportunity for housing affordable to low- and moderate-income households.

Mount Laurel is a South Jersey township in Burlington County. Comprising twenty-two square miles, it had been rural for most of its existence. In 1950, developers discovered it. The population doubled by 1960 and again by 1970. During the latter decade, the township was sued over exclusionary zoning, which the suit maintained kept affordable housing from being built.

The state supreme court got the case in 1975 and declared Mount Laurel's zoning practices were contrary to the general welfare requirements of the state constitution. The left-leaning court said New Jersey municipalities had to provide their share of affordable housing.

A second case, known as Mount Laurel II, affirmed its original decision and created mandates for the state's municipalities. In 1983, the legislature passed the Fair Housing Act to replace judicial framework with legislative guidance. A part of that was creation of the Council on Affordable Housing (COAH) to determine a town's fair share of affordable housing.

Mount Laurel made no one happy.

In theory, the Mount Laurel rulings were supposed to outlaw discrimination in housing, but they had limited success because towns evaded the rules, which upset affordable housing advocates.

A suit brought by West Windsor, backed by the New Jersey State League of Municipalities, alleged Mount Laurel was no more than a weapon used by builders to overturn zoning laws that limited development. "The state is spending hundreds of millions of dollars to acquire open space, and meanwhile, the judiciary is doing just the reverse through the builder's remedy," said Mike Herbert Sr., an attorney for West Windsor.

The court gave developers the "builders' remedy," which says a builder can bring suit if it thinks zoning allows too few units on a parcel of land. If zoning only allows four houses per acre, for instance, the builder can bring suit for, say, twenty units per acre—allegedly so that it can build affordable housing. This usually involves condos and apartments since builders wouldn't want affordable housing among their high-priced McMansions. Usually the threat of a suit is all it takes for a town to modify its zoning. If the issue never makes it to court, there is no order forcing the builder to provide any affordable housing although he does get the more dense zoning, which can be used solely for market-rate housing.

Environmentalists said Mount Laurel contributed to sprawl. "Although it's not the biggest factor in sprawl, Mount Laurel does lead to construction on environmentally sensitive areas," said Jeff Tittel, New Jersey Sierra Club director.[48]

When former Jersey City mayor Bret Schundler was running for governor, he said of Mount Laurel, "It's been a total failure. Builders go out to suburban areas, sprinkle a few houses in the mix and get to cut down trees."

There is also the matter of transferring housing credits. The law allows a municipality to pawn off up to 50 percent of its affordable-housing obligation to another town for $30,000 for each unit.

Not far from where it all started, the Township of Mount Laurel, a hostile audience jammed a planning board meeting in Evesham to hear a developer explain his plans for luxury apartments on a 15.5-acre site. There would be no low-income housing, the builder assured the audience. The court-mandated affordable-housing requirement would be met by buying housing credits in another town—allowing the affordable housing to be built in someone else's backyard.

In 2007, an appellate court upheld a municipality's right to buy credits in another town but said the Council on Affordable Housing's mandates for municipalities were so far out of whack that they had to be redone.

Superior, or county, courts aren't much better than the Supremes. Because most things in New Jersey government are based on political connections, not merit, some of the superior court judges leave a lot to be desired.

A memo leaked to the press during the Jim Florio administration gave the public a look into the blatant politics of judicial appointments in New Jersey. Kathleen Bird's *New Jersey Law Journal* article on the memo started with this Garden State joke: "What's the definition of a judge? A lawyer who knows a politician."[49]

The staff memo written to Florio's chief counsel, Andrew Weber, talked about the governor's need to "horse trade" judicial selections with state senators, who, through the age-old senatorial courtesy system, had to give their approval to judicial appointments inside their turf. "As you know, Mr. (Eugene) Austin is the quid pro quo which Senator (Gerald) Cardinale requires to release the Patrick Fitzpatrick nomination," the memo states.

Even more offensive is the memo's highlighting of the connection between judicial appointments and political fund-raising. The memo notes that the political supporter of a Somerset County lawyer for a judgeship has "not been as active in his fundraising" and that the administration should "give this some thought" in reviewing the lawyer's "qualifications" for a judgeship.

And the memo highlighted what has always been apparent in New Jersey—that judicial appointments were used to move people out of coveted posts in state government, especially posts that involve investigating the administration. The Florio administration was hoping—if it could placate Burlington County Democrats—to make Jim Morley, then executive director of the State Commission of Investigation, a judge in order to put someone else in the top SCI spot.

Let's meet a few other New Jersey judges:

Former state Superior Court Judge Stephen W. Thompson was convicted by a federal jury in 2005 for sexual exploitation of children. He traveled to Russia to produce a videotape of him having sex with a teenage boy and then brought the tape back to the United States. The federal judge sentenced Thompson to ten years in prison.[50]

After four days of hearings in 2000, the state supreme court's special disciplinary committee voted 4–3 to censure Superior Court Judge Rosemarie Williams and require that she continue psychological counseling for her "bad judgment."[51]

The discipline grew out of two restaurant fights with former boyfriend Wes Bridges, an investigator with the Mercer County Sheriff's Department. Judge Williams was charged with judicial code violations for her tavern spats with Bridges and his date.

Court documents indicated Judge Williams was having dinner when Bridges and his date entered the restaurant. After Williams confronted the duo, they left without being seated, going to a second restaurant. Williams followed and unleashed a second profanity-laced diatribe.[52]

Trentonian reporter Tony Wilson, a veteran of the capital city streets, probably thought he had seen it all until this one. He wrote that Patrick Monahan, the lawyer presenting the Williams case, said the judge lied about the two encounters. "Her prevailing attitude throughout was arrogance and the emotion she displayed . . . was jealousy which quickly developed into a jealous rage."[53]

Two members of the disciplinary panel voted to remove Williams from the bench: "Judge Williams has demonstrated by her untruthfulness that she cannot be trusted to tell the truth ahead of her personal convenience. She should be removed from judicial office."

Williams, who is twenty years older than Bridges, defended herself by claiming to be a victim of battered woman's syndrome, saying it was Bridges who was abusive to her, but the judicial panel didn't buy it.[54]

The state supreme court, which has the final say on discipline, suspended Williams for three months in 2001. She came back before the disciplinary committee again five years later after she pleaded guilty to drunken driving. Again, the committee recommended a light sentence—that she be censured.[55] The state supreme court went along even though when stopped by police, Williams recorded a blood-alcohol level of .16, twice the legal limit.[56] In 2006, Williams decided not to seek reappointment to the bench.[57]

Judges tend to go easy on each other even when it comes to drinking and driving. The *Star-Ledger* reported that "five state judges have been sanctioned by the supreme court following drunken driving convictions. Three were publicly reprimanded, one was censured and one was suspended for 60 days after he was convicted of a second driving-while-intoxicated charge."[58]

One of the more bizarre judicial cases, even for New Jersey, involved Administrative Law Judge Florence Schreiber Powers, who was convicted of shoplifting two twenty-nine-dollar watches from T. J. Maxx.[59] She admitted taking the timepieces but claimed diminished mental capacity because of a variety of problems including an "ungodly" vaginal itch. The *Star-Ledger* reported she also blamed menopausal hot flashes, problems with a wallpaper job, and a toilet that would not stop flushing.

Found guilty, she was fined $250. And that was the end of it. Judge Samuel Lenox explained, "I find no reason to believe the defendant cannot continue to perform the functions and duties of her office in a manner consistent with her oath." Especially if that toilet quiets down. Florio did not reappoint Powers to the bench, but she returned to state government as assistant chief of municipal court services.[60] Only in New Jersey.

Harsh treatment was saved for Superior Court Judge Wilbur "Wild Bill" Mathesius, an outspoken former prosecutor who didn't take any bribes or steal watches but did take controversial stands and spoke his mind. The supreme court's disciplinary committee recommended six months' suspension for him, including three without pay.[61]

He was hauled in on charges of castigating a jury for failure to convict a man on a weapons charge, dismissing a jury for the day without trial lawyers present, and complaining about an appeals judge who reversed a criminal conviction. He also said, in one of his opinions, that the death penalty is costly and never enforced and therefore ineffective. That apparently irked the almighty state supreme court even if it is true.

It should be noted that when the unusually strong six-month suspension was recommended, Judge Mathesius had already rejected the state's motion to dismiss the case of the whistle-blower who contended the McGreevey administration influenced the parole board in the bizarre early release of mob capo Angelo Prisco, whom we'll meet later. The case involved some highly influential, politically connected people. Some felt the charges were an attempt to intimidate Mathesius or delay the case. Mathesius also was hearing a lawsuit by state troopers against former attorney general Peter Harvey involving allegations of retaliation over what troopers found when they investigated former state police superintendent Joseph Santiago. With the politically charged cases pending, the supreme court decided to suspend Mathesius for just thirty days—without pay.[62] The author of the Mathesius disciplinary opinion was Justice Rivera-Soto, who had yet to face his own discipline.

But with panache and humor Mathesius got back at the high court when he responded to its request for him to reflect upon the way he handled authority. He described meeting former Supreme Justice Deborah Poritz like this: "The Chief swept in, clad in diaphanous tulle and a high-fashion shahtoosh. Her diamante' Harlequin glasses provided interesting accent. The picture collectively brought to mind a hint of a mature Andrea Dworkin with a touch of Dick Cheney. Under her arm she carried the mega-hit treatise 'Modern Management Theory' by Kim Jong-il." Mathesius cited New Jersey justices and judges who "become inured to a daily showering of reverence such that it mutates into an entitlement." And he railed about the court's policy against judges speaking their minds, labeling it "enforced intellectual servitude" and a violation of constitutional rights. The *New Jersey Lawyer*, which published the Mathesius tirade, said "Rarely, in fact if ever, has a previously disciplined sitting judge publicly unloaded so heavily on his superiors and further belittled some of the operations and policies of the courts, especially rules that he says keep judges from speaking their minds."[63]

In one particularly odd judicial appointment, a Republican earned a spot on the bench from a Democratic governor after serving a less-than-stellar tenure as both a county and federal prosecutor. Lee Solomon began as a Republican assembly member from South Jersey. After he was defeated by Boss George Norcross's Democratic Camden County machine, Governor Whitman named Solomon acting Camden County prosecutor. He later became an assistant federal prosecutor for South Jersey and, as we'll see, eventually a superior court judge.

During Solomon's tenure as a federal prosecutor, there was a big roundup of teenagers awaiting trial in Camden County.[64] That caught the attention of Superior Court Judge Louis Hornstine, a straight shooter, who asked authorities to investigate. Officials wondered if the roundup was performed in an attempt to boost state and federal funding for programs at the Camden County Youth Detention Center—funding determined by the jail population on one day of the year. The arrests came just days before the annual jail census on October 15. Many of the fifteen picked up and sent to jail were wearing electronic monitors at home. Most of the teenagers were released shortly after the census.

Insiders told the *Courier-Post* that filling the detention center before the census was an annual routine, and central to the investigation was whether the center's director, Assemblywoman Mary Previte, was aware of the possibly illegal sweep. Previte cultivated for herself an image as a child advocate and wrote books about her experience with troubled teens. She had been the center's director for some thirty years. In 1997, she was elected to the assembly with backing from the Camden County machine and thus joined the ever-growing double-dippers club in state government.

It would seem a serious matter, a violation of protection provided by the U.S. Constitution, to round people up and put them in jail for no reason other than to boost funding, but Assistant U.S. Attorney Solomon passed a federal investigation into the matter on to New Jersey Attorney General Harvey, known for lackluster results in probes involving politicians. The best Solomon could manage as an explanation was that it was better suited to be a state investigation, as if federal constitutional rights were of no real concern.

Previte stepped down as the center's director, and she decided not to seek reelection, but for some time nothing came of the investigation Solomon passed on to Harvey.

Two years after the roundup incident, a unit of the attorney general's office issued a report saying wrongful acts occurred, but no laws were broken because no individual benefited financially.[65] Previte and the woman in charge of electronically monitored juvenile offenders, Eva Johnson, did not cooperate with the investigation. They demanded immunity from prosecution, and the state refused to give it.[66]

After Solomon handed the investigation to the state and not long after another candidate beat him out for a federal judgeship, Solomon was nominated by Gov. Dick Codey for a state superior court job.[67] The unusual appointment of a Republican by a Democratic governor won swift approval.

6

The Run for the Roses Starts in the Boondocks

If state government in New Jersey is the major league for corruption, local governments are the farm teams with players yearning for the day they can make the big time with multiple public jobs and fat pensions.

Leading the league, Republican division, is Monmouth County. Though fourth in the state in population, Monmouth has the second largest government payroll, and many employees got there the old-fashioned way—their political connections. In 2004, at least thirty county employees and five county counsels were Republican Party officials or partners of party officials. It would be hard to choose the pennant winner in the Democratic division, although it is safe to say Camden County, which, even more Democratic than Monmouth is Republican, is the poster child for what's rotten in the state of Jersey. Editor William "Skip" Hidlay's *Asbury Park Press* investigation of Monmouth government resulted in a series called "Club Monmouth: Perks, Patronage and Property

Taxes."[1] It began by asking: Where else can a county employee
make up to $100,000 a year in overtime and be provided with such
perks as free golf and an all-expenses-paid car for commuting to
work? It's all on the taxpayers, who have no choice but to fork it
over through their property taxes.

"In fact, among the 21 counties, Monmouth now collects more
tax dollars from its residents, spends more to run its government
and oversees a larger county payroll than all except Essex, the
home of Newark," wrote reporters Bob Cullinane and Nina Rizzo.
"A review of spending by the *Asbury Park Press* found that decades
of single-party control by the GOP, combined with a windfall of tax
dollars from soaring property values, have produced a culture of
perks, patronage and fiscal excess."

An unholy union of crooked politicians and developers willing
to cross the line can be found in the scum at the bottom of most
New Jersey political barrels. Millionaire developer Anthony Spalliero, for instance, was indicted on federal charges that he paid
$140,000 in bribes to Monmouth officials to secure contracts for
his business.[2] Included were trips and entertainment at his sons'
go-go bars. His story took a Jersey turn for the weird while he was
awaiting trial. An armed Spalliero, then in his sixties, forced his
way into the car of a twenty-two-year-old female student, described
as an ex-girlfriend, on the first day of classes at Brookdale Community College in Lincroft, according to his grand jury indictment for
attempted kidnapping and aggravated assault.[3] According to the
indictment, Spalliero stuck a gun in the girl's ribs and threatened
to kill her if she didn't follow orders. A college police officer heard
screams and went to investigate as the developer fled in another
car. Spalliero pleaded not guilty.

Spalliero's name was synonymous with suburban sprawl. Starting in 1992, he cultivated a relationship with Mayor Matthew Scannapieco of Marlboro, a desirable town within commuting distance

of New York City.[4] The Spalliero clan had wide-ranging interests. Two of Spalliero's sons and a son-in-law separately owned four area go-go bars. In addition to two of the watering holes, one son also owned a cemetery, an idea developed by his father. Besides bending an elbow together at one of the sons' adult entertainment establishments, developer Spalliero and Mayor Scannapieco also saw each other while on separate vacations in Florida. Marlboro's attorney at the time was John Bennett, who also was a state senator, among other public jobs, and as senate co-president issued a senate birthday proclamation for Spalliero, a flashy guy who wore a diamond-studded watch and drove to township meetings in a stretch black limo.

As the town's attorney—recommended for the job in 1992 by Mayor Scannapieco—Bennett worked on agreements related to developer Spalliero's many housing projects, and over the years the Spalliero family gave $24,450 to Bennett's campaigns. Bennett and Spalliero told *Asbury Park Press* reporters James Quirk and James W. Prado Roberts no special treatment was given the developer. Camilla Modesitt of the National Civic League's New Politics Program disagrees. She said Marlboro officials "have crossed the line of propriety and have entered into a conflict-of-interest relationship."

In April 2005, Mayor Scannapieco pleaded guilty to accepting $245,000 in bribes from Spalliero.[5] The amount is large even by New Jersey's larcenous standards. He also pleaded guilty to tax evasion, especially for failing to pay federal taxes on the bribes. Ironically, Mayor Scannapieco double-dipped as a member of the state's Victims of Crime Compensation Board. Following his plea, Assemblywoman Loretta Weinberg and Assemblyman Michael Panter called for the $107,000-a-year positions on the victims' board to be eliminated.[6] They said New Jersey was one of only two states that have paid victims' boards—not a surprise, really, since the board is more of a patronage dump than a legitimate attempt to help crime victims. The fiscal 2008 budget made the board positions unpaid.

In December 2007, Spalliero pleaded guilty to paying Scanna-pieco $100,000 in bribes in an effort to build homes on airport land. The project was never built, and the feds dropped other charges related to $77,500 in bribes, the *Asbury Park Press* reported. In June 2008, Scannapieco was sentenced to twenty-one months in prison.

Another ironic scenario on the Democratic side that came out of the federal investigation of Monmouth County involved John E. "Jack" Westlake, who pleaded guilty to a federal tax evasion charge, alongside his business partner, former state senator and party boss John Lynch.[7] Westlake was president of the county's board of taxation, the outfit that considers tax appeals.

Westlake did more than help Lynch hide his bribes from local officials. At the same time Westlake was securing a state pension with his tax job, he was the lobbyist for a Philadelphia firm raking in Camden County contracts—something that's OK in New Jersey's free-for-all political climate.

Courier-Post reporter Tim Zatzariny Jr. and coauthor McClure teamed for a story revealing another chunk of change for Westlake.[8] Because he owned an interest in the deal, Westlake reaped $672,000 when Gary Taffet and Paul Levinsohn, poised to be top aides to incoming Gov. Jim McGreevey, sold their billboard interests just before entering state government. Westlake also helped run New Directions Through Responsible Leadership, the political action committee controlled by Lynch, who stuck his nose into the local billboard deals when it really counted. Just before McGreevey was elected—at a time when Taffet and Levinsohn were trying to boost the value of their billboards by securing government approvals and advertising—Lynch, then a powerful state senator, telephoned the chief executive of NJ Transit and asked him to "speed up the approval" for one of their billboards along the Atlantic City Expressway, the *Star-Ledger* reported.[9]

"Lynch's call expedited the approval process, and a lease for the billboard was approved on Dec. 14, 2001. With that approval in hand, the two aides turned around and sold the sign on Jan. 10, 2002 for $848,800," wrote *Star-Ledger* reporter Josh Margolin. Former assembly member Jeff Warsh, executive director of NJ Transit at the time, said the special attention given to the application for the billboard, located on transit land, resulted from a phone call, but he would not say who placed the call, Margolin reported.

Five years later—even with Lynch headed to jail—the corrupt network attached to local government was still cranking out money for the politically connected.

Asbury Park Press reporter Cullinane discovered that an assistant Monmouth County counsel and his law firm were paid $50,000 by the county in 2006 to help prepare a report that ultimately concluded the county should continue to pay its attorneys by the hour.[10] County administrator Louis Paparozzi said he didn't see a conflict in a county counsel paid by the hour gathering and analyzing legal fee information for a report to determine if county counsels should be paid by the hour. Paparozzi and two elected officials wrote the report.

Local government in Monmouth County took an even more bizarre turn in 2007 when the former mayor of Lake Como, Lawrence Chiaravallo, a Republican, acknowledged that he had shredded documents related to his secret negotiations with the government of Kuwait for a $3.7 million grant to build a new police station, the *Asbury Park Press* reported.[11]

When reporter Erik Larsen questioned Chiaravallo about destroying what should have been public documents, the ex-mayor asked Larsen if he was familiar with Italian culture and then threatened to send him a dead fish.

Chiaravallo apparently turned to Kuwait for money after Oprah Winfrey and Bill and Melinda Gates spurned his requests. Just to prove that Chiaravallo is not an anomaly in New Jersey, the new mayor of Lake Como, Michael Ryan, a Democrat, said that while contacting the Persian Gulf country for money was unusual, if the rich country wanted to give the town money without any strings attached, it would be a unique way to lower property taxes. In an effort to demonstrate how different he is from Chiaravallo, Ryan said he would use the money not for a police station but for a firehouse and to pay the town's debts. Borough lawyer William B. Gallagher said the borough was not interested in investigating Chiaravallo's contacts with Kuwait.

As we'll see later, in the Soprano State, the mob usually goes after big targets. But it also likes to share in the goodies that freely flow into the hands of local officials. Camden Mayor Milton Milan and Council President James Mathes linked their own greed with organized crime and found the feds knocking on their door.

Here's how the *Courier-Post* described Milan's plight:[12] "Milan was indicted March 29, 2000, by a federal grand jury in Camden. A jury convicted him of 14 of 19 counts of mail and wire fraud, conspiracy and money laundering, making him the third Camden mayor in 20 years to be found guilty of crimes.

The jury found, among other things, that he accepted as much as $30,000 in payoffs from former Philadelphia/South Jersey mob boss Ralph Natale between 1996 and 1998; laundered a $65,000 cash loan in 1994 from now-convicted drug dealer Jose 'JR' Rivera; used part of $7,500 he skimmed from campaign funds to pay for a trip to Puerto Rico with friends and supporters in 1997; and staged a burglary at his business, Atlas Contracting, in 1995 to collect insurance money.

Milan was stripped of his office the day after his conviction.

Later, federal prosecutors took taped conversations into the courtroom to nail Council President Mathes. The U.S. attorney's office described how it happened:[13] "During the trial, jurors heard more than 200 secretly recorded tapes of conversations in which, among other things, former Boss Ralph Natale of the Philadelphia La Cosa Nostra organized crime family (LCN) discussed with LCN family associate Daniel Daidone a conspiracy to corrupt Camden City officials in order to gain city contracts.

"During the trial, Natale testified that he was the boss of the Philadelphia LCN from 1994 to 1998, and that he had Daidone make payments to Mathes and former Camden City Mayor Milton Milan. Natale testified that he arranged for a Philadelphia jeweler to provide Mathes with a diamond ring for his girlfriend. Natale also testified that approximately two months after Milton Milan became president of Camden City Council, Natale, through Daidone, made his first payment to Milan."

U. S. Attorney Chris Christie said, "These convictions strike a blow at the two most insidious types of criminals—organized crime figures and corrupt politicians."[14]

Milan was released from prison and sent to a halfway house in October 2006.

Appointed by President George W. Bush after raising money for his campaign, Christie is a prosecutor—despite all the controversy over political firings of federal prosecutors—who wasn't afraid to go after Republican officials whether it was in Monmouth County or Essex County. He hooked a big fish with Essex County Executive Jim Treffinger, who thought he was heading to Washington as the next U.S. senator. That was before disclosure that Treffinger—whose hair was so perfectly quaffed some people thought he wore a wig—had put his hairdresser Cosmo Cerrigone on the payroll with what prosecutors called a no-show job.

Treffinger, a lawyer and former Fulbright Scholar, came to power in an upset victory in 1994 for county executive, the top official in

one of the state's most populous counties, which is heavily Democratic. He ran on a platform of integrity, singling out the no-show
jobs that are a staple of New Jersey's political corruption. "But instead of wiping out the practice," wrote Diane C. Walsh and Nikita
Stewart of the *Star-Ledger*, "federal authorities say he raised it to a
new art, doling out 'perfect attendance awards' to two $38,000-
a-year staffers who hardly ever reported to work."[15] Instead of
working in the Hall of Records, the two recent college grads toiled
in Treffinger's campaign headquarters. Another no-show, according to a federal indictment, was Cerrigone, the hairdresser and old
chum of Treffinger's who once vacationed with him in Italy.[16]

Treffinger was caught when the feds wiretapped Gerald Free, a
salesman for the sewer repair company United Gunite who used
bribes, travel, and gifts to win more than $50 million in work
statewide.[17] Free pleaded guilty to bribery charges but ended up
with six months of home arrest after cooperating with the feds.[18] In
a secretly recorded 2001 conversation, Treffinger bragged he was a
candidate for U.S. attorney for New Jersey and said when he got
the office, the probe was kaput. "Then, this whole thing goes
away," he allegedly told a friend. "Plenty of mobsters to go after;
you don't have to go after all these poor politicians plying their
trade."[19] That was a telling insight into a guy who climbed the lad-
der from a small-town city council to a race for the U.S. Senate.

Treffinger didn't get the U. S. attorney job, unfortunately for
the state's crooked politicians, because the man who did, Christie,
demonstrated with gusto what an honest, hard-driven G-man can
do. Three Treffinger aides or associates secretly taped him and
agreed to testify. One of them, a former county engineer, said Treffinger ordered him to arrange campaign contributions from United
Gunite.

Treffinger's indictment also said he conspired to make thousands of anonymous phone calls to South Jersey Republicans to

damage the campaign of one of his opponents for the GOP U.S. Senate nomination, State Sen. Diane Allen. In the calls, made during the Super Bowl weekend of 2002, a female voice attacked Allen's stand on abortion. The calls were done in such a way as to make them appear to be from another U.S. Senate candidate, State Sen. John Matheussen. And yet Treffinger tried to project a Snow White image to the point of being silly. He and County Sheriff Armando Fontoura actually banned *The Sopranos* from filming scenes on Essex County–owned property, the Associated Press reported. HBO wanted a permit to shoot a gunfight in the South Mountain Reservation. Treffinger, who is half Italian, said he did not want HBO to use public property "to perpetuate harmful stereotypes."[20]

But rather than TV shows, it is politicians like Treffinger who mold the national image of New Jersey. In thirteen months Treffinger went from promising U.S. Senate candidate to common criminal. He admitted coaching others to lie to federal investigators and created phony documents to hide $10,000 in campaign contributions from United Gunite.[21] His defense asked the judge for leniency, citing his fall from the heights of politics to being an unemployable lawyer who had converted from Catholic to Baptist and worked as a part-time church secretary. Prosecutors, dismissing the religiously reborn persona, said it was just one more campaign by a politician. "The only difference is the goal, which has turned from garnering votes to staying out of prison."[22]

In the end, Treffinger signed a six-page plea agreement. In return, eighteen of the twenty counts against him were dismissed. He got forty-one months—three more months than party boss John Lynch—and agreed to pay restitution to the county.[23] David Chase had the last laugh on Treffinger in the final episode of *The Sopranos* when he inserted a reference to political corruption and the prosecution of a county commissioner named James Treffolio.[24]

When Treffinger emerged from ten months in prison, he enrolled in Princeton Theological Seminary. He told Diane C. Walsh of the *Star-Ledger* that he had gone through an "epiphany" and now wanted to help other prisoners.

The feds captured another county politician just as big in Hudson County. As Treffinger arrived in court, Robert Janiszewski, a longtime Hudson official, was testifying as a government witness in another room in the same building.[25] Known as "Bobby J.," he pleaded guilty to extortion after the FBI caught him in its net. A former state assemblyman and Port Authority commissioner who ran Bill Clinton's Jersey campaigns in 1992 and 1996, Janiszewski was chief executive for fourteen years in Hudson County, one of the most powerful boss-run machine governments in the state.

The Janiszewski saga played out like a *Sopranos* episode. It involved Union City psychiatrist Oscar Sandoval, whose tape-recorded conversations put Donald Scarinci, longtime associate of U.S. Sen. Bob Menendez, on the hot seat. Sandoval had valuable Hudson County contracts and according to court testimony paid bribes to Bobby J. The woman passing the bribes from Sandoval to Janiszewski was Nidia Davila-Colon, the longest-sitting county freeholder, with nineteen years in the job, as well as the first Latina freeholder in the state. Davila-Colon met psychiatrist Sandoval as his patient. Although he was married, they became romantically involved after the therapy ended, she testified, but he kept prescribing antidepressants.[26] The problem was that no one knew Sandoval was secretly taping conversations for the FBI.[27] And he wasn't alone. So was Bobby J., who abruptly resigned and disappeared, to be discovered five months later by the *Jersey Journal* working in a ski shop near Hunter Mountain, New York.[28]

Leaving the slopes behind, Janiszewski returned to plead guilty to taking more than $100,000 in bribes. He was hit with $40,000 in fines and forty-one months behind bars, the longest possible under his plea bargain. The judge cited "corruption of unbelievable depth and duration." Davila-Colon was indicted on charges of passing the cash bribes from Sandoval to Bobby J. And Hudson County Freeholder William Braker of Jersey City resigned, saying he was not guilty but news reports said indictments were expected.[29] A week later, in true New Jersey style, Davila-Colon and Braker were reelected to another term as county freeholders. The day after the election, Braker, thinking he was in the clear, rescinded his resignation. But he was wrong. A month later, he was arrested and charged with extorting Sandoval and demanding "cash and Viagra." He pleaded guilty, admitting he extorted $3,000, and was sentenced to forty-one months in prison.[30]

Davila-Colon, who never pocketed any of the bribes, went to trial. A jury convicted her of delivering two cash-stuffed envelopes to Bobby J. During the sentencing another psychiatrist testified Davila-Colon, while being treated for depression, became dependent—not on the drugs but on the doctor/boyfriend, Sandoval. She was sentenced to three years in prison, less than she could have received, because the judge said Davila-Colon—like the mob and political bosses who argue for leniency—had done exceptional charity work.[31]

Believe it or not, Hudson County once had a reformer, Jersey City Mayor Glenn Cunningham, a former cop and Marine veteran. Cunningham, a Democrat, challenged the establishment candidate for a state senate seat in 2003 and surprised the heck out of everyone by capturing the primary, along with his two assembly running mates, in a victory over longtime assemblyman Joe Doria and his running mates, who were endorsed by the Hudson County Democratic Organization. Cunningham won the general election in November, but five months after he was sworn in, he died suddenly of a heart attack. While the defeated Doria, who also was mayor of Bayonne, got appointed to the senate seat, Cunningham's wife, Sandra, vowed to keep the reform movement going.

Three years later, in 2007, Sandra Bolden Cunningham announced her candidacy for the senate seat and laid out an anticorruption platform opposing the dual officeholding even her husband had participated in. "Not long ago, there was a voice of integrity, but when that voice silenced another rose. This voice will continue what that voice started," the *Waterfront Journal* reported. A month later, in a surprise move, Doria dropped out of the race. He and Senate Majority Leader Bernie Kenny, chairman of the Hudson County Democrats, joined roughly a dozen state senators announcing their retirements.

Even with so many senators departing, there wasn't much optimism the situation was going to improve greatly. Some of them were being replaced by members of the assembly moving up, and the ones who weren't were political insiders raised on the system.

Sandra Cunningham won the Senate Primary race, but by then she had smashed the reformer logo to pieces, once again proving there is no hope for improvement in New Jersey. The *Star-Ledger's* Tom Moran blasted Cunningham before the election as among the worst New Jersey politics has to offer. Moran cited the convicted child rapist working for her campaign, her drunken driving conviction in 2005, and a *Jersey Journal* report that a charitable foundation she runs spent most of its money on parties and things like her salary.[32]

There wasn't much hope the assembly would improve appreciably, either. Some eyeing the seats of those leaving for the upper chamber were retreads who had served in the assembly and wanted another bite of the apple.

The only hope to weed out some of the bad apples in the legislature was an ongoing federal probe into whether New Jersey lawmakers traded their votes for goodies for themselves and their districts.

In New Jersey's affluent areas, the taxpayers are supporting their own local greedy politicians. In places like Camden and Newark, the local pols give away the treasury, which is stocked with taxpayers' money from other parts of the state, since local taxes can't support the patronage-ridden and corruption-plagued governments.

Contractual agreements with former Camden police chief Edwin Figueroa allowed him to retire in February 2006 with a severance package worth more than $256,000, including $149,000 for unused vacation pay, $40,000 in unused sick leave, and $39,000 for longevity bonuses.[33] That's right, some civil servants have contracts that pay them additional money if they stay on for specified periods. At fifty-seven, Figueroa had been on the police force for thirty-two years but chief for only two. Camden was running a $47 million deficit while crime rates were soaring. The prior chief left with a severance package worth more than $153,000. (Those examples are not even close to a Jersey record. When Parsippany Police Chief Michael Filippello retired in '06, he was paid $469,000 in unused sick and vacation days.[34] On top of that he got a $95,000 annual pension. When Newark Mayor Sharpe James and twenty-one former members of his administration left city government, they got checks for unused vacation and sick time totaling $658,187.[35] Seems like Jersey pols never get sick or take any time off.)

Camden's two-year-tenured police chief's departure happened as the state was engaged in a partial takeover of the city in what was ballyhooed as an effort to get corruption and crime under control. To oversee the cleanup, the McGreevey administration hired a former Camden mayor, Randy Primas, who was well connected to the

South Jersey Democratic machine run by Boss George Norcross and already had a reputation as a machine guy. After his earlier term as Camden mayor, Primas took a state job with another politician out of Camden, former governor Jim Florio.

Primas served as Florio's Department of Community Affairs commissioner and chairman of the state Housing and Mortgage Finance Agency, which supervises municipal financing and bonding. Leaving state government in 1992, Primas quickly aligned himself with Commerce Capital Markets, a company allied with Norcross. But what spurred a scandal in Trenton was Primas's joining Cypress Securities, Inc., in Cherry Hill, where he became managing director. The firm's majority owner was Florio fund-raiser Vernon Hill II, founder of Commerce Bank. The newly created Cypress Securities, despite its lack of experience, began raking in state and local no-bid contracts, raising questions by Republicans in the legislature at a time when the federal government was investigating bond issuance in New Jersey.[36]

"After Primas came on board, Cypress was picked as a co-underwriter of the state's controversial $1.8 billion refinancing package," the *News Tribune* wrote. "Underwriters were picked without competitive bidding, and the state never sought proposals from bond dealers. Cypress had never participated in a bond issue bigger than $35.6 million and had only worked as an underwriter in six earlier issues. . . . Cypress also was picked without any bidding to serve as a financial adviser to the state Transportation Trust Fund Authority, which was preparing for an April,1993 sale of $500 million in new road construction bonds."

Making matters worse was the business Cypress landed with the Housing and Mortgage Finance Agency, where Primas previously served as chairman. In one lucrative deal, Cypress was among the highest paid without selling even one bond. "The fledgling Cherry Hill firm was paid $111,218 for its role in the sale of

NJHMFA bonds, records show," the *Record* reported. "The firm didn't sell a bond, but only three of the 25 firms in the deal, some of which sold millions of dollars worth of bonds, made more than Cypress."[37]

When Republicans cried foul, Cypress president David B. Thompson told the *News Tribune* that it was the firm's expertise, not its political ties, that landed the lucrative contracts. In reality, the revolving door between government and the private sector rakes in millions for the politically connected. But even when they head to private industry, they hang on to their state pensions.

Fourteen years after leaving Florio's cabinet, Primas resurfaced big-time. He was hired as Camden's overseer at $175,000 a year, the same pay a New Jersey governor gets, and given czarlike powers to veto actions of the city's council, agencies, and boards. Howard Gillette's book *Camden After the Fall* says Primas was the only candidate interviewed for the job.[38] "All this is exploitation of a poor city and poor people," said Colandus "Kelly" Francis, head of the Camden chapter of the NAACP.

Primas signaled what he thought of Camden's "revitalization" chances by his choice of residence. He didn't live in Camden. He didn't even live in New Jersey. Investigative reporter Alan Guenther of the *Courier-Post* found that Primas resided in Delaware, a state with lower taxes and less crime.[39] Primas purchased a condo there in 2004 for $399,025. In his four years as overseer, Primas did little, if anything, to curb the patronage and corruption that rule the town and helped bring it to its knees. Kelly Francis, who also works with the Camden City Taxpayers Association advocacy group, told the *Philadelphia Inquirer*'s Dwight Ott, "Primas has taken the city backwards, not forwards."[40]

There's budgetary evidence to back that up. The state approved $175 million—in bonds, borrowed money—to rebuild Camden in 2002. The city's deficit went from $9.8 million at the launch of the "revitalization" to $47.1 million in the 2005–6 budget year without a lot to show for it, leaving observers asking: Who got the money?

Not surprisingly, Primas was chiefly supported by other elements of the Norcross machine, like Assembly Speaker Joe Roberts, who coauthored the takeover legislation and represents the district that Camden is in. He said Primas "has done a good job under very challenging conditions."

During the "revitalization" the Camden mayor was Gwendolyn Faison, an octogenarian who once felt it necessary to show a rally for U.S. Senators Barack Obama of Illinois and Bob Menendez of New Jersey that she could dance with her new artificial hip.

Faison signed a memo of understanding with the state giving more fiscal control to the Department of Community Affairs in Trenton. Then, when she realized the county political machine was unhappy, she did an about-face, wrapped in a blanket of more Camden righteous indignation:[41] "It is an insult to me and the residents of Camden that they would try to impose this." Asked why she signed it, the mayor said she didn't realize what she was doing. That document, which gave Community Affairs Commissioner Susan Bass Levin strict control of Camden's hiring and spending, became the focal point of a feud between Primas and the commissioner, who said if Primas didn't sign, the money flow to Camden would stop.

Primas maintained he and Levin were equals and refused. Governor Corzine backed his commissioner, and on October 12, 2006, Primas called it quits as overseer.[42] That left Faison, little more than comic relief for the past few years, in charge.

The Camden takeover idea originated in the Christie Whitman administration. Senator Bryant at first opposed it. When Democrat McGreevey succeeded Republican Gov. Donald DiFrancesco, who replaced Whitman when she joined the Bush administration, South Jersey Democrats realized what a gold mine a takeover could be since they were in control. McGreevey wanted to put the revitalizing money in the state budget, which would have required it to be renewed every year. Bryant would have no part of that. "It will not pass my house," he said, meaning the state senate.[43] He told the weak-kneed governor it would be borrowed money and the entire $175 million would be available from the start. McGreevey caved, and the taxpayers will pay for it for decades.

The recovery act appears to have been little more than a scheme to distribute additional state money to the usual suspects. As for Camden, despite millions of dollars, it shows next to no improvement. Its people still suffer, which, sadly, should come as no surprise. There was ample recent history for McGreevey to have known the likely result. State takeovers don't have a good track record.

Under Whitman, the state took control of Newark's school district. Beverly Hall was brought in from New York to run things. During a three-month period in 1996, Hall's staff spent $92,000 for food and catering.[44] The district was warned to no avail. During the same period the next year, it spent $84,000 for catering. Newark school officials also built an addition to Arts High School without bothering to get a permit. Yet Whitman's education commissioner, Leo Klagholz, waited for thirteen months before he wrote to Hall in 1999 to say "shortcomings" had been found. Two months later Klagholz was gone, leaving to teach at a state college. Hall was history in three months; she went south to run Atlanta's school system.

The devastating result: a $73 million budget shortfall.[45] But no one was found liable for any criminal activity. An education spokesman explained, "Because of lax controls in the business office, they were spending money they may not have realized they didn't have."

When the state took over the school district, its coffers were flush with $58 million. It went through that and $58 million more for a total of $116 million, leaving Sen. Robert Martin to lament that more than $100 million was now missing. "Where did the money go?" he asked.[46] Not only had the state-run school district spent money it did not have, $9 million in unpaid bills were found in school district drawers.

School districts are a favorite way local pols take advantage of taxpayers. They pad the payroll with unnecessary administrators and their assistants who have assistants, which they justify by claiming, "It's for the children." After years of state oversight and taxpayer money poured into the state's large city schools, an audit in 2007 showed millions were wasted. In Camden alone, $13 million in spending was questioned, including apparent payments to the dead.

"A number of employees were on the payroll after their deaths, including 10 who were issued a total of $380,000 in compensation after dying," the *Courier-Post* reported.[47] "One employee, hired in 1966 and dead since 1974, was listed as retired in 2006. He was issued checks of $130,000 after taxes. Many employees lacked personnel files, while three employees have birth dates sometime in the future—such as Sept. 17, 2048." The school district responded with its own report saying the dead and yet-to-be-born employees really had not been paid, but the bookkeeping was so sloppy and antiquated that it appeared that way.[48] In the future, the school district vowed, it would promptly remove the dead from its payroll records and flag payments to those too young to work—a novel idea.

The State Commission of Investigation issued a report in 2006 called "Taxpayers Beware."[49] It showed that the Hopatcong school superintendent, Wayne Threlkeld, had a base salary of $182,847, but his total compensation was actually $221,880—a difference of $39,033, or 21.3 percent. The SCI report said New Brunswick Superintendent Ronald Larkin received $487,000 in compensation in his final year working for the city, although his official reported salary was $226,000.

The average reported salary among administrators in 71 of the 615 districts the SCI examined was $181,000, while the actual compensation neared $252,000—all this at a time when New Jersey governors were paid $175,000 annually.

In October 2006, seven months after the scathing SCI report, the state Department of Education posted online a database listing salaries for 1,518 top school district administrators.[50] It said eleven state school districts paid superintendents base salaries of more than $200,000 and dozens more were not far behind. The education department should get an F on that report. It didn't mention the names of the administrators, nor did it list the generous perks and benefits the SCI report said distorted what the public was told about school district compensation. "They don't include the types of things that our work revealed," said Lee Seglem, SCI spokesman. Salaries for top school administrators grew by 31 percent from 1997 to 2004, while the average teacher salary grew by about half that. The education department's report was based on a survey of salaries as of October 15, 2005. It took the department a year to make it public, limited as it was, and had it not been for the SCI report, the limited information probably would not have been posted on the Web at all.

Coincidentally, made public the same day was a list of New Jersey's two hundred most prolific "tackers" in 2005—people who string together government jobs and boost their pensions.[51] It was requested by Republican Sen. Bill Gormley as lawmakers looked at ways to take control of government employee pensions in an effort to cap the highest property taxes in the nation. Eight state lawmakers were on that list. Sen. Nicholas Scutari, D-Union, who had two public jobs, wanted to limit the reforms. He said people with expertise, such as health inspectors or lawyers (like Scutari himself), should be able to work in several towns.[52]

Gormley's suggestion was simple and logical. "Limiting public employees to a single pension based on one job is a common-sense approach to ending this fiscal mess."

Senator Nicholas Sacco, D-Hudson, earned the No. 4 position on the list with a combined salary of $247,558 from jobs as North Bergen mayor, assistant schools superintendent, and senator, which paid $49,000.

You may wonder how school superintendents and other public employees earn their pay and future pensions when they spend time in Trenton as legislators. How could they get that much work done in a day? The legislature, in its infinite wisdom, passed a law that says public employees who also are state lawmakers must be paid for their public jobs back home while they're cavorting in the statehouse. It's another way New Jersey taxpayers are shortchanged to the benefit of multiple-job-holding politicians, who, of course, passed the law to benefit only themselves.

Union County Assemblyman Neil Cohen, who made $182,432 from five jobs, offered up another excuse, saying if tacked-on pensions were banned, other people would be filling the positions. If pensions were paid only to full-time employees, holders of the part-time jobs wouldn't get pensions. That's especially true of lawyers or judges who work in several small towns. One from the list worked in eleven towns and made $171,777.

That's the real reason lawmakers want to keep 566 separate municipalities in the nation's fifth smallest state by land area. Every little burg and hamlet needs a judge, a police chief, a mayor, and the like—and they all get in on the pension bonanza that includes paid health care for life.

Union City Mayor—and state lawmaker—Brian Stack was after more than pension money, according to ongoing lawsuits accusing him of making sure his political contributors who were contractors got the approvals they needed from the city zoning board.[53] Within a two-year period, developers with cases before the zoning board gave $146,000 in contributions, leading developer Ralph Lieber, who did not contribute and who got rejected, to declare, "Simply put, zoning board approvals are for sale." Stack told the *Star-Ledger* that Lieber's comments were "sour grapes." However, another lawsuit, filed by the state Schools Construction Corporation, quoted a former zoning board member who said Stack orchestrated votes on the board.

One of the biggest downsides of Jersey's archaic machine political system is the need to keep the faithful employed at any cost. One example is William Krebs.

After he lost his job with a pharmaceutical company, Krebs found a paycheck at the South Jersey Port Corporation, which operates the Camden port on the Delaware River, as an assistant to the port's executive director, a post created for him by the port's board. Krebs also is a Gloucester County freeholder, an elected county official, with ties to people like State Sen. Steve Sweeney, who also double-dips as a Gloucester County official and is part of the Norcross machine based in Camden County. Krebs was paid $90,000 a year, but a probe by the *Courier-Post*'s Eileen Stilwell revealed a flagrant disregard for the port's security ID system for workers and an erratic work schedule.[54] Between May 1 and September 1, 2006, Krebs failed to swipe his ID card fifty out of seventy-five workdays. He frequently arrived after 10:00 A.M. and left at 4:00 P.M. with a lunch break in between.

The port's directors decided to eliminate Krebs's job in April 2006, officially because he didn't have enough work to do. But more importantly, he also appeared to have fallen out of favor with

Gloucester County Democrats. Krebs, a two-term county free-holder, was dropped from the 2006 ticket.

Months after his port job was eliminated, however, he still was on the port payroll and driving a state-issued car.[55] After his term as freeholder expired, he had ten years in New Jersey's Public Employees' Retirement System. If he doesn't return to the public payroll or even if he never works again, he is entitled to an annual pension of $19,000 at age sixty. That's based on his $17,000-a-year salary from the county and that $90,000 port job that was determined to be unnecessary.

Unnecessary jobs are the stock-in-trade of political machines. When four Camden County government workers became too sick to work, they were transferred to no-show management jobs, costing taxpayers $162,000, wrote investigative reporter Alan Guenther of the *Courier-Post*.[56] Another employee too sick to work got health benefits for eleven years at a cost of $66,460. The five were politically active Democrats. Another forty county employees who apparently didn't have the right connections lost their salaries because they were on extended sick or maternity leave. When Guenther asked how the freeholders board decided on the four who kept their pay, he was told that was done behind closed doors. Another with a no-show job when sick was Joseph Springle, former chief administrator of the Camden County prosecutor's office, who was kept on salary for sixteen months, ending with his retirement, in a deal worked out by then-prosecutor Republican Lee Solomon, who later was nominated for a state judgeship by the Democrats. Without the special treatment, salaries and benefits would have expired and the employees would have had to apply for disability payments, which typically are about 66 percent of a worker's pay. Moving the sick workers into management jobs gave them thousands of extra dollars during the illnesses. The money came from Camden County taxpayers, some of the most overtaxed in the state.

"I suppose there is a question of fairness," said Karl Walko, president of Council 10, the union that represented four of the workers before they were transferred to management jobs. "The rules should apply to everybody."

Questions were referred to Jeffrey Nash, a tool of the Norcross machine who as a freeholder is an elected Camden County official and also double-dips as vice chairman of the bistate Delaware River Port Authority, which runs some of the toll bridges over the Delaware River. Nash still found time to be a member of a law firm. Reporter Guenther sent Nash eleven questions to which Nash responded with one paragraph, a part of which fell back on Camden-style righteous indignation: "Any suggestion that the county's actions are motivated by politics is inaccurate and offensive."

It was all about compassion, Nash said, to which Robert Levin, an attorney for the nonpartisan state Office of Legislative Services, responded: "There is nothing in the law that allows public money to be spent for acts of compassion by the freeholders." Ingrid Reed of Rutgers University's Eagleton Institute of Politics said awarding pay out of compassion "is not an acceptable way" to manage public money.

Camden County also provided lifetime full health benefits for a large number of people who lacked enough time on the job to qualify.[57] As the cost of insurance soars, so does the price of the county's mistake. Through the end of 2005, wrote reporter Guenther, the cost had reached at least $46 million. Nash declined to be interviewed but issued a statement objecting to use of the word "illegal" in describing benefits that exceed New Jersey law.[58]

Public records show that about 57 percent of the county's retirees didn't work long enough to earn their benefits. State law requires government employees to work for twenty-five years or to work fifteen years and be sixty-two years old before they qualify for lifetime paid health benefits when they retire. Soon after Nash was elected to the Norcross-Democratic-machine-controlled freehold-ers board in 1991, the county agreed to pay full benefits for re-tirees with as little as five years of government service.

In 1993, during Nash's first term on the board, county employ-ees were given a health benefits package more generous than any ever offered in New Jersey. While he was a failure when it came to watching taxpayers' money, Nash was full of himself for other rea-sons: "Since I became director, the county Democrats have not come close to losing an election, and I'm very proud of that."

John Hanson, who ironically in his former job as leader of the Camden County Republicans was responsible for recruiting and leading candidates in challenges to Nash and the Norcross ma-chine that rules the county, said, "I came to have great respect for his [Nash's] desire to serve the public and help the public."[59] Han-son wasn't successful in recruiting GOP challengers, but he did manage to land a cushy job as chief financial officer at the very po-litical DRPA, where Vice Chairman Nash heads the New Jersey del-egation.

In Jersey's tangled web of local politics, there are strange things happening even in the offices of county sheriffs. Take Union County's Sheriff's Officer Christopher Coon, who bought a $49,500 Mercedes and sued because he was unhappy with the vehi-cle.[60] He won and was awarded more than $142,000 in damages and attorney fees. The dealership appealed but failed to post the necessary bond. Sheriff's deputies showed up at the dealership and seized three vehicles—a Porsche, a BMW, and a Volvo—with a retail value of more than $100,000. They were slated to be sold at auction to satisfy the outstanding judgment. The dealer tried to buy back the cars, bidding more than $110,000, but failed to pro-duce a certified check as auction rules required.

In the end, Coon and his mother, Marlene Froehlich, who cosigned for the Mercedes purchase and is married to Coon's stepfather, the county sheriff, bought the three cars for $300. The dealer still owed the $142,000 judgment minus the $300, and if he didn't pay, he was liable for another seizure.

As Ted Sherman of the *Star-Ledger* pointed out, the only announcement of the car auction for the three vehicles was a notice posted in the sheriff's office. Only one other bidder showed up.

Henry Furst, the lawyer for Coon and his mom, said his clients received no favoritism. Perhaps, but if that auction notice had been posted on the Internet or around town in public places, somewhere besides the sheriff's office, there certainly would have been more bidders.

U.S. District Judge William Walls summed up the condition of New Jersey's local government in August 2007 when he sentenced former Monmouth County mayor Terrance Weldon to fifty-eight months in jail. Weldon, who pleaded guilty to taking $64,000 in bribes, helped the feds arrest and convict an auditor, a developer, and a local sewerage authority chairman and also helped arrest an engineer whose trial was expected to begin in December, the *Asbury Park Press* reported. Prosecutors said one restaurant owner who refused to pay a bribe to Weldon found inspectors at his doorstep and a dead chicken over his door.

Tired of New Jersey politicians "hell-bent on corruption," Judge Walls was not impressed with Weldon's cooperation and likened it to Al Capone helping the feds nab his driver.

7

Speaking Authoritatively:
No Oversight

New Jersey's government authorities are perhaps the biggest boondoggles and burying grounds for deadwood and unemployed relatives. There are more than 300 state and local authorities, independent bodies that can float bonds and spend money without outside control. Basically, they're about getting around the state constitution's requirement that borrowing has to be voter-approved and are an example of how politicians have reduced the control the general population has over its government. The contracts they generate also can help friends and allies.

State Inspector General Mary Jane Cooper investigated forty-five New Jersey authorities and found perks even overindulged state workers in other offices don't enjoy. She discovered employees at the Atlantic City Convention Center Authority spending up to $125 per person on business dinners. And one executive at the Casino Reinvestment Development Authority had a state car for commuting but socked the state with another $1,700 for gas in his own car.[1]

The state Casino Reinvestment Development Authority, or CRDA, was created in 1984 to develop blighted areas through funding from a surcharge on casino profits. Democrat Gov. Jim McGreevey raised eyebrows when he named Republican Curtis Bashaw CRDA executive director, a plum political post that usually goes to the party in power. Both McGreevey and Bashaw are gay, but Bashaw said there never was an intimate relationship.

Strange things started happening under Bashaw's leadership. Over a six-year period, Sun National Bank of Vineland had loaned Bashaw and his business partners $18 million in mortgage money for their Congress Hall hotel in Cape May. Two months after Bashaw was appointed to CRDA, the authority board passed a resolution giving Sun National Bank's affiliate development company nearly half a block, eleven lots assessed for $322,700, for just $10 total.

Coauthor McClure picks up the story:[2]

The April 2004 resolution added new development rights to the project, giving Sun National Bank's affiliate, Vineland Construction, an entire block for development of a five-story office building at Indiana and Atlantic avenues, where a new bank branch, a post office and a parking deck will be located.

Bernard A. Brown, chairman of Sun Bankcorp Inc., parent company of Sun National Bank, is president of Vineland Construction, the developer.

Five months earlier, in November 2003, the CRDA agreed to pay Sun National Bank $4.2 million, more than twice the $1.54 million assessed value, for its Atlantic City bank building at Atlantic and Arkansas avenues.

Bashaw was on the bank's Cape May County advisory board, and his financial disclosure form showed he owned between $5,000 and $25,000 of the bank's stock. Bashaw told McClure he left the bank board when he went to CRDA but had not recused himself from Sun National Bank issues because he was an administrator, not a board member, and it's the board that makes decisions.

Lloyd Levenson, Vineland Construction's politically connected lawyer, said the $10 for the eleven lots was not a bargain because some of the lots have environmental contamination, although he didn't know what the contamination was. Fred Munford of the state Department of Environmental Protection said the site required removal of underground tanks.

When Gov. Dick Codey succeeded the disgraced McGreevey, he wanted someone else at the helm of CRDA. Bashaw resigned but planned to continue as chairman of the Jersey Shore Tourism Corporation, a newly created nonprofit that operated outside state government but had $500,000 in CRDA money to promote tourism.

In a June 2004 speech at Asbury Park, Bashaw warned about conversions of existing buildings and businesses into condominiums. "We need to make sure that the voracious appetite for condos and second homes doesn't neuter our towns of attractions and transient places to stay," he said. "We need our motels and our mini-golf courses and hot dog stands and boardwalk commercial zones."

Nevertheless, Bashaw was a partner in two development projects converting Cape May motels into condominiums, the Sandpiper and the Driftwood.[3] Under the name Sandpiper Beach Associates, Bashaw converted what was once the Sandpiper Beach Inn, with sixty-five motel rooms, into fifty-two Sandpiper Beach Club condos. The Web site for the project refers to the condos as second homes and shows scenes of a waterfront view and a suite decorated by Colleen Bashaw, Curtis's sister. Bashaw's Washington-based lawyer said there was no inconsistency in what he said and what he did because changing an existing motel to a condo-motel is not the same as shore areas losing other commercial properties like mini-golf or custard stands. (Condo-motels have hotel amenities and are sometimes rented.)

Public disclosure forms show that Jamie Fox, who was McGreevey's chief of staff before the governor—on his way out the door—appointed him to the Port Authority of New York and New Jersey, invested $50,000 in the Sandpiper.

Among investors in both of Bashaw's projects are Sandy Keziah, who was president of a Colorado company hired by CRDA for a survey on shore tourism that included concerns about the conversion of hotels to condos, and David Von Savage, chairman of the Cape May County Republican Party. Three other investors in the projects either sat on Cape May city boards regulating development or were married to people who did.

When Bashaw left CRDA, he also resigned as chairman of the Jersey Shore nonprofit after news stories raised conflict of interest questions about his heading a group receiving CRDA funds.

He was replaced at CRDA by Thomas D. Carver, who announced CRDA under Bashaw had spent all its grant money and depleted its future project money by spending revenues it had yet to receive.[4] For the next three years, Carver said, $120 million in anticipated revenues had been committed. At the last minute, $1 million went to the Cape May zoo and $3 million to a convention center in Cape May near Bashaw's hotel.

"For years, this organization was flush with money," Carver said. "And guess what? They spent it."

The lucrative revolving door between government and private industry continued in New Jersey. Bashaw quickly went into the casino development business in Atlantic City.[5] Thomas Auriemma, director of the Division of Gaming Enforcement—the agency charged with keeping the casinos honest—joined Penn National Gaming, Inc., owner of sixteen casinos and horse tracks, as vice president and chief compliance officer.[6] The moves apparently met the lax state rules on postemployment conflicts because Bashaw's projects would take several years before they were up and running and Penn National had yet to play in the Atlantic City market.

The $120 million CRDA blew was nothing next to the $8.6 billion the state Schools Construction Corporation (SCC) went through in record time. With much fanfare and a wink from the state supreme court, the New Jersey Legislature created the SCC, supposedly to build and repair schools but more realistically to pay back the education lobby, trade union lobby, and various other hangers-on and dim-wit supporters and their families who needed a paycheck. Its $8.6 billion budget was to last ten years. Amid scandal and corruption, it ran dry in about three years with less than half the projects done.

The state supreme court, nevertheless, wanted the taxpayers to ante up for the rest of it. That's about $13 billion more to complete plans laid out in 2000 if they were done right away. New proposals have been added. If it takes ten years to complete them, inflation and interest are estimated to balloon the cost to $29 billion.

The Office of the Inspector General (OIG) investigated the SCC and in an April 2005 report said problems broadly fell into two areas:[7]

1. Weak internal management and financial controls and questionable personnel practices.
2. Lax and/or nonexistent oversight and accountability.

The agency did not have a chief financial officer, comptroller, or other senior official responsible for the oversight of an operating budget of up to $40 million. It employed 270 and paid $16 million in salaries.

"Questionable personnel practices include, in addition to regular salaries and raises, bonus payments for certain employees—a highly unusual perk for government entities. According to a review of the corporation's records, for calendar year 2003, $113,500 in bonuses was paid to 43 staff. Of that amount, $32,000 was split between the chief operating officer and two managing directors. For calendar year 2004, essentially the same amount of bonus money was dispersed, but the amount of bonuses was lowered and the bonuses were dispensed more widely: 68 staff received bonuses and the COO and certain high level managers received the maximum, $4,000 each," the OIG said.

Most of the SCC employees were housed in a six-story building in Trenton that cost SCC $10 million to renovate and furnish, but the agency operated three regional offices in close proximity to each other. State-owned vehicles were assigned to seventeen SCC employees, and until Acting Governor Codey put a stop to it, forty-one SCC employees were allotted mileage allowances of $450 a month.

The 270 employees were insufficient, apparently, so at least twenty-two individuals were hired under a three-year contract, worth up to $25 million, with an outside employment agency. These outsiders were paid about three times what SCC would pay comparable state workers.

Beyond the overstuffed payroll, there was the question of land acquisition, the OIG report said. "Sites targeted for school construction have been found to be environmentally contaminated, requiring substantial additional expenditures for clean up and remediation. In others, relocation costs alone have turned out to be triple the price of the land parcel itself."

In 2003, New Jersey Treasurer John McCormac gave Joseph

Jingoli & Son the final nod as construction manager on four projects costing the school construction program $250 million.[8] Jin-
goli, a major Democratic donor, had given the party $150,000 the
month the award was made, the *Star-Ledger* reported. McCormac
and officials at the Schools Construction Corporation said the donations had nothing to do with the award. GOP State Senator Peter Inverso disagreed. "Clearly there is a nexus between what firms
contribute and what they get," he told the *Star-Ledger*. After the
problems were aired, New Jersey Inspector General Cooper recommended changes in SCC procedures and a resumption of
spending of the remaining funds.

For waste and corruption it's hard to beat Camden, and it's also
hard to know where to begin. So we threw a dart and it landed on
the Housing Authority—a high-profile agency in one of the nation's poorest towns with a waiting list for a place to stay that can
stretch for four years or more, a wait so long the authority won't
accept new applications. Alan Guenther of the *Courier-Post* reported that was not a problem, however, for Geronimo Santana,
son of the authority's executive director, Maria Marquez.[9] He lived
in public housing three years rent-free, then bought the unit from
the authority and sold it a short while later for a $40,000 profit.

Marquez's daughter-in-law Betzaida Santana, who works at the
authority, received a $10,000 boost in salary to $35,000 annually
even as the authority considered Marquez's proposal to lay off
more than thirty workers because of a deficit of between $700,000
and $1.3 million, plus $1.8 million in unpaid water and utility bills.
Marquez announced the layoffs as she was planning a trip to Den-
ver with five other Housing Authority members. Meanwhile, Housing Authority administrator Kathryn Blackshear, who made
$69,000 a year and also served on the local school board, lived in
public housing.

Places like Camden are ripe for authority abuse. So much

money is poured in from Trenton. So many hangers-on are ready to take it. So little oversight is involved.

Why would a place with as many social and economic problems as Camden need an authority to handle parking? Money and patronage. In the early '90s the guy running it was Ted Hinson, who just happened also to be head of the city's Democratic Party, a unit of boss George Norcross's county machine. He drove a Lincoln Continental with two telephones and pulled down an $87,000 annual salary.[10] The authority ordered flowers to hand out and had fancy catered lunches. Hinson and his pals lived high on the hog in a town where many families had trouble getting enough pork to season their beans.

Imagine the insensitivity it takes to drive amidst that much poverty in a fancy car with two telephones. Not to mention the fact that the authority was going broke.

After a tough editorial campaign by Ingle, Gov. Christie Whitman sent in state auditors. Ingle wrote, "Grateful taxpayers can thank the Local Finance Board (LFB), a part-time state agency which waded through enough political claptrap to down a horse, and in the end, reached the only logical conclusion—the authority is beyond helping itself."[11]

The state came in, took Hinson's Lincoln Continental with the two phones, and reduced his pay by $37,000. Under Hinson, the authority lost $1 million. After the state moved in, the authority would make an estimated $425,000. Incredibly, as Hinson was stepping down, Parking Authority commissioner Vernon Hill (no connection to the Commerce Bank founder) tried to push through a $130,000 parting gift for him. An investigation of Hill showed his appointment to the commission was illegal under New Jersey law because he was on the city payroll when Camden Mayor Arnold Webster named him to the authority.

Ingle picks up the story: "Hill calls himself the mayor's son, although he is not related to Webster. His city job was in the Department of Community Affairs, run by Novella Hinson, related to Ted Hinson by marriage—she's his wife. And, that's just one example of why the employee flow chart for Camden government looks like a family tree."[12] Hinson's handpicked party committee reelected him to run the city party. Then Boss Norcross's county machine nominated Hinson to sit on the county board of elections, a part-time job that pays $10,000. It was arranged by County Democratic Chairman David Luthman.

"Luthman and the back-room crowd feel they have to bail out Hinson because, every election, he gets Camden residents to turn out and vote Democratic," Ingle wrote.[13] "That allows the machine to stay in power and get first crack at jobs and lucrative contracts. Unfortunately, the Camden people living in poverty are ignored, shunned and stepped on until their votes are needed again."

Six years later, Camden's parking authority was back in the news. Joseph Bowen, who had been hired by the authority's then-chief, Anthony Scarduzio, to do maintenance work, filed a lawsuit against the agency saying it was a den of patronage, bid rigging, and corruption. It didn't take a genius to notice that, but it really ruffled the feathers of Scarduzio, who worked the system to rise through the ranks, a system that relies on being blind to public rip-offs and loyal to benefactors.

Then the rift turned violent.

Andrew Jacobs of the *New York Times* said investigators believed Scarduzio shot Bowen four times and nearly beat him to death as he did landscaping in Gloucester County.[14] "Minutes later," Jacobs wrote, "the police found Mr. Scarduzio sprawled on the floor of a friend's home less than a mile away, a shotgun by his side, his face obliterated by a single blast to the head."

Apparently, the state had taken special notice of the authority again, and Scarduzio was in the spotlight once reserved for Hinson.

"State officials would not detail the charges they were preparing against Mr. Scarduzio," reporter Jacobs said. "But Mr. Bowen claimed that Mr. Scarduzio had awarded lucrative contracts to friends and condoned widespread patronage at the Parking Authority, one of the few money-making agencies in Camden. In 1999, Mr. Scarduzio joined Mayor Milan on a golfing trip to Arizona that was paid for by a consultant to the authority. In February, investigators said, they received a copy of a fax that Mr. Scarduzio had sent to the consultant, asking him to claim that he had been reimbursed for the trip." His death was ruled a suicide.

One of the ripest areas for authority abuse is New Jersey's toll road system. Only in New Jersey would roads need such vast bureaucracies to operate. In most other states, roads seem to work just fine with minimal oversight. At one time the New Jersey Turnpike, the Garden State Parkway, and the Atlantic City Expressway had separate authorities behind them. Under McGreevey, the Parkway and Turnpike bureaucracies were combined. The South Jersey Transportation Authority, which oversees the Atlantic City Expressway and the Atlantic City International Airport, was left out so the South Jersey pols could continue to use it as one of their patronage mills. But Governor Corzine pulled the plug on South Jersey boss Norcross when he announced in 2007 that the state transportation commissioner, Kris Kolluri, would chair both the Turnpike and South Jersey authorities, likely clearing the way for the state to do what New Jersey does to balance its state budget: sell things, like either the Turnpike or the airport, to someone—say, the Port Authority of New York and New Jersey.

Kolluri, an Indian émigré, had raised questions when he commuted 130 miles from Trenton to Georgetown University in Washington to finish his law degree at the same time he was chief of staff at the state transportation department.[15] His boss was then-Commissioner Jamie Fox, who left that job to be McGreevey's chief of staff, then went to the Port Authority, then resigned to start a firm with offices in Washington and New York to advise clients on transportation issues. So Kolluri has the right connections.

So did Susan Bass Levin. When Fox left his job as deputy director at the Port Authority of New York and New Jersey, Corzine appointed Bass Levin to the post that pays $250,000. But that wasn't enough. While Corzine was bad-mouthing those in the Legislature with dual positions to pad their pensions, he did the same for Levin, who would go to the port authority without enough time in the state pension system to qualify for free health benefits upon retirement. Corzine appointed Levin to a five-year term on the Local Finance Board (ironically the ethics watchdog for local government) for another $12,000 a year, allowing her to stay in the state pension plan long enough to tap into the free health benefits for life. Who got Bass Levin's top spot at the Department of Community Affairs? Former senator Joe Doria of gold-badge fame. Once again, only in New Jersey.[16]

Transportation authorities in New Jersey aren't about actually running roads and collecting tolls; they're about hiring people and handing out contracts to the well-connected. When the Turnpike was built, New Jersey said the tolls would come off when it was paid for. That was proposed in the 1950s, but the tolls lived on after politicians found out what a patronage pit they had. The authorities float bonds without having to ask the public at the ballot box. Bond floating itself creates plenty of contract work. The bonds require tolls to stay in place until the bonds are paid off. They never will be. It's a cycle that guarantees plenty of employment.

McClure reported for the *Trentonian* as far back as 1992 that Attorney General Robert Del Tufo was pressing an investigation into contracts awarded by the Turnpike Authority. "Sources close to the governor say Florio insiders want Del Tufo to leave the authority alone because they see it as a rich source of patronage and contracts for campaign contributors and friends of the administration.

"Florio people, patronage-wise, are up to their eyeballs in the turnpike," a source told McClure. "If he (Del Tufo) won't back off on the turnpike authority, it's the final straw. It's the real jar of honey."[17]

All this bureaucracy certainly doesn't guarantee an efficient operation. The E-ZPass system, in which a gadget on the windshield automatically deducts toll money from an account, eliminating the need to stop and fork over cash to some overpaid attendant with a hand out, was efficiently installed and worked well everywhere in the Northeast but Jersey. McGreevey determined he would change that.

He announced reforms during a news conference in which Transportation commissioner Jamie Fox summed it up: "E-ZPass is a good system, but it has been hobbled by too many contractors who have dodged responsibility for its many problems and former state officials who misled the public about its financing."[18]

The original contractor was MFS Technologies of Nebraska, which had battled with Lockheed for the $500 million contract. The Whitman administration was convinced that income from fiber-optic rentals and fines of twenty-five dollars per violation could pay for the system. Either Whitman was poor at math or she thought New Jersey residents are a lot more dishonest than they are, because in order to get the money for the annual debt payment 1.8 million cheats would have to be caught each year. Reasonably, half would get by with it. So they would need 3.6 million cheats. Some of them would have to be repeat offenders. That situation would put officials in the position of hoping for lawbreakers. This is not unlike the ever-increasing cigarette tax situation, in which most of the revenue is used to plug budget holes but some goes toward a stop-smoking campaign. Imagine the chaos if the campaign were successful.

The state couldn't get the violation-processing system working, and motorists were billed for faulty violations. The Whitman administration was relieved when the contract was taken over by WorldCom, which later filed for bankruptcy, the largest such filing in U.S. history, after accounting scandals. Eventually, WorldCom CEO Bernard Ebbers was sentenced to twenty-five years in prison on a variety of charges, including fraud. The state senate empaneled a group of investigators to get to the bottom of Jersey's version of the emperor's new clothes on both E-ZPass and the state's emissions testing program. The investigators dug in, and it wasn't looking good, what with the bipartisan task force calling for subpoena power so that witnesses could be forced to testify. Whitman, meanwhile, had escaped the E-ZPass disaster and New Jersey to become President Bush's Environmental Protection Agency chief. Senate President Donald DiFrancesco, also a Republican, was acting governor.

In timing that was questionable, DiFrancesco not only refused the subpoena power for the legislative committee, he shut down the task force he had helped create. The *Courier-Post* editorialized:[19] "He made a terrible move. One that will offend the legislators who were prepared to examine these contracts. One that will send a message that N.J. government is open for bad business. And one that steals away the citizens' right to an open investigation of those tainted endeavors."

Delays, lawsuits, and empty promises continued for four years until the system had a $469 million deficit. McGreevey was elected, and he ordered Jamie Fox to fix E-ZPass, a task Fox launched by firing WorldCom. By 2004, at last, the electronic toll collection system operated the way it was supposed to, the way it already had in other states for years.

The good didn't last long.

McGreevey appointed Joseph Simunovich as chairman of the

Turnpike Authority, saying, "I have the utmost confidence in Joseph Simunovich's ability to serve in this critical position. It is an honor and privilege to have an individual of his character and integrity serve as chair of the New Jersey Turnpike Authority." That was in May 2002.[20]

In July 2006, the state Ethics Commission said it appeared Simunovich, who also was finance chair for U.S. Sen. Bob Menendez's campaign, violated ethics laws when he took free trips aboard a jet co-owned by one of the road's biggest contractors.[21] (New Jersey's ethics code forbids state employees and officers in a state agency from accepting gifts from people who do business with that agency.) Ethics Commission Director Rita Strmensky cited use of an aircraft owned in part by Joseph Sanzari or his company, which had won at least $52 million in turnpike jobs since 2004. That made the firm the sixth-largest contractor in that time period. After the trips became public in a report by the the *Record,* Simunovich reimbursed Sanzari $7,125.[22]

The Ethics Commission levied its largest-ever penalty, $50,000, against Simunovich in 2007.[23] He agreed to pay, but with arrogance typical of New Jersey pols, he refused to admit guilt. He agreed only that "his conduct could be construed to be a violation" of ethics rules. Two of the airplane rides were for his grandchildren. The third trip to Florida was for Simunovich and his wife and was—get this excuse—"in order to avoid potential health issues associated with commercial flight." He resigned in 2007.

Another state board with independent authority, the state Board of Public Utilities (BPU), is charged with keeping the price paid for gas, electric, water, wastewater, and phone service reasonable. But while energy prices in New Jersey soared, members of the BPU traveled the world for conferences and workshops. They're paid for by trade associations—whose dues cost the state hundreds of thousands of dollars.

Board members say the travel keeps New Jersey's utility rates down because of what is learned. Coauthor McClure reported that in 2000, BPU board members went to Macedonia, Croatia, India, Hungary, Belgium, and Bulgaria, among other places.[24] In 2003, board member Fred Butler made trips that included Bulgaria and Rome. In 2004, he went to West Africa and Australia. In 2005, he took twenty-nine trips, all of them in the United States. That year three BPU board members traveled for 183 days on sponsored trips. With all that learning going on, it's a wonder New Jersey utility rates have remained so high.

Board President Jeanne Fox also traveled about, as did board member Connie Hughes. A Hot Springs, Virginia, meeting in 2005 must have been a doozy since three of five board members attended that one. McClure obtained records showing trade associations and other sponsors paid at least $108,000 over a four-year period for Fox, Hughes, and Butler to travel. The BPU likes to point out the state doesn't pay for the trips, the associations do. But the BPU paid $1.1 million in association fees from July 2002 until January 2006, including $327,366 in fees to the two trade associations which paid the costs of many of the conferences. Fox said the membership fees have no correlation to the trips, but Republican State Senator Pete Inverso said they were an indirect way of passing the costs on to the BPU, funded by money from the federal government and from utilities, which passes the cost on to ratepayers.

The umbrella agency for many of the BPU trips is the National Association of Regulatory Utility Commissioners, or NARUC, whose members are government agencies that regulate utilities. The NARUC Web site shows that those attending NARUC events are not just government officials but also representatives of the utilities they regulate and vendors, suppliers, consultants, etc.

Fox has connections. She is married to political consultant Steve DiMicco, who handled campaigns for Governor McGreevey and Corzine, U.S. Senator Menendez, and a number of other Democrats. Appointed to the BPU in 2002 by McGreevey, Fox was kept on by Corzine and was not required to appear before the senate judiciary committee to answer questions at a confirmation hearing. The official reason given by the Corzine camp was that she didn't need to because she was a holdover. Other holdovers, however, did.

One reason she may not have appeared is that questions were being asked about the BPU's Clean Energy Fund, which was established with ten to twenty dollars a year from each customer's power bills to provide what the BPU said was "education, information and financial incentives for renewable energy systems and energy efficiency measures."

McGreevey's state treasurer, John McCormac, wrote Fox saying he had heard the BPU created, without his knowledge, a bank account to disperse money from the fund. A 2004 Treasury audit of that unit followed and was kept secret after Attorney General Peter Harvey went to a superior court judge and requested it be sealed. Word began to leak that the audit was a disaster for BPU management. Coauthor Ingle devoted a segment of his column to the secret audit:[25]

Audit: Waiting for that audit of the Board of Public Utilities to be released. Attorney General Zulima Farber says that can be done as soon as certain "formalities" and "packaging" are complete.

Observes Sen. Peter Inverso, R-Mercer: "It is simply not good enough to hide behind ill-defined notions of formalities and packaging when it comes to what might be a $100 million scandal involving the public's money. . . . In his State of the State address, the governor called upon all of us to join him in an historic effort to end the toxic mix of politics, money and public business. We can begin this effort with the full disclosure of the suppressed Treasury audit."

Reportedly, the audit found a $100 million bank account outside the state's financial systems with no controls. One of the vendors that allegedly got money from the unusual account was an organization to which Farber was an adviser. Scott Weiner, Corzine's chief of the Schools Construction Corp., heads the outfit Farber advised.

Ingle had it right. On July 25, 2006, growing public pressure forced the Corzine administration to release the audit. It showed top BPU executives created a private bank account worth more than $80 million outside state purview and lacking basic controls. Gannett State Bureau newsmen Tom Baldwin and Gregory J. Volpe reported, "In one of the many problems cited by the audit, bids went out for BPU consulting work, and 'in each case, the person getting the contract was a former BPU employee.' "

Their story continues:[26]

Here are some of the condemnations in the audit by Jeffrey Seifert, chief auditor of the State Treasury Department. He used "OCE" for the Office of Clean Energy.

- Money going in or out could not be entirely accounted for—"And OCE's outstanding balances owed could not be determined."
- OCE "kept inadequate accounting records; lacks an encumbrance system for reporting purchases/contracts; lacks detailed policies and procedural manuals; lacks a system of internal controls."
- OCE "hired consultants with limited or no competition; paid grants based on time rather than percentage of project

completed; paid questionable items on invoices that should
have been disallowed."

- OCE "made payments to a consultant without a contract
  through another consultant's contract."

The litany runs to 34 pages, saying such things as OCE got a
bad rate on its investment; or a former OCE employee left
the job with OCE files on a laptop, and then popped up as
a consultant to OCE with access to the same file-packed
laptop.

"Few written policies and procedures are maintained
over accounting functions," said the audit, which reported
that at least once an OCE employee named Ron Jackson authorized payment of $25,019.55 to a "World Water" while no
Ron Jackson appears among those allowed to draw on the
secret account.

The $80 million account was held at Wachovia Bank, which was
charging the state $1,000 a month while loaning out the funds and
making money on it. "My bank gives me free checking and I don't
have $80 million, even on payday," Ingle quipped in his column.

Turns out BPU board member Butler—that's "Galloping Fred"
Butler, who visited fifteen countries, six continents, and ten U.S.
states in a three-year span—owned between $250,000 and $500,000
in Wachovia stock, according to his public disclosure forms. He
said, however, that he had no influence in the choice of Wachovia.
Nevertheless, the state Ethics Commission told Butler to pay five
hundred dollars for approving the bank deposit while he owned
the stock.[27]

Fox maintained for weeks that the bank account was not secret,
that it was set up with the help of an assistant attorney general who
was attached to the Treasury Department. When asked why she

didn't tell the senate and assembly committees about the bank account during budget hearings, Fox said, "They never asked me that question." Reporters did, though. Why didn't she tell them? "I did tell one reporter, but it wasn't included in the story."[28]

When Gannett reporter Gregory J. Volpe pressed for the paperwork, Fox finally admitted the assistant AG was actually attached to her and the BPU, not Treasury. When asked if Fox lied, her spokeswoman said Fox "misspoke."[29]

The investigation of potential criminal activity was left to Attorney General Zulima Farber, which appeared to be a conflict of interest since she was adviser to an agency that got money from the secret $80 million account.[30] On August 23, 2006, things got serious when federal agents subpoenaed BPU records.[31]

While the feds investigated, a second state audit showed more corruption inside the BPU.[32] The audit revealed former BPU executive director Michael Ambrosio had been hired by the agency as a grant adviser at a cost of $16,000 per month—more than the BPU's president earned. Ambrosio drew down the BPU fee at the same time he was representing clients vying for BPU grants. The audit said the state could have saved the money paid to Ambrosio by using its own staff to evaluate grant applications. The agency, of course, disagreed.

The hero in the fight against corruption and waste inside the BPU was Joe Potena, the BPU's chief fiscal officer, who blew the whistle on the secret bank account. Potena filed a lawsuit charging that once he alerted the state treasury to the bank account, Fox and others at the BPU retaliated. Attorney General Peter Harvey responded with a belated investigation and by hiring politically connected lawyers to defend the state. The law firms, including former governor Florio's, quickly racked up more than $1.4 million in fees before a trial ever began. The private law firms were used instead of the state's own lawyers to avoid conflicts

of interest, but instead created one. Fox was defended by promi-
nent Democratic lawyer Angelo Genova, who had teamed with
Fox's husband, DiMicco, when they were key advisers on the
Menendez campaign.[33]

Assemblywoman Amy Handlin told Gannett's Volpe, "We have a
David vs. Goliath situation, the whistle-blower versus the state be-
hemoth, and I don't think taxpayers would appreciate knowing
that their resources are being used to scare off the little guy who is
trying to shine a light on potential violations of procurement policies, nepotism and cronyism." Believe it or not, in early 2008,
Corzine nominated Fox for another six-year term on the BPU
board. The senate refused to hold her confirmation hearing until
the whistle-blower case concluded, Gannett reported. But with
Corzine's support, she remained in the powerful post, pending
confirmation.

The BPU has been a patronage pit for years, with questions of
ethics, evidence of inappropriate gifts from those the agency regu-
lates, and cases of political favoritism. Christine Whitman did her
part to uphold the agency's bad reputation after she was appointed
its president by Gov. Tom Kean. Just days before she expected newly
elected Gov. Jim Florio to replace her with a Democrat, Whitman
rammed through an illegal decision opening protected land—
some of the last undeveloped land in northern New Jersey—to development. Robert Kean, the governor's brother, sat on the board
of the parent of the realty company and the water utility that benefited from the decision.[34] Whitman held two meetings within a half
hour. Between 2:00 P.M. and 2:30 P.M., she cast one of two votes on
a BPU watershed review committee and then convened an unusual
meeting of what was then a three-member BPU board.

"Via a conference telephone call made by Whitman from the
public meeting room at the BPU's Newark office, she and [board
member] George Barbour, who was on the other end of the tele-

phone line, ignored the BPU's standard competitive bidding process for land sales and voted two-to-zero to allow the sale of the 287 acres," McClure wrote in her biography of Whitman. (Barbour was already in trouble and paid an $855 fine to the state Ethics Commission after he allowed a consultant for a county utility authority to pay for his dinner a week before the BPU granted a rate increase for the utility.) The Environmental Defense Fund sued over the decision to sell the 287 acres. The court ruled that the BPU's watershed review board broke state law, the BPU board violated bidding rules, and it had all been prearranged. Whitman blamed everything on bad advice from her staff.

Another golden egg for New Jersey politicians is the state's Sports and Exposition Authority. Florio's administration seized control of the Sports Authority in 1992 when a lame-duck legislature allowed the authority to issue an unlimited amount of bonds for Atlantic City, a new Rutgers University stadium, and a convention center study for Asbury Park. The expanded bonding was expected to cost taxpayers at least $1 billion. Coauthor McClure wrote for the *Trentonian* in August 1993 that the intent was to "suck campaign money from law firms, bond underwriters and others who might benefit from" projects the bonds paid for. She said:[35]

In March 1992, when the first bonds were issued, the *Trentonian* reported that $2.2 million in fees went to 21 underwriters who contributed thousands of dollars to the state Democratic Party.

Former authority chairman Peter Levine said the list of underwriters came directly from the governor's office.

Federal investigators from the SEC and the U.S. Attorney's Office in Manhattan are already reportedly probing whether brokerage giant Merrill Lynch made improper payments to a Camden County securities company owned by

Florio's former chief of staff Joseph Salema in order to obtain state Turnpike Authority business.

Salema was a master at milking authority money. He started as Florio's driver in 1974 and served as his chief of staff for nine years when Florio was in the U.S. House of Representatives. While Florio was in Washington, sources told McClure, "Little Joe" Salema was running things in Camden County. "He used Florio's clout to place loyalists in elected and appointed positions and to control county policy."[36] Lawyers, consultants, and others who reaped hundreds of thousands of dollars in county contracts in turn contributed to Florio's congressional races.

In the mid-1980s, Salema and Nicholas Rudi, a former Camden County administrator and finance director of Florio's failed 1981 gubernatorial bid, resigned from public jobs and formed Consolidated Financial Management (CFM). "Almost immediately," McClure reported, "the consulting firm landed hundreds of thousands of dollars in county contracts."[37]

The trend continued after Florio's election, when the firm nearly doubled its business. When he replaced Florio's first chief of staff in 1990, Salema said he put his assets in a blind trust. Nevertheless, by May 1993 CFM had more of New Jersey's financial consulting market than any other firm.

"In terms of turning government into a moneymaking proposition, they turned it from a fine art into a science," Republican Camden County Freeholder Lee Solomon, later an assemblyman, a prosecutor, and state judge, told McClure.[38]

After a three-month *Trentonian* investigation that took McClure to small towns across the state and into Florida, she reported that CFM raked in its money by turning Salema's and Rudi's government clout into fat consulting fees, sometimes at taxpayers' expense.[39]

Officials with several political subdivisions said CFM submitted unacceptable bills. A review of bills from eleven counties, municipalities, and authorities found bills without backup materials in six cases, McClure reported.

At the Lacey Municipal Utilities Authority, the attorney labeled CFM's bill "loosey goosey." "Amid charges that a political deal had been cut to get the contract for CFM, officials asked CFM to back up its bill for $12,500. The backup never came," McClure reported.

CFM also used an amendment to state law to encourage school districts to use a lease-purchase method for building new schools—without the need for voter approval of bond issues. School districts, without public approval, built buildings that in some cases were viewed as unnecessary or too large.

When Salema came under scrutiny, he used the defense that his assets were out of his control and in the blind trust. But McClure reported the blind trust was not as blind as it appeared, as Salema had signed a deed of sale on a Glassboro property after it was put in the so-called blind trust.[40]

When CFM took its methods into Florida, the feds took note, and so did McClure.[41] "Although the company operated primarily in New Jersey, it made at least one foray into another state where it used the services of a character court testimony has tied closely to organized crime," she reported. "CFM's efforts to get a toehold in Florida ended when it was fired for submitting inflated and unsubstantiated bills." "Many of CFM's bills, $62,510 in six months, did not have receipts required by Florida state law."

St. Lucie County commissioner Judy Culpepper and two others said Randy Avon convinced the county to give CFM a financial consulting contract. Culpepper said she was told by a CFM employee that Avon was getting 10 percent of whatever was paid to CFM.

"Now Avon—and CFM's activities in St. Lucie County—are being investigated as part of an ongoing statewide probe by the FBI and Florida officials into political corruption and bond financing," McClure reported. "Florida lawmen became interested in Avon in the mid-1970s when he was linked to Tom Farese, a reputed member of the Joseph Columbo crime family in Brooklyn. Farese is serving a 24-year federal prison sentence for running a marijuana smuggling operation out of Fort Lauderdale. Fort Lauderdale police officer Leonardo Olivieri testified in 1976 that the bugging of Farese's Fort Lauderdale restaurant linked Avon to a bribery scheme to obtain a restaurant's liquor license." The case was not prosecuted, and Avon denied having anything to do with Farese.

Salema said Avon was not on the payroll of CFM's Florida staff, which included two Camden County Democrats, one of them Salema's cousin, Joseph "Big Joe" Salema, a Florio congressional aide for nearly ten years who retired as Camden's public safety director. The other CFM employee was Ray Hoban, a former Camden County Democratic Party official who left his job as Camden County Municipal Utilities Authority fiscal officer to handle the St. Lucie account.

But the Florida probe wasn't the biggest problem. In New Jersey, the U.S. attorney's office zeroed in on CFM's activities and investigated whether Salema used his influence to direct bond business to favored brokerage firms. Of particular interest, the *New York Times* reported, were Turnpike Authority bonds, especially the role Armacon Securities—owned by Salema and Rudi—played. The Turnpike Authority floated the bonds to refinance its existing debt, among other things.[42] The $1.8 billion in bonds was underwritten by forty-nine companies with Merrill Lynch as managing underwriter. Merrill Lynch opened a joint securities trading account with Armacon, and some questioned why the nation's largest brokerage firm would hook up with a newly formed company in South Jersey. Three Merrill Lynch executives, all Florio contributors, were suspended.

But it was a bond deal at the Camden County Municipal Utilities Authority (CCMUA), another patronage dump, that finally took Salema and Rudi down. Salema pleaded guilty to securities fraud and paid $324,000 to settle Securities and Exchange Commission charges. Rudi was acquitted of criminal charges[43] but agreed to pay $86,000[44] to settle the federal case accusing the two of taking more than $200,000 in kickbacks to help First Fidelity Bank get a $237 million municipal bond contract with the CCMUA. "Salema could have spent up to 10 years behind bars for steering government bond business to First Fidelity in exchange for payments in a scheme that netted him hundreds of thousands of dollars," the *Trentonian* reported.[45] U.S. District Judge Sonia Sotomayor instead sentenced him to six months in a halfway house and six months of home detention, fined him $10,000, and gave him 1,400 hours of community service.

The Florio administration was knee-deep in the process of issuing bonds for various authorities. "Huge state bond deals handed out under Gov. Florio have opened a pipeline that's pumped more than $1 million from Wall Street financial firms and bond lawyers into state Democratic Party's coffers," wrote Dave Neese, a veteran reporter and editorial writer for the *Trentonian*.[46] "Altogether, according to a check of state records by *The Trentonian*, financial firms and bond lawyers in the Turnpike and Sports Authority deals or deals with Armacon and CFM have contributed at least $1,161,930 to the Democratic State Committee since 1990," Neese reported in early 1993. "The Democratic contributions show a departure from previous practices by many of the Wall Street firms, which were once closely linked solely to conservative Republicans. Now, it appears, the firms have realized that political contributions net big government business—regardless of the party in power."

The late Sam Perelli, a strident advocate for New Jersey's hard-working citizens and then head of the United Taxpayers of New

Jersey, told Neese, "One of the reasons we're borrowing ourselves into oblivion is that bond issues are how the politicians pay off their investors—that is, their contributors."

McClure teamed with reporter Phyllis Plitch in an investigation of an obscure state authority, the New Jersey Health Care Facilities Financing Authority, created to make sure bonding for hospital construction was done properly. McClure and Plitch found that an agency no one was watching had been turned into a cash cow for friends of the Florio administration and the state Democratic Party.[47]

"Bond companies that, by all accounts, had given hospitals solid advice for years are gone, replaced by firms that have given Florio and his party generous campaign contributions," their *Trentonian* story read. "The authority's board of directors has been peopled with Democratic fund-raisers. When legal advice has been needed, law firms with a history of Democratic giving have gotten the jobs. A role has even been found for construction firms whose names appear prominently on lists of Florio and Democratic contributors. And hospitals that have tried to continue work with the firms they trust have been told in no uncertain terms to switch to the friends of Florio. It's a story that has to be pieced together, much as a quilt is sewn from scraps of cloth, because the only people who have direct knowledge of what's been said by whom believe they'll be fired if they say anything. Interviews with those people, all of whom work for the authority or have intimate dealings with it, reveal that the directive that turned their agency into a political duchy came initially from two longtime Florio friends. Those sources say former gubernatorial chief of staff Joe Salema and incumbent chief of management and planning Brenda Bacon made the calls that brought the administration's friends into the authority and exorcised others."

Prompted in part by the Salema bond scandal, the Securities

and Exchange Commission banned campaign donations by firms doing bond work. But firms found loopholes. A decade later, the love affair between investment bankers and the state's politicians had rekindled, Joe Donohue of the *Star-Ledger* reported in May 2004.[48] "After virtually disappearing from state races since the mid-1990s, employees of banks that underwrite state debt have returned in force, ponying up nearly $1 million to various state campaign committees since 2001. In addition, they have spent more than $2.7 million during the same period for lobbyists and consultants to press their interests in Trenton."

(Salema and other aides to Florio were not the only ones who parlayed their jobs in government into lucrative private sector work. McGreevey's aides did the same thing. Kevin Hagan, McGreevey's deputy chief of staff, moved from that job to director of the Democratic State Committee to lobbyist. One year after McGreevey left office, Hagan had a client base of only thirteen but earned $487,500, the *Star-Ledger* reported.[49] Two years after McGreevey departed, the influential Fox, also former transportation commissioner before Port Authority deputy executive director, along with Eric Shuffler, former gubernatorial counselor, and George Warrington, the outgoing director of NJ Transit, announced the creation of a consulting firm specializing in transportation.)

In 2005, even Salema showed up again in the news when *Courier-Post* investigative reporter Alan Guenther checked into a politically connected land developer who paid the salaries of public officials. These same officials negotiated contracts involving the developer in two Camden County towns, Camden and Pennsauken.[50] (Salema was hired as a consultant by Cherokee Investment Partners. Also making an appearance was David Luthman, who as head of the county Democrats gave then Camden Parking Authority director Ted Hinson his $10,000 county job at the board of elections.)

In Pennsauken, a local subsidiary of Cherokee provided about $80,000 to pay the township's attorney, Luthman, who told reporter Guenther he saw no conflict in being paid with funds provided by the company involved in contract negotiations with the township. When, as township attorney, he worked on Cherokee-related business, he doubled his fee from $125 an hour to $250 an hour.

Guenther continued:

In Camden, Cherokee provided financial relief to the cash-starved Camden Redevelopment Agency. In November 2002, Arijit De was hired as the agency's executive director, with a salary of $125,000 per year. But after his hire, the agency lacked the money to pay him for months.

Toward the end of 2003, Cherokee agreed to pour $250,000 into an escrow account. The money came shortly after the agency, with strong backing from De, selected Cherokee as the developer for a $1.2 billion project in the city's largely Hispanic Cramer Hill neighborhood.

The money Cherokee paid into an escrow account provides between 15 and 20 percent of De's salary. De said the money did not influence him when he endorsed Cherokee's plan to build 6,000 new homes in Cramer Hill.

A good government group in Washington, D.C., said De had compromised his position.

"If 20 percent of his salary is coming from a company with an interest in the negotiations, then he's certainly not a neutral party. He's an agent of the developer," said Bill Allison, spokesman for the Center for Public Integrity.

About Luthman doubling his salary, Allison said: "I'm just kind of astonished by it. . . . It's hard to imagine anyone doing that and thinking it's OK. The fact that he doubled his income only increases the level of scrutiny this project should have."

Guenther reported Cherokee was aware of Salema's criminal past when the developer hired him as a consultant. "We knew about his background," said Richard Ochab, Cherokee spokesman. "But he's been a part of the South Jersey community for decades." He said Salema provided "valuable advice on following regulatory processes."

Didn't this arrangement between Cherokee and the Camden authority violate even New Jersey's weak ethics laws? Not according to Albert Porroni, director of the nonpartisan state Office of Legislative Services. Porroni said ethics rules don't apply when government spends money placed into escrow by a developer.

8

The Gospel According
to the Mob

I f the Mafia were a religion, the first song in the hymnal would be
"What a Friend We Have in Jersey."

From the early days, it was a mobster's dream, a state filled
with crooked officials on the take, a wide-open Atlantic City with
undercover gambling, speakeasies, prostitution, smuggling, and
the nearby Pine Barrens with its more than one million acres of
deep isolated woods, perfect for the occasional hit. Except for the
small number of eccentric locals, called Pineys, the large expanse
of pine forest is devoid of human habitation and tailor-made for
constructing illegal stills during Prohibition and dumping bodies
anytime. Ironically, a portion of the acreage is named the Brendan
T. Byrne State Forest after the former governor and judge who told
the Mafia to keep its dirty hands off Atlantic City when gaming was
legalized in 1978.

Atlantic City's mob history goes way back. Its Ambassador Hotel was convention headquarters for a 1929 meeting that brought

together some of the biggest names in crime—Meyer Lansky, Al Capone, Lucky Luciano. Since crime families from Philadelphia, Jersey, and New York liked to partake of what the city by the sea had to offer, it was a neutral zone of sorts, sans the bloody family feuds that raked places like Chicago, New York, and, later, nearby Philly.

Ironically, one of the higher-profile mob-connected guys didn't spend his life in Jersey but is often rumored to be spending eternity in the Garden State: former Teamsters Union president Jimmy Hoffa.[1] When Robert Kennedy became attorney general, his focus was rooting out organized crime in labor unions. Anthony "Tony Pro" Provenzano, thought to be a member of the Genovese crime family, was a member of a Teamsters local in Union City, New Jersey, and a Hoffa loyalist. After going to jail for jury tampering and manipulating a union pension fund, Hoffa was freed by President Richard Nixon in 1971. To calm critics who said Nixon exchanged Hoffa for union support, Nixon barred Hoffa from a leadership position with the union until 1980. Hoffa wanted his old job back and wasted no time in greasing the skids. First, he had to make nice with his onetime friend Provenzano, who had fallen out with Hoffa when they spent time together in prison.

In 1975, Hoffa called for a meeting to bury the hatchet with Provenzano. Instead it was Hoffa who was interred. There are several versions of the confab afloat, and it is not known for sure if the meeting was supposed to be with Tony Pro himself or others with connections to Provenzano. What is known is that on July 30 Hoffa drove to a restaurant in Bloomfield Hills, a Detroit suburb. He reportedly called his wife and said he had been stood up, which was probably an error on Hoffa's part because that was the last time anyone heard from him, on the record at least.

The cops thought Provenzano was Suspect No. 1, but conveniently on July 30 Tony Pro had an alibi. He was meeting with

Teamster associates—in New Jersey. Mobster Frank Sheeran claimed he had a role in Hoffa's fate but gave different versions of what it was.[2] In one, he implicated Salvatore Briguglio, a subordinate of Provenzano, and Russell Bufalino of the underworld in Pennsylvania and New York state, and said he himself offed Hoffa. In another, he said he only disposed of the body. After Sheeran died in 2003, his family questioned the statements. Provenzano died in 1988 in prison, where he was serving time for labor racketeering while being a New Jersey Teamsters boss.

We may never know Hoffa's final resting place, but Jersey just keeps cropping up. It has long been rumored to be under Giants Stadium in the Meadowlands of North Jersey. The exact location changes as often as those who claim to have had a hand in his murder. Lynda Milito held a Florida news conference in which she claimed her late husband, Louie, told her he killed Hoffa in Michigan and dumped his remains near New York's Verrazano-Narrows Bridge.[3]

Danny Provenzano, Tony's nephew, carried on the family tradition. Danny was sentenced to ten years in prison after pleading guilty in 2003 to racketeering.[4] He was among eight named in a forty-one-count indictment charging beatings, kidnapping, and murder threats to extort $1.5 million from a dozen victims. Danny admitted ordering an employee to break the thumb of a salesman suspected of stealing $9,000 from Provenzano's printing company. He also admitted pummeling a man in a dispute over a $181,000 printing bill. Prosecutors said they caught Provenzano on tape boasting of his Genovese crime family ties.[5]

A B-movie filmmaker who denied ties to organized crime, Danny Provenzano used those two violent incidents in the movie *This Thing of Ours,* which he cowrote, directed, and starred in as the nephew of a mob boss. (Frank Vincent and Vincent Pastore of *The Sopranos* had major roles in the film.[6] Provenzano promoted it on

The Jimmy Kimmel Show, where his response to the violence was "No remorse.") The Provenzano case was prosecuted by then–Deputy Attorney General Robert Codey, brother of former governor Dick Codey. Robert also nabbed Gerald Zecker, longtime Republican state assemblyman and former Clifton mayor, as an unindicted co-conspirator, *the Record* reported.[7]

The indictment charged Provenzano with an attempted strong-arm takeover of the insurance agency where Zecker was office manager. Questions were raised by prosecutors about meetings Zecker attended with Provenzano and a reputed mobster, according to the *Record.* Zecker said he knew nothing about the extortion and was just trying to save the business.

The roots of illicit activity often are traced to trash in New Jersey. In the past, that meant mob-related turf wars. More recently, it meant pulling strings at the highest levels inside the New Jersey statehouse in Trenton.

Top lawyers in New Jersey's Criminal Justice Division, sources told coauthor McClure, were getting ready to ask a grand jury to indict Linden Mayor John Gregorio (a longtime Democratic power in Union County despite being convicted in 1982 for conspiracy related to hiding his interests in two Linden go-go bars) and Domeinick Pucillo, his son-in-law, for alleged conspiracy involving a venture to set up a trash-transfer station on the Linden waterfront.[8] Partners in that deal included Paul M. Weiner, a Parsippany attorney and law partner of State Sen. Ray Lesniak—a Democrat power broker from Union County, host of fund-raisers for Bill Clinton and longtime confidant of Jim McGreevey—and Agnes Villani, wife of Benny Villani, who has been banned for life from New York City's trash business because of alleged ties to the Genovese crime family.[9] Benny Villani was one of seven individuals named in a sixty-one-count indictment in 1996 that charged racketeering, tax conspiracy, and extortion, among other things. Prosecutors alleged the seven used threats of violence to maintain control over customers and keep out rival trash haulers.[10]

Gregorio not only had been mayor since 1967, but he had served concurrently in the state assembly and then the senate. Under terms of his go-go bar conviction in 1982, Gregorio was forced to vacate the mayor's office and his senate seat. At Gregorio's request, Lesniak approached then-Gov. Tom Kean, a Republican, about a pardon, which Kean granted on his last day in office in 1990.[11] That cleared the way for Gregorio to return to elective politics. Six months later he won the Democratic primary for mayor.

Gregorio shepherded the trash-transfer station through city approvals in Linden without first mentioning his son-in-law's connection. The push began ten months after Pucillo and Judi Gregorio were married in West Orange, Kathy Barrett Carter reported for the *Star-Ledger.*[12]

Those involved in the trash deal were set to make millions on the plan to bring New York City trash to Linden on barges and then transport it by train from New Jersey. The head of a firm doing trash consulting for Linden told Carter the whole scheme was the mayor's idea. "Gregorio did not inform the council about a competing offer from another waste disposal company that would have brought the city a much higher host fee," Carter wrote. From beginning to end, those with political connections were involved.

Paul Weiner, as the deal was being put together, was municipal attorney for Woodbridge, where McGreevey was mayor before becoming governor. Candidate McGreevey fired Weiner when his involvement was revealed because Woodbridge was publicly opposed to the trash-train project. Gregorio's lawyer during the grand jury investigation was Jack Arseneault, McGreevey's favored choice for attorney general. Arseneault was a longtime friend of McGreevey and Peter C. Harvey, whom McGreevey eventually named attorney general.

State prosecutors were so sure there would be an indictment in the Linden trash-transfer matter that they planned a news conference for March 19, 2002, the day after the indictment was expected.

It never happened. McGreevey's administration, just taking over, ended the indictment drive, much to the chagrin of prosecutors and investigators who had been working the case for two years under the prior Republican administrations. No indictment was sought, and the grand jury that spent eight months hearing testimony was dismissed. This one was blatant, even by New Jersey standards.

Officially, the decision to end it came from Harvey, who was director of the Division of Criminal Justice before McGreevey named him attorney general. Originally, Harvey appeared OK with the probe, but then he reversed himself, saying he and other lawyers found the case lacking.

Disagreeing with them was Deputy Attorney General John Musarra, the investigation's lead attorney. He wrote a four-page memo to his boss in Special Prosecutions, fighting to continue the case and recalling Harvey had been aboard at first. The *Star-Ledger* obtained a copy:[13] "At the conclusion of that meeting to my recollection all present expressed the opinion that the case was worthy of prosecution, and Director Harvey even used a blackboard to sketch out his suggested theory of the case and provided suggestions for remarks in opening and summation."

There was some sentiment for holding the news conference in Linden, maybe on the city hall steps to drive it home, so to speak. That was a fatal mistake; gossip travels quickly in a town like Linden. Inquiries were made to police and other agencies concerning permits and such. "I assumed it was about the mayor because the mayor was under fire," city clerk Val Imbriaco told reporter Carter. Word spread fast that a call from Trenton sought a place for a news conference in the Gregorio case, Linden Councilman Richard Gerbounka said.

Only McGreevey administration higher-ups know for sure what happened next or what strings were pulled, but Musarra's memo indicated he learned Harvey had canceled the grand jury presentation, ostensibly because of a conflict with a McGreevey press conference. The monumental McGreevey event in question was to declare a tax amnesty for people who thumbed their noses at the state treasury. That a grand jury presentation couldn't occur the same day as a brief gubernatorial press conference defies all logic. Nevertheless, the grand jury was rescheduled to April 1, then rescheduled again for April 15. On May 13, the last day of the grand jury's term, a meeting was held to discuss whether to go forward. Harvey didn't bother to attend, and the grand jury was dismissed without handing down an indictment. Musarra asked permission to present the case to a new grand jury, arguing, "Gregorio's stranglehold on Linden can only be strengthened by his being able to brag that he got away with it yet one more time."

Musarra lost the fight, but the Local Finance Board, a state agency, fined Gregorio a mere $2,000, charging that the mayor used his office to benefit son-in-law Pucillo.[14] Harvey's boss, Attorney General David Samson, recused himself from the Linden case because up until just before McGreevey appointed him, he represented a lobbyist, Alan Marcus, who had helped broker the Linden deal on behalf of his client, Browning-Ferris Industries. Reporter McClure later found Harvey could have recused himself as well because his old law firm, when he was a partner there, had represented Pucillo's waste companies.[15]

Jersey mob ties to politicians go well beyond trash collecting. In 1968, New Jersey Assistant Attorney General William J. Brennan III said that three members of the state legislature were "entirely too comfortable with organized crime."

Chris Baud of the *Trentonian* reported:[16]

Brennan, the son of Supreme Court Justice William J. Brennan Jr., was directing a Mercer County grand jury investigating organized crime and corruption in local government.

Saying that crooks had infiltrated numerous industries and labor unions, Brennan added: "Too many local governments are responsive more to the mob than to the electorate that put them in office."

Brennan's statements came on the heels of a series of *Life* magazine articles about organized crime, charging that the Mafia wielded great influence in New Jersey . . .

Within a month of that speech, New Jersey created the State Commission of Investigation to keep tabs on and battle organized crime and corruption. It was tough and aggressive, and sometimes cooperating with the SCI was dangerous. Consider the case of George A. Franconero, brother of '60s singing star Connie Francis. Franconero told the SCI about alleged crime links to union dental plans and testified for the government in a bank fraud probe.[17] On March 6, 1981, two thugs shot him to death in his driveway in North Caldwell as he scraped ice from a car's windshield. No one thought it was a random act of violence or a robbery gone bad, since he was shot from about twenty feet away, and afterward the two men got into a car that had been circling the block and fled. Previously, he had told authorities he feared for his life but had declined police protection. Franconero for a short time had been a law partner of Brendan T. Byrne before Byrne left to run for governor, serving in the post from 1974 until 1982. Franconero took a different path. He was convicted of land fraud in Morris County in 1980 and had pleaded guilty to bank fraud charges in 1978. He admitted to authorities he was part of fraudulent loans and kick-backs to officials of Teamsters Local 945.

The SCI was hell on wheels for crooks until the '90s, when Gov. Christie Whitman, a Republican, roped it in by requiring the agency to immediately report anything that seemed criminal to the politically charged attorney general's office, where things often fall into a black hole never to be heard from again. Before Whitman's interference, the SCI's potentially criminal probes could be kept confidential for a time, making it more difficult for the politically connected under investigation to cover their tracks.

The SCI continues to issue reports on organized crime and is one of the few state agencies generally devoid of political hacks. Its last update on the mob was issued in May of 2004, when it reported that seven La Cosa Nostra (LCN) crime families operate in New Jersey:[18]

Bruno: Based primarily in Philadelphia and South Jersey, it "has been decimated by factional violence, internal treachery and a succession of wide-ranging state and federal prosecutions." Officials doubt the organization will ever be strong again.

Bonanno: "As recently as 2002, a number of law enforcement authorities characterized the group as the most stable LCN faction in the New York/New Jersey region." But, the report continues, defections have plagued the family, with at least five members becoming government witnesses.

Colombo: "More than 40 members and associates are active in New Jersey. . . . The group occasionally coordinates criminal activities with other LCN groups and has participated in more sophisticated schemes involving motor-fuel tax evasion and securities fraud." The longtime head

of the family, the late Giuseppe "Old Joe" Profaci, owned
a 328-acre estate in Central Jersey.

DeCavalcante: Based in Union County's Elizabeth, and also
known as the "Jersey family," this is the only group indige-
nous to the Garden State. "It is rather small and consists
of approximately 40 members, including many who are
incarcerated, and at least 50 criminal associates."

The family garnered national attention in the early '80s when
Francesco "Frank" Polizzi and twenty other men were charged in
what became known as the "Pizza Connection case."[19] Authorities
said they smuggled in billions of dollars' worth of heroin over a ten-
year period and distributed it through a network of pizza parlors in
the Midwest and Northeast. The trial lasted seventeen months and
was highlighted by testimony from Mafia turncoat Tommaso
Buscetta, who at the time was the highest-ranking mobster to testify
for the prosecution. Polizzi was a major crime figure, officials said,
because of his ties to Simone Rizzo "Sam the Plumber" DeCavalcante. Thirteen defendants appealed their convictions, maintaining, among other things, that the trial was so long no jury could
have rendered a reliable verdict and that violence outside the courtroom prejudiced the outcome.[20] During the trial, a defendant from
Oregon was shot and wounded. He was the lucky one. Another defendant, Gaetano Mazzara, was murdered, his body stuffed in a
garbage bag and left on a street corner in Brooklyn.

Later, in 1992, self-appointed acting boss John "Johnny Boy"
D'Amato was rubbed out by family members, in part for naming
himself boss and stealing money from the group, but mostly for en-
gaging in homosexual activity. The family felt the latter would
make it a laughingstock among other crime families. D'Amato's
girlfriend disclosed the activity took place in New York sex clubs. In

a 2003 trial, Anthony Capo testified he killed D'Amato because "nobody's gonna respect us if we have a gay homosexual boss sitting down discussing La Cosa Nostra business."[21] After D'Amato's death, the family decided all future members had to be New Jersey residents, probably thinking there were no homosexuals in Jersey, which makes one wonder what they thought that day Mc-Greevey gave his "I am a gay American" resignation speech. Years after the D'Amato embarrassment, the DeCavalcantes felt their respect had been restored. They were caught on FBI tape comparing themselves to the Sopranos.[22] Finally, something to be proud of.

> **Lucchese:** "The most recent formal induction, or 'making,' ceremony, of which authorities are aware involving elements of the Lucchese group reportedly occurred sometime in 1996. The event, which apparently concerned the swearing-in of just one new member, was celebrated in New Jersey." It has about fifty members in the Garden State.

According to *The Boys from New Jersey* by Robert Rudolph, defense lawyers headed by Michael Critchley defended the entire Lucchese family hierarchy from indictment and won more than seventy-five "innocent" declarations in 1988.[23] Their luck ran out in 1991 when the state attorney general's office indicted the family again. Michael Taccetta, described by law enforcement as a capo (mob lingo for captain), was sentenced to twenty-five years. Court TV's online Crime Library describes the five-foot-seven, 215-pound Taccetta as the real-life Tony Soprano.[24] Ironically, Taccetta wanted to be known as a reading man, so he carried a copy of Machiavelli's *The Prince* in a back pocket. (There it is again.)

Gambino: In 1992 a leadership void developed when John J. Gotti, called the "Teflon Don" because prosecutors couldn't make charges stick, ran out of luck. With the testimony of turncoat Salvatore "Sammy the Bull" Gravano, Gotti got life for murder and racketeering but spent only ten years behind bars. He died in 2002. On his death, son John A. "Junior" Gotti became acting boss, but he pleaded guilty to racketeering and went to prison in 1999. "[Arnold] Squitieri, who resides in Englewood Cliffs, N.J., is presently in charge of family matters in New Jersey." In May 2008, twenty-three reputed members and associates of the Gambino family were indicted, including what the feds described as one of its highest ranking officers, Andrew Merola. The feds charged Merola with accepting bribes from companies wanting to use non-union labor, with running a Web-based gambling operation and with manufacturing phony bar code labels to pay less at Lowe's and other stores. In case you think New Jersey's mob days are over, the feds said the racketeering occurred from 2002 to the present.

Genovese: "The Genovese group is the most active, powerful and resourceful LCN family in New Jersey. . . . Historically, more high-ranking members of the Genovese family than any other LCN group have called the Garden State their home, and it was the first of the five New York–based families to expand its rackets to New Jersey decades ago. Today, there are five main Genovese crews headquartered in New Jersey."

One who allegedly paid tribute to the Genovese crime family was Elvis Presley impersonator Robert D'Alessio, who wears long sideburns and slicked-back hair and prefers to be called Elvis. Authorities agreed he was the king all right, but not of rock 'n' roll.[25] They charged him in February of 2006 with running a sports gambling ring that operated in three states and brought in $1 million a week. Officers seized his Corvette and discovered a collection of Elvis memorabilia, which they left behind because they surmised it wasn't all that valuable. Also charged, after a series of raids, was the manager of a strip club in Lodi called Satin Dolls, which is used as the Bada Bing Lounge in *The Sopranos*.

Not even Jersey's legendary diners are exempt. After a three-year federal investigation, fourteen alleged members of the Genovese crowd were charged in August of 2005 with shaking down Greek American diner owners.[26] U.S. Attorney Chris Christie said the fourteen threatened to hurt the diner owners if they didn't pay high interest rates and protection money. Christie, known for his no-nonsense crime-busting ways, told reporters that *The Sopranos* may glamorize mob life but family members are no more than common thugs who would rather steal than work for a living. "It's no more glamorous than that."

A Bridgewater motel was the site of both an infamous Genovese mob hit and a sex taping. The Red Bull Inn, where the prostitute lured the brother-in-law of Democratic fund-raiser Charles Kushner, was the scene of more than sex in 1977. On Easter Sunday of that year, a mob hit at the motel generated the most colorful of Genovese crime family quips when, according to a mob informant, the .22 carried by Michael "Mikey Cigars" Coppola misfired and Johnny "Cokes" Lardiere responded, "What're you gonna do now, tough guy?"[27] Coppola's alleged answer was to pull a .38 revolver from an ankle holster. This time the gun worked well—five times. Lardiere, who was on a one-day furlough from prison, where he was serving time for refusing to cooperate with the State Commission of Investigation, took a permanent vacation and missed his date with a hooker.

With the guns, a holster, and a hat left behind and the testimony of the mob informant, Coppola was listed among America's Most Wanted until March 2007, when he was picked up in New York City.[28] Prosecutors said Coppola, whose last known address was Spring Lake at the Jersey Shore, conducted Genovese family business and appeared to have unlimited funds while on the lam. Coppola pleaded innocent to mob work and murder charges, with cash bail set at $1 million.

In 1988, John DiGilio, identified by authorities as a capo of the Genovese family, oversaw the mob's interests on the Bayonne waterfront. A former middleweight boxing champ, DiGilio was a little too flamboyant as an underboss, plus he publicly insulted his superiors. On May 5, 1988, a friend and former driver and bodyguard, George Weingartner, picked up DiGilio in a new Lincoln Continental, and they drove to the Truck Haven Rest Stop in Kearny.[29] As they sat talking in the parking lot, a third man in the rear seat pulled out a .38-caliber handgun and shot DiGilio five times in the back of the head—mob execution style. With incredibly good timing, a Kearny police officer on routine patrol came upon the scene. According to New Jersey Deputy Attorney General Robert Leaman, the third man tried to hold up what was left of DiGilio's bloody head while Weingartner, a former Bayonne police officer who resigned from the force when his mob ties became apparent, jumped out of the driver's seat and schmoozed with the cop, who eventually went on his way, leaving the two men to clean up. DiGilio's body was stuffed in a bag and dumped in the Hackensack River, where it wasn't found for weeks.[30]

The man in the rearview mirror was Louis Auricchio of Holmdel Township, an admitted mobster, who pleaded guilty in 1994 to aggravated manslaughter in DiGilio's demise. He also admitted to two other mob slayings and racketeering. After twelve years behind bars in Virginia, he was returned to New Jersey in

October 2006 to finish what's left of a thirty-year sentence.[31] As you may recall, Auricchio's brother-in-law is former senate president and jailed political boss, John Lynch. He was a key backer of Gov. Jim McGreevey and still called the shots in the center of the state—until, as we've seen, Lynch was indicted, pleaded guilty, and was sentenced to thirty-nine months in federal prison in 2007.

After DiGilio's death in 1988, state prosecutors say, the Genoveses' Bayonne turf was taken over by Genovese capo Angelo "the Horn" Prisco.[32] In 1994, following a three-year investigation, Prisco and twelve other men were charged with murder, arson, extortion, and the illegal sale of automatic weapons. Prisco also was accused of sanctioning a plot to bomb an occupied apartment building in Philadelphia. That never happened because the man assigned to do the deed was a state policeman working undercover.

In 1998, Prisco pleaded guilty to arson for hire and conspiracy in the burning of a Garfield, New Jersey, bar. He showed up in a Toms River courtroom in brown leather boots, mauve-tinted glasses, and blue jeans. Not once in his conversation with Superior Court Judge Edward J. Turnbach did he mention his colleagues in the mob or any other activities. But the State Commission of Investigation said the Genovese family was involved in labor union and construction industry racketeering in New Jersey's Hudson, Bergen, Essex, and Union counties and was extending its reach into Morris, Middlesex, Monmouth, and Ocean counties.

Prisco was sentenced to twelve years in prison. The next year, 1999, he pleaded guilty to extortion in a federal case with codefendant John A. Gotti and was sentenced to two years, concurrent with his state sentence. Asked by a state sentencing judge if he realized his actions were helping further organized criminal activity, Prisco replied, "I guess so."

Considering what the prosecutors said about his career, it is no surprise that the two times Prisco applied for parole he was rejected.

Then, miraculously, after McGreevey became governor, the state parole board reversed itself just four months after the last parole denial in what insiders called a highly unusual move. Records show there was none of the customary paperwork that would have indicated that someone in the appeals unit had reviewed the case.[33]

"It appears to me that it didn't go through the normal channels," said Edward Ocskay, chief of the parole board's appeals unit. "Normally, the process is that the appeal comes to my attention and either I, myself, or a member of my staff investigates. We would make a recommendation to the panel or to the full board."

Vacating a parole denial is rare and usually happens when inmates are denied the right to speak at their hearing or their release dates have been calculated wrong. Neither was the case for Prisco. His parole was denied in January 2002 based on his alleged organized crime status and his failure to admit it. That denial was vacated in May 2002 and his parole granted a week later.

Prisco's original turf was the Bayonne waterfront, where International Longshoremen's Association Local 1588, long associated with the Genovese crime family, operates. Seven weeks before Prisco got paroled, campaign records show, the International Longshoremen's Association, based in New York, donated $85,000 to the Democratic National Committee's nonfederal account. The union donated $5,000 to the Hudson County, New Jersey, Democrats the day the parole board withdrew its denial of Prisco's parole. Donald Scarinci of the Scarinci & Hollenbeck law firm signed the Hudson County Democratic Committee's report as its treasurer.[34]

Scarinci is a Democrat fund-raiser known to run Hudson County for then-Congressman and now U.S. Sen. Robert Menendez. Scarinci had also served as general counsel to McGreevey's 2001 transition team, had been named "Politician of the Year" in 2000 by PoliticsNJ.com, and in the early 1990s was legal counsel to the state assembly Democrats. After McGreevey was elected, Scarinci & Hollenbeck became lawyers for the Casino Reinvestment Development Authority, a job worth millions of dollars in legal fees.

Prisco hired the Scarinci firm to help spring him from the joint.[35] Robert Levy, a former state deputy attorney general with the organized crime unit whose wife was a lawyer in the state attorney general's office, handled the case for Prisco.

When coauthor McClure launched an investigation for Gannett New Jersey newspapers, Scarinci denied there had been any contact with the McGreevey administration about Prisco. But there had been contact just two weeks before Prisco's fortunes changed. Here's what McClure reported:[36]

Lyndhurst lawyer Donald Scarinci communicated with McGreevey's then–chief of staff, Gary B. Taffet, and told him it was "very important" that the State Parole Board reconsider its decision to deny Prisco parole. In the May 7, 2002, letter, Scarinci indicated that he was "reminding" Taffet of a meeting he [Scarinci] had the next day with then-chairman of the parole board, Mario Paparozzi.

A day later, the date of the scheduled May 8, 2002, meeting, state computer records show the parole board, which denied Prisco parole four months earlier, logged in a plan for Prisco's release, even though Prisco was not eligible for parole for more than a year.

Former parole board executive director Kenneth Connolly filed a whistle-blower lawsuit, alleging he lost his job status and was transferred because he told state police about the circumstances surrounding Prisco's release.[37] Connolly said he was demoted three times and transferred to a job ninety miles from his home.

In court papers, Connolly said that Mario Paparozzi, then parole board chairman, emerged from his office with a telephone message bearing the name of Jim Davy, a trusted McGreevey aide who had worked with the governor since the latter had served as mayor of Woodbridge Township. Connolly quoted Paparozzi as saying, "I got a call from the Governor's Office. Davy said it would be good to have the appeal granted." Paparozzi was asked about that under oath during a deposition in March 2006.[38] He invoked his Fifth Amendment right against self-incrimination no less than seventy-five times. He even refused to say if he had been contacted by law enforcement investigating the issue. Scarinci was quoted in a McClure story saying he never talked to Paparozzi about Prisco, although he might have spoken to him about other matters. According to Scarinci's later deposition in the whistle-blower case, he arranged a face-to-face meeting with Paparozzi and Prisco's application for a new parole hearing was discussed.[39]

In May 2003, the parole board notified Connolly that his director of operations job was being eliminated for "reasons of economy and efficiency." His lawsuit says his was the only position eliminated. Later that month, Connolly was transferred to Northern State Prison in Newark, and he was demoted to Hearing Officer II. Ironically, while other parole board members were called before a grand jury looking into the Prisco matter, sources close to the matter say Connolly—the guy who started it all and thus presumably knew the most—was not.

Davy was McGreevey's chief of management and operations. The administration and Davy denied he made the call to the parole board.

Coauthor McClure's investigation found that at the time the parole was granted, the board was indeed communicating with Davy on some politically sensitive personnel matters.[40]

- Parole Board Chairman Paparozzi reported to Davy's office on the disciplining of the parole officers' union and on hiring at the parole board.
- Davy agreed to waive a hiring freeze to employ someone recommended by Sen. Wayne Bryant.

Attorney General Harvey said he could find no wrongdoing on Davy's part, just in time for Davy to clear senate confirmation to become the state's human services commissioner.[41]

Harvey's alleged investigation of the Prisco case, which he took over from state police—taking responsibilities from the highly respected state police was commonplace during the McGreevey administration—was controversial. Harvey's minions somehow dropped a parole board computer, believed to contain e-mails about the case, and later said nothing could be obtained from the wrecked hard drive.[42] Sources told McClure federal officials went to the attorney general's office and took possession of the computer, but there was no public word on where it wound up or what they found, if anything.

As he left office in January 2006, Davy was under investigation by the feds for a series of e-mails he had sent county human services directors, offering himself as a consultant on grants his agency handed out.[43] Davy's consulting company was to start when he left office. During the Prisco brouhaha, Davy said, "I'm from a family background that believes public service is a noble calling and that ethical public service is a standard we have to maintain and live up to."

An SCI report indicated that after Prisco's unusual early release in 2002, when he had served only about one-third of his term, he was believed to have returned to running his mob crew.[44] Incredibly, one month before that report was released, Prisco was given a lenient parole status, having to report to his parole officer four times a year instead of monthly because of his "clear record." That status is granted to only 5 percent of parolees. When asked to identify another parolee afforded such lenient status, parole board spokesman Edward Bray called the request "preposterous."[45]

While the parole board did not bar Prisco from associating with anyone while on parole, the Casino Control Commission banned him from Atlantic City casinos based on his background. Even after his release, Prisco was believed to head of one of five main Genovese crews in New Jersey, the SCI said. "Of all the LCN, the Genovese criminal organization poses the greatest threat to New Jersey. It has a proven record of resiliency that has enabled it to maintain a grip on lucrative segments of the legitimate economy despite repeated assaults by law enforcement."

After the SCI report, the parole board did yet another about-face, tightening Prisco's reporting schedule to twice a month. That didn't keep him out of trouble.

Prisco was arrested in February 2005 for a parole violation—leaving the state—and returned to state prison to complete his sentence.[46] That action by state officials likely interrupted a federal wiretapping operation they had no knowledge of. After New Jersey released Prisco in September 2005, he was free for only six months before the U.S. attorney's office arrested him and two other men on extortion conspiracy.

That led to a federal courtroom showdown in Newark over bail. United States Attorney Steven D'Aguanno played secretly recorded conversations in which Prisco—silver-haired, overweight, and appearing shopworn at sixty-six—said he was getting $2,500 in extortion money every two months from an electrical contractor for lighting Manhattan's famous San Gennaro street festival in Little Italy.[48]

He also described how unglamorous his underworld life was. "Outside of you being the boss, this life sucks." On the mob's lack of retirement plan: "You gotta take care of yourself. Anything I got, I earned. I got through myself. The family don't give you nothing." And unlike in the mob movies, "honor, that's all a crock of shit. They wait on line to rat. They take a ticket like in the bakery."

The conversations were secretly recorded for the FBI by a driver identified only as "Jeff." Jeff's wire picked up Prisco talking about actor Steven Seagal's connection to Prisco's early parole in New Jersey. Seagal testified during a New York mob trial that he had visited a mob peacemaker in East Jersey State Prison in Wood-bridge Township to ask for protection from members of the Gam-bino crime family who later were convicted of shaking him down. That peacemaker was Prisco, even though McClure and others looked for his visitors' sign-in sheets at East Jersey State Prison and found them missing. Prisco chatted with Jeff about Seagal's prison visit.

Prisco said he had relayed the Gambinos' sentiments to Seagal. "I said, 'Steven, I can't help you. Maybe when I come out I can.' "

One of the taped conversations featured Prisco telling of a visit from a lawyer who wanted him to convince Seagal not to cooperate with the government but didn't want to tell Prisco who sent him, resulting in a scene with violence and language worthy of Tony Soprano.

"You can't tell me, you motherfucker. . . . You want to come and talk to me, don't tell me who it is." Prisco said he grabbed the lawyer by the tie and twisted until the visitor turned purple and dis-closed it was reputed mobster Anthony "Sonny" Ciccone. Prisco was not in a cooperative mood. "When I sent you the message that you're pushing this guy [Seagal] to the wall, I was told to mind my fuckin' business, you know? You know what, get the fuck out of here, tell him to go fuck himself, I'm minding my business."

When Prisco was sitting in state jail, his chief concern was another chance at parole. Hollywood teamed with political connections to come to his rescue. Seagal testified during the mob trial that when he sought Prisco's help, he paid Prisco's lawyer $10,000 to speed the mobster's release from jail.[49] The link between Prisco, Seagal, and the politically connected lawyer Scarinci was Prisco's cousin Robert DeBrino, a rough-talking Hollywood movie producer and former New York police officer. DeBrino was known to others in New Jersey—including McGreevey. Coauthor McClure obtained a letter signed by McGreevey, then governor-elect, to DeBrino telling him it was a pleasure meeting him in connection with a fund-raiser for families of Port Authority officers who died on 9/11.[50] The DeBrino connection was confirmed when Scarinci had to produce documents for the whistle-blower lawsuit. That's when it was revealed a fully executed retainer agreement had been sent from Scarinci to DeBrino two months before Prisco was paroled.

What set the Prisco case apart from others in New Jersey was the tendrils that reached toward the top. In what can only be described as an incredibly stupid move, amid the Prisco parole investigation, McGreevey allowed the International Longshoremen—under federal probe for ties to the Genovese family—to pay for a five-night trip to Puerto Rico for him and his family, where McGreevey would attend the union's national convention, and deliver a speech. The invitation came from Albert Cernadas, then president of Local 1235 in Newark and executive vice president of the International Longshoremen's Association (ILA), which made him one of the top five honchos in a union that has tens of thousands of members, including about 3,000 in New York and New Jersey.[51]

A Brooklyn, New York, grand jury later described Cernadas as an associate of the Genovese crime family who handled union jobs and contracts for organized crime. His son Albert Cernadas Jr. is an assistant prosecutor in Union County.

Albert Cernadas Sr. was indicted along with ILA leaders Harold

Daggett and Arthur Coffee and reputed Genovese capo Lawrence Ricci, who supposedly earned a living as a dairy salesman but, according to the FBI, in reality milked waterfront businesses for decades.[52] They were charged with steering a union health care contract to a company with mob links. Cernadas pleaded guilty to wire and mail fraud conspiracy but was sentenced to only two years probation. That's because, as you recall, his lawyer, Jack Arseneault—friend of Harvey and McGreevey—presented U.S. District Judge I. Leo Glasser with 292 letters asking for leniency.[53] The judge explained he had never seen such an outpouring of support. Daggett and Coffey were acquitted, as was Ricci, although he disappeared midtrial only to be found two months later shot to death and stuffed into the trunk of an abandoned car at a New Jersey diner, thus never knowing of his good fortune.[54]

When the Puerto Rico trip controversy flared, McGreevey cut the freebie short and returned to New Jersey, but not because of how it looked or questions about its ethics or even with an apology for his giving his state yet another black eye. A spokesman said the governor had to come back for the funeral of a close friend's daughter.

The National Legal and Policy Center in Falls Church, Virginia, which has tracked mob ties to labor unions since 1977, said the trip was a red flag that something was wrong inside the McGreevey administration.[55]

"If he is taking gifts of hospitality from the union, which is documented to have problems vis-à-vis the Genovese family, this represents a conflict of interests," said center chairman Ken Boehm. "In this case, you don't have to connect too many dots. His Parole Board has done favors for the Genovese family. And a union that is very closely tied to the Genovese family has done favors for him. It looks like a quid pro quo.

"Getting their key figures out of prison has always been a major objective of organized crime for which they have been willing historically to use political chits," Boehm said. "[McGreevey] should be so sensitive to that sort of thing."

The union defended McGreevey. James McNamara, a spokesman for the ILA, said raising questions about the trip in light of the Prisco parole and union corruption probes was unfair. "I think the press is unfairly taking a cheap shot at an outstanding young Democrat [with] whom we hope we have a long-standing relationship. There are a lot of people in the ILA that hope we are not calling him Governor McGreevey, that we are calling him President McGreevey."

Since he left office in disgrace, supposedly because of a homosexual extramarital affair, one wonders what the dockworkers call the former governor of the Soprano State now.

Connolly's whistle-blower lawsuit over the Prisco parole was settled in April 2007 right after the jury was selected and just before what was expected to be explosive opening statements from Connolly's attorney. With Davy, Scarinci, and Taffet set to go on the stand—and with the possibility McGreevey would be called to testify—Governor Corzine stepped in and ended what many in Trenton thought would be a good show. Connolly got $480,000 and a new state job closer to home. He said that despite some "very, very dark moments" since he picked up the phone and called state police in late 2002, "it was worth it."[56]

Attorney General Stuart Rabner's aides said the lawsuit was settled because the state was expecting to lose big-time, but they were unable to explain why the case wasn't pursued from a criminal standpoint. Three weeks after the Connolly settlement, U.S. Attorney Chris Christie dropped this bombshell: When the time is right—after Prisco's sentencing in the pending extortion case— the feds may take another look at Prisco's early release in New Jersey. Christie said he turned the Prisco parole case over to the state at the request of former attorney general Peter Harvey. "I felt like I got burned by backing off," the U.S. attorney said.[57]

Ten days later, Prisco pleaded guilty, not to extortion conspiracy with a maximum of twenty years in prison, but to a lesser conspiracy charge. The crime, conceived at an Edgewater, New Jersey, restaurant, was plotting to use a bat to encourage a competing contractor to drop the contract for the annual festival lighting so Prisco's pal could have it. The feds stepped in before the bat was wielded. The plea bargain supplied New Jersey readers with more Soprano-style entertainment.[58]

To begin with, Prisco was asked to put his hand on a Bible and swear to tell the truth before he entered a guilty plea, an unusual circumstance made all the more difficult since he was wearing handcuffs. Also, the judge asked repeatedly if the mobster had concerns that one of his lawyers, Paul Bergrin, who has worked as a federal and local prosecutor in New Jersey, was under indictment in New York for promoting prostitution in connection with an escort service called NY Confidential. A former New Jersey state trooper and a law student were charged along with Bergrin.

In September 2007, the sixty-eight-year-old Prisco was sentenced to five years in prison. A year later, in a ten-count indictment, the feds charged Prisco with racketeering, robbery, and extortion.

The state parole board had a bad reputation for letting mobsters and racketeers out of jail—both before and after Prisco. And the state Department of Corrections kept some of those inmates comfortable over the years.

One of the state's major mobsters, the late Samuel Corsaro, got two breaks from Republican governor Tom Kean and his appointees—first a pardon by Governor Kean, and later a speedy release by the man Kean appointed to the state parole board and Gov. Christie Whitman made its chairman.

"Samuel Corsaro, known to authorities as a major figure in the Gambino crime family, was paroled Feb. 14, [2000,] after serving the bare minimum before becoming eligible for early release," *Record* reporter Thomas Zolper wrote. "Unlike other violent criminals who sometimes wait months or years for a parole hearing, Corsaro was heard within weeks of his eligibility."[59]

Corsaro's speedy parole surfaced during the 2000 state and federal probe of Parole Board Chairman Andrew Consovoy, who was appointed to the parole board by Kean and had friends who had friends in the mob. In the wake of the investigation, Consovoy quit his job, left the state, and was never charged. But plenty of juicy details were revealed in the press before his departure, and it read just like a *Sopranos* script. Consovoy's woes—including accusations that he eased the release of mob-connected inmates and a judge's son—highlighted an earlier Kean connection to the Corsaro case.

Zolper of the *Record* wrote:[60] "The Corsaro case marks yet another instance when the mobster has received favorable treatment from the state, said Donald Belsole, who prosecuted Corsaro for the slaying of a Morris County liquor store employee in 1974. Corsaro was pardoned for that murder in 1983 by then-Gov. Tom Kean after serving only nine years of a life sentence. Cary Edwards, the governor's chief counsel at the time, has said publicly he did not know of Corsaro's mob connections when he recommended the pardon to Kean." (Edwards went on to become attorney general, a gubernatorial candidate, and chairman of the State Commission of Investigation.)

When "Little Sammy" Corsaro of Clifton was pardoned, Consovoy was a major player on Kean's staff as the top adviser on gubernatorial appointments and the patronage mill that entails. Consovoy started as Kean's driver during his run for governor in 1981, when Kean won a squeaker against Jim Florio. Consovoy played a much larger role in Kean's 1985 landslide victory. Kean owed Consovoy big-time, as he was credited with bringing in the GOP vote in Hudson County, hard-core Democratic turf. Consovoy was in and out of the governor's office and worked for various GOP campaigns and the Republican State Committee before Kean appointed him to the parole board in 1989, Kean's final year in office.[61] Republican Governor Whitman appointed Consovoy its chairman in 1998. Reporter Zolper told this amazing story about the celebration for Consovoy when Whitman made the appointment:[62]

Zolper described a summertime party, a private event where friends of Consovoy took over a white-tablecloth Italian restaurant in Trenton where some of the finest Italian food in the country is still served. The group was celebrating Consovoy's elevation to chairman of the parole board. Several guests were astonished by the man sitting at the bar and watching and greeting the guests.

"Dennis Steo had spent 23 years in prison for two murders, described by police as cold-blooded, 'gangland-style' executions," Zolper wrote. "One victim was his own business partner, and the other an elderly gambler. Steo wasn't the only one at the restaurant with a checkered past. The man who apparently paid for the buffet for at least 25 people—antipasto, sausage and peppers, ziti, and more—has his own links to the mob, and his own bizarre employment history, according to court documents, other public records, and interviews."

The man Zolper said was footing the bill was Joseph "Gus" Ferrera, who used his job as a county corrections officer in the late 1970s to help an inmate "come and go" so he could meet women and grab some pizza and fast food, according to the inmate's lawyer. Ferrera, convicted of official misconduct, spent seven month in prison before he was paroled. But his misconduct at the county level didn't stop him from getting a state job in corrections while he was still on parole for the county offense. At age seventy-two, he was hired by the state with a salary of $73,000 a year. He admitted knowing people in the mob and was the cousin of a top New Jersey mobster.

Ferrera's cousin was Michael Taccetta, former New Jersey boss of the Lucchese family. The inmate Ferrera allowed to grab fast food and fast women was Robert Spagnola, who later ran the Lucchese crime family's sports-gambling operations in New Jersey, the *Record* reported.[63] It wasn't against state law for the state Department of Corrections to hire Ferrera while he was on parole. For seventeen years, he worked from an office in a storage room next to the chapel at the Passaic County Jail in Paterson, the *Star-Ledger* reported.[64]

Steo—the man at the bar for Consovoy's celebration—used to be an enforcer for the Philadelphia mob, law enforcement officials told reporter Zolper. The New Jersey Parole Board released him in 1995 after twenty-three years of a life sentence, and Consovoy was one of two parole board members on the preliminary panel that considered Steo's release, the *Record* reported. Final decisions at the parole board are often rubber-stamped after the preliminary decision is made.

Consovoy, who called Ferrera a friend, said he attended the wedding of Ferrera's daughter and used his condo on Marco Island in Florida. Consovoy told the *Record* this about Ferrera:[65] "Does he know people who are in (the mob)? Sure he does. But a guy's your friend; a guy's your friend. If he's involved in organized crime, it's a surprise to me. If he knows people in it, it wouldn't be a surprise to me. I make no bones about my friendship with Joe."

Ferrera allowed the *Star-Ledger* to interview him: "He acknowledges he has spent his life socializing with mobsters, crooks, killers, wise guys. 'I know them all,' Ferrera says. 'That don't mean I'm part of 'em.'" To prove his point, Ferrera said he did not hang out at the Bada Bing, the fictional strip club and mob hangout on *The Sopranos*.[66]

The probe into Consovoy's role in the speedy release of those with organized crime ties came at a time when he was singling out cases for himself and doing work normally handled by hearing officers, not parole board members. His handiwork was uncovered just as it was discovered that the parole board had a backlog of nearly three thousand cases, making the fast exit for mobsters even more questionable. A class action lawsuit was filed by inmates in an effort to cure the backlog. Joyce Couch, a union official representing the rank-and-file employees at the parole board, told the *Record* that Consovoy was making parole decisions on his own at home on the weekends.[67]

Consovoy drove to Bayside State Prison and handled work normally done by a hearing officer when he recommended the release of Lucchese crime family member Michael Perna in 1993. Consovoy listed Perna, who ran the Lucchese crime family's New Jersey operation while other mob leaders were in prison, as "crime free for 20 years" even though he had been indicted four months earlier on racketeering charges.

"State and federal authorities had charged him with conspiring to commit 11 murders, looting public funds from Newark, and a general reign of terror lasting two decades," Zolper wrote. "But just as it appeared that Perna would be eating prison food for decades to come, he saw the light of freedom—albeit briefly—thanks to the state Parole Board."[68]

Investigators also looked into how reputed Genovese crime family associate Vincent Ravo was able to skip ahead of the thousands on the waiting list for parole, the *Star-Ledger* reported. Ravo was among those indicted with Angelo Prisco.

There have always been rumors in New Jersey that paroles were for sale at a cost of $10,000. Ferrera, in an interview with the *Star-Ledger*, said investigators asked him about a meeting he had with Consovoy and a convicted sex offender at the Six Brothers Diner in Little Falls.[69] "Ferrera says the authorities want to know whether the convicted man gave Ferrera and Consovoy $5,000 each before he was sentenced in the hopes of getting favorable treatment when his parole hearing eventually came up." Ferrera told the *Star-Ledger* he bumped into the convict at the diner and the man gave him two Yankee tickets, but no favors were exchanged.

As if it couldn't get any worse, Ferrera confirmed finding jobs for Consovoy and others at the Parole Board. "In 1992, when Consovoy, then a Parole Board member, was strapped for cash amid his second divorce, Ferrera says he called his old friend Anthony Proto, business agent of Laborers Local 342 and reputed organized crime member. The call helped Consovoy get a night job removing debris from a Newark cogeneration plant that had been hit by fire. At the time, Proto and 14 other reputed members and associates of the Gambino crime family were awaiting trial on a 70-count racketeering indictment," the *Star-Ledger* reported.[70] Through Proto, Ferrera also procured jobs for Consovoy's son and the son of former Parole Board member Peter Loos.[71]

Before Consovoy moved to Virginia, investigators, using a search warrant saying they suspected bribery, went to his home and removed a dozen boxes of parole board and personal records.[72] After two years of investigating, in April 2002, less than four months after McGreevey took over and with First Assistant Attorney General Peter Harvey in charge of prosecuting criminal activity, the state dropped the case against Consovoy.

Little seems to have changed with the parole board and mobsters. In 2006, on Governor Corzine's watch, Danny Provenzano—the filmmaker who played himself in a movie just before he was sent to jail for ten years for violent racketeering—was enjoying the low security of a prison farm one year after he was sentenced and entered a halfway house just six months later.[73]

Continuing his movie career right into New Jersey prison life, Provenzano lived at the Harbor halfway house in trendy Hoboken and was allowed to travel to the Newark office of his lawyer, who runs a film company. Provenzano's prison job was working on set designs, and the production was getting so large, his lawyer asked if he could report to a newly purchased warehouse for his work. That might seem like outrageous good fortune for a racketeer, but it got better for Provenzano.

Despite a strong and lengthy objection from the state attorney general's office, which described Provenzano as a violent offender, unrepentant, and likely to commit other crimes, the state parole board met in July 2006 and said he could be released in October. Only another movie-like incident the next month kept him from getting his ticket out.

Gannett reporter Jonathan Tamari found that one day instead of heading to his job location, Provenzano went to his Upper Saddle River home, where a car driven by his brother-in- law ran into him, pushed him into the garage, and landed him in the hospital. The police report said that it was an accident and that his brother-in-law thought he had the car in reverse when it was in forward. A Department of Corrections report said the brother-in-law's foot slipped off the brake.

Provenzano said he had permission to go home, but the halfway house said no way. Parole board officials were already in a panic. In light of the Prisco scandal, they knew the release of Provenzano could blow up, and Danny had provided them with a way to save face. His release was canceled, and his movie days were over, for a while. But it was not as if he was going to do hard time for long in the Soprano State. By spring 2007, he was out of East Jersey State Prison and into Talbot Hall, the transition stop back to a halfway house. By summer, he was there.

9

On the Boardwalk: Sand, Sea, Sun, and Scandal

Just yards from the Atlantic Ocean, along streets off the original Monopoly board, gamblers feed slots and try to beat the house at poker tables and roulette wheels, hoist a few drinks, and catch a glitzy show. Unlike the old days when Al Capone, Meyer Lansky, and Lucky Luciano came to Atlantic City to enjoy the Jersey Shore and take a break from the brutal and often bloody business back home, there hasn't been any organized crime in the area since gaming was legalized—if you believe Jersey politicians. If you've gotten this far in our tale, you know better.

Gov. Brendan Byrne led the drive to legalize gaming in Atlantic City—voters approved it in 1976, and the first casino, Resorts International, opened in 1978—to rejuvenate a town that had fallen on hard times. Another goal was a cash flow for the state's ever-greedy coffers—$468 million in fiscal 2007.[1] Critics warned that all that cash would attract the mob. To appease those critics, Byrne made a big production of publicly telling organized crime to keep its filthy hands off Atlantic City as the town opened its doors to gambling.[2]

A great photo op, perhaps, but it was too late.

"When the governor issued that warning to the mob to keep the hell out of Atlantic City, they were already laying the groundwork," said Frank Lentino, who would know, since for years he was the link between the Bruno/Scarfo Philadelphia mob and both organized labor and local government in Atlantic City.[3]

"A friend of mine from Philadelphia contacted me and said certain people from New York would like to meet with me. We met in Little Italy. They were powerful guys, the bosses of bosses. One was flamboyant and the other conservative. They gave me a proposition. But [Atlantic City–based mobster Nicodemo "Little Nicky"] Scarfo hears about it. That's how it all started," Lentino, at age eighty-two, said in a 1993 interview, until now unpublished, with coauthor McClure at the dining room table in his Mays Landing home.

Nicky Scarfo's telephone list, written in code, listed Lentino as "Frank Gray," according to a 1990 signed statement from Scarfo nephew and admitted mob hit man Philip "Crazy Phil" Leonetti after he entered the federal witness protection program.[4] Leonetti literally grew up with the Mafia, with five family members in La Cosa Nostra. Leonetti said when he was nine years old, his uncle "Little Nicky" Scarfo took him for a ride in a pickup truck that had just been used for a murder. Scarfo told him having a little boy in the truck would make the mobster appear less suspicious if the police stopped him.

The Scarfo and the Bruno crime families, ensconced in southeastern Pennsylvania across the Delaware River from Jersey, weren't about to let the New York bosses waltz undeterred into the South Jersey gambling halls. Atlantic City was no longer the safe haven of sun and surf from the Al Capone days. It was a place where money was to be made, enough money to murder for. Scarfo wanted Atlantic City for his own. Scarfo and Phil "Chicken Man" Testa served as under bosses to Angelo "the Gentle Don" Bruno, a traditional kind of guy who opposed drug trafficking and respected compromise. Testa figured he could rake in tribute from his iron-fisted control over unions and construction. Lentino told McClure it was Testa who told him to go to Local 54, the restaurant workers union the mob used as its foothold into the city.

Bruno, however, was murdered in 1980, shotgunned by two assassins dispatched from New York, as he sat in his car just after buying a newspaper.[5] Testa moved up to big boss and soon faced the challenges and testing that come with being the top wiseguy in town. Atlantic City roofers union chief John McCullough engaged in a war of wills with him and Scarfo over Testa's attempts to control city labor. McCullough lost. He was shot to death. Testa remained top dog for about a year, then was replaced by Scarfo following Testa's murder in a bomb blast that destroyed the front of his home.

The family operated in Philadelphia, North Jersey, and South Jersey, according to Leonetti, who managed Atlantic City for the Bruno crime family and was considered one of the most powerful mob figures in Philadelphia and Atlantic City. Lentino was his associate.

"At Local 54, I was supposed to be a consultant, but I did everything," Lentino told McClure. "It was cash and carry. They are so greedy. Scarfo got kickbacks from services to the union, like health care."

Lentino was first arrested at age twenty-five for running a bookie operation. But he beat the rap. A year later he hid as a patient in Philly's Temple University Hospital and then in California when he got caught skimming profits. In 1938, he got ten years hard labor for robbing a numbers joint in Atlantic City run by the

Jewish mob. He served only three because he believed someone had pulled strings for him. He joined the Operating Engineers, where he recalled Italians and Irish fighting for control before he moved to the Seafarers Union, where he said he saw a bloody battle over control of the New York and Philadelphia docks. And then he became a Teamster.

Lentino was eventually caught by the feds for extortion and conspiracy. His lawyer, Robert Madden, tried to get Lentino's ten-year sentence reduced. The government successfully argued otherwise. Executive Assistant U.S. Attorney Peter B. Bennett told the Associated Press: "He is a mob figure. He worked for the mob right up to his arrest. He assisted the mob in purchasing the mayor's office of Atlantic City."[6] A federal undercover agent spent a year and a half infiltrating the Atlantic City mob and sidling up to Lentino, who was caught on tape in hundreds of hours of secretly recorded conversations. Atlantic City Mayor Michael Matthews, indicted in 1984, took a $10,000 bribe from the undercover agent Lentino treated like a son. Undercover agent James Bannister acted like he was part of a mob-related plan to buy twenty-one acres in the Marina section of Atlantic City. Lentino and the mayor were each to get $10,000, plus a hidden interest in the property, for their support of the project.[7]

A former Atlantic County elected official and state assemblyman, Matthews was sentenced to fifteen years in federal prison, spending most of the five years he served in solitary confinement since the feds said he needed to be protected. "The people of Atlantic City thought they were electing a mayor, not a crook," U.S. District Court Judge Harold Ackerman said at the sentencing.[8] (But Atlantic City had elected crooks before, and has since. It had happened earlier with Mayors William Somers and Richard Jackson who were two of seven city officials, past and present, indicted for kickbacks and payroll-padding. All were convicted or pleaded guilty.[9] After Matthews, Mayor James Usry was accused of influence peddling but pleaded to campaign finance irregularities.[10] Mayor Lorenzo Langford admitted to trying to influence an election by coercing subordinates to improperly collect absentee ballots.)[11]

Leonetti told the feds about more than murder. He detailed Scarfo's control of Local 54 of the restaurant and hotel workers union in Atlantic City from the start of gambling and even after the Casino Control Commission replaced Local 54's president, Frank Gerace.

He explained to the feds: "I met with Scarfo and Gerace in 1977 at Lillian Gerace's apartment on Mississippi Avenue in Atlantic City. At the meeting, Scarfo told Gerace that he would be required to get Scarfo's approval for any significant decisions made in Local 54. No appointments, jobs, union cards, or other favors were to be made or given without Scarfo's approval. Gerace agreed to Scarfo's terms and suggested to Scarfo what he (Gerace) said were opportunities to make a lot of money with Scarfo." At the time, Bruno was still in charge, and Scarfo did not have permission to approach Gerace.

Lentino said Bruno, who emigrated from Sicily in 1911, was less violent than some in the organization. "He was willing to sit down and talk, not shoot all the time. He was a gentleman. He did not like to resort to violence if he could avoid it."

But not when it came to Atlantic City. In the summer of 1978, Scarfo saw one of Bruno's hit men outside his North Georgia Avenue apartment. Scarfo told Bruno he would kill the hit man if he saw him again and built a wall around the rear of his place, Leonetti told the feds. By 1980, when mob bosses were dropping like flies passing through a DDT cloud, Bruno was gunned down as he got into his car. To the end, Bruno admitted nothing when it came to Atlantic City even though he was apparently ready to kill for it.

As for Scarfo, Leonetti described his rise to power: "Phil Testa was murdered in March 1981. Scarfo became the boss of the Family within a week after Testa's death. Scarfo made Salvatore 'Chuckie' Merlino his under boss. Scarfo also made me and Lawrence Merlino 'capos'. During this period and since late 1978, when Resorts Casino opened, Gerace delivered money to Scarfo each month. Gerace said that the money was taken from the union's welfare plan by a man we called the Cakeman."

Leonetti said in his sworn statement that Scarfo protected a number of bars and restaurants from the union in exchange for payments or free meals and drinks. The cost was hundreds of dollars a week—beginning in the late 1970s—for sweetheart deals with the union. According to Leonetti, two of those bars were Memories, in Margate City, near Atlantic City, and Scannichio's.

Memories was owned by Jerry Blavat. Known to Philadelphia and South Jersey radio fans as "the Geator with the heater," Blavat began his showbiz career at age thirteen when he was a dancer on the original *Bandstand* show with Bob Horn, who later was replaced by TV staff announcer Dick Clark after a series of scandals. The show was renamed *American Bandstand* when it went on the ABC network. Later, Blavat was a road manager for the rock group Danny and the Juniors and, in what surely was one of his greater challenges, served as a valet for comedian Don Rickles.

A New Jersey State Commission of Investigation report in 1995 discussed Blavat's alleged association with Philly mobsters, based on statements by Leonetti. Blavat got a liquor license, issued by the local municipality, in 1974 under the corporate name New Gold, Inc., for Memories. He still has it.

A week after the SCI report became public, Blavat asked on live television. "Where'd this stuff come from that I was associated with the mob?" He denied what Leonetti told the SCI.

In 1984, the New Jersey Casino Control Commission, set up to keep the mob out of town, forced Local 54 president Gerace to resign because of his ties to Scarfo. But Leonetti claimed nothing changed. "In 1987, and 1988, I and Scarfo met with his son, Nicky Jr., in jail," Leonetti said from protective custody. "During that time, Nicky Jr. showed us a record of accounts and carried messages to and from Scarfo regarding Local 54. Nicky Jr. told Scarfo that he was receiving the regular payments on Scarfo's behalf from Gerace."

The feds charged Gerace and two construction executives with embezzling $52,000 from a union hall renovations project. In 1985, the executives were convicted, but Gerace was acquitted after the jury deliberated for eight hours.[12]

Among the conversations secretly taped by the feds in their investigation of crooked mayor Matthews was a conversation in which Lentino said he had personally delivered campaign cash— never disclosed to election officials as required—to then–New Jersey Senate candidate Steven Perskie, known as the father of casino gambling because he authored the legislation that set it up.[13] He later became Gov. Jim Florio's chief of staff and chairman of the Casino Control Commission before returning to private practice and then a superior court judgeship in Atlantic County.

Perskie called Lentino's claim "outrageous lies." And Lentino later signed an affidavit saying that he had lied and was exaggerating his importance to the undercover agent.

When gaming was made legal in the old mob-gathering place, the powers that be, eager to show organized crime didn't have a prayer in Atlantic City, created the Casino Control Commission. But the state's reputation as a crime watchdog was reduced to lapdog from the start. The late Ovid Demaris, author of *The Boardwalk Jungle*, pointed to a serious violation of the public trust in Governor Byrne's appointment of the late Joseph Lordi as the first chairman of the Casino Control Commission. Byrne used his vow to keep organized crime out of Atlantic City as the slogan to win reelection, but his opponent noted that during Byrne's decade as

Essex County prosecutor he failed to tackle the corruption in his own backyard. His assistant and then successor as prosecutor was Lordi. From *The Boardwalk Jungle*.[14]

"What was remarkable about this appointment [to the Casino Control Commission] was that Byrne named Lordi even after State Police Superintendent Clinton Pagano told him that Lordi had failed their background check because of serious questions about past associations and actions," Demaris wrote.

One of the problems for Lordi was New Jersey mob underboss the late Gerardo "Jerry" Catena of the Genovese family, according to Demaris. While Lordi was county prosecutor, he approved a gun permit for a friend who was a Catena soldier. While director of the State Alcoholic Beverage Commission, he hired a Catena associate as a commission investigator. One of Lordi's brothers worked as a bartender in what Demaris described as a "Catena restaurant." Lordi frequently visited bars and restaurants that were "reputed hangouts" for the mob. But Demaris said the most damaging connection to Catena was that Lordi's law firm represented Best Sales, a food brokerage business "fronted by Jerry Catena's brother Gene."

Through Best Sales, the Catenas tried to enter the legitimate business of detergent, but they withdrew from the field after high-pressure tactics with the A&P, including two murdered managers and $60 million in arson, attracted the attention of the feds.

Lordi, like Newark's Joseph Santiago—Gov. Jim McGreevey's failed pick as state police superintendent twenty-five years later amid allegations that he, too, was too close to organized crime—called the state police reports politically motivated. Demaris wrote of Lordi's reaction: "The mere fact that you rub shoulders with somebody or eat in his restaurant doesn't make you an associate," Lordi said at a news conference. Lordi did not deny the allegations but talked about what it was like living in the Ironbound section of Newark. "I am sure that there are other bars that I went to that might be controlled by organized crime. . . . Don't ask me to identify them." Lordi said his law firm had only represented a member of the Catena family on civil matters. The media did not ask him about Best Sales, Demaris wrote. Pagano, appointed to his post by the governor, changed his mind on Lordi and endorsed him for the appointment to the Casino Control Commission. The Senate Judiciary Committee, chaired by Martin Greenberg, a former law partner and adviser to Byrne, confirmed Lordi.

The Lordi family is still in New Jersey politics. Linda Lordi Cavanaugh, Joseph's daughter, worked on Gov. Jon Corzine's U.S. Senate campaign and was elected an Essex County freeholder. President Bill Clinton appointed her husband, Dennis Cavanaugh, a federal judge. As for Lordi, a scholarship at the Seton Hall Law School bears his name and honors him as an outstanding public servant.

There was an interesting member of the legislative commission that studied gambling before its entry into Atlantic City. It was the late William V. Musto, state senator, Union City mayor, and mentor, you recall, to U.S. Sen. Bob Menendez (who later testified against Musto) and politically connected Democratic lawyer Donald Scarinci. Demaris described Musto as an old friend of the Atlantic City machine and the commission's most evangelistic proponent of gambling.

"It was Musto's theory that legalized gambling would not only increase revenues but would reduce organized crime." Demaris noted that in 1977, Musto was charged with using his power to protect an illegal baccarat game operated at a bar owned by the wife of another city official. The case was dismissed. But four years later Musto was convicted of racketeering and sentenced to seven years in prison. Ironically, the very next day, he was re-elected Union City mayor.

Politicians are to blame for Atlantic City corruption. And not much has changed. The state set up a system to scrutinize liquor license applications in the city to keep unsavory characters like mobsters out. Here's how coauthor Ingle described a run at a liquor license in his June 20, 2005, "Politics Patrol" column:[15] "Used to be people applying for a liquor license in Atlantic City were investigated by the state police, an august no-nonsense agency of professionals. Then came former Gov. Jim McGreevey, who took the troopers off the job."

Coauthor McClure found a Dover Township man, Brian Petaccio, convicted of running an illegal video poker operation in the wake of an indictment alleging organized crime, had a liquor license pending.[16] When the state police were involved, even Petaccio's mother's liquor license application was denied.

But Brian Petaccio got his record expunged and applied for the liquor license right after McGreevey took the troopers off investigating Atlantic City liquor licenses.

Who then handled liquor license reviews? The Division of Alcoholic Beverage Control, which was under the eye of Attorney General Peter Harvey. Convicted with Petaccio was his father-in-law, Carmen Ricci, whose lawyer in 1991 was Jack Arseneault, whom we met earlier as a political ally of McGreevey, old personal friend of Harvey, and lawyer for convicted political boss John Lynch.

After coauthor McClure started asking questions, Robert Schiff, co-owner of the Boardwalk building where the bar was to be located, said, "The deal is off." The Petaccio bar would have been located at the prime Boardwalk spot off St. James Place near Cathy Burke's popular Irish Pub.

Also falling under McGreevey's administration was the strange case of Interstate Industrial Corporation, whose affiliates have been banned from doing business by two New York agencies, which cited allegations Interstate had done business with those involved with the mob. New York City's Business Integrity Commission also recommended rejection of an application by an Interstate affiliate for a trash transfer station permit.

This is how the Web site AmericanMafia.com reported New York City and federal investigations of Interstate:[17]

The City investigation was prompted by a $30 million contract sought by the DiTommaso brothers' business to assist in the closing of the Fresh Kills landfill on Staten Island. This illegal Mob-controlled landfill was allowed to operate for decades until the people of New York City elected as Mayor a former Mafia Prosecutor, Rudolph Giuliani, who shut the operation down. As a result of the city's investigation, the $30 million dollar contract with the DiTommaso brothers' business was canceled.

The Federal investigation of the DiTommaso brothers concerned their purchase of a Staten Island waste station controlled by Edward Garafola, who is married to the sister of former Gambino Family Underboss Sammy "The Bull" Gravano. Garafola was indicted in March 2000 along with Lawrence Ray, an executive of Interstate Industrial Corporation, and Daniel Persico, nephew of Colombo Family Godfather Carmine "The Snake" Persico, on Federal charges involving a $40 million stock "pump and dump" scam.

New Jersey Casino Control Commission member Michael Fedorko, however, recommended the commission grant a license to Interstate and its sister company Interstate Drywall Corporation of Clifton, New Jersey. Those working in Atlantic City casinos need a license. The system was set up to keep the mob out. Fedorko, a career state trooper and former acting state police superintendent, was appointed to the CCC as a consolation prize by Gov. Christie Whitman after someone else was named to run the state police.

McGreevey appointed Fedorko to another five-year term just after, as the hearing officer, he recommended approval of Interstate's license to do business in Atlantic City, a sure road to full
commission approval. Ironically, as a former member of the governor's security detail, Fedorko was beside Governor Byrne in the
'70s when Atlantic City opened for business and the mob was told
to stay out.

The Interstate case wasn't the only time Fedorko ruled in favor
of a firm accused of mob ties. He praised the owners of Mazzocchi
Wrecking, also known as Maztec Environmental—a demolition
company state investigators reported had contact with mob figures. Fedorko said he found that Grace Mazzocchi and her
brother, Nicholas, had "good character, honesty and integrity," according to a story in the *Star-Ledger* by Judy DeHaven.[18]

"I couldn't have hoped for anything better," Mazzocchi's lawyer,
Lloyd Levenson, told DeHaven. She wrote: "After a four-year
probe, [gaming] division investigators concluded Grace Mazzocchi came into contact with mob figures through the Laborers International Union of North America Local 1030. Among them
were two reputed soldiers in the DeCavalcante crime family."

Grace and Nicholas, whose company did recovery work at the
World Trade Center after the terrorist attacks, said they did business
with the union because it was the only one specializing in asbestos re-
moval. Fedorko believed all the brother and sister had to say. De-
Haven reported he found their statements "credible" when they said
they had no idea—despite warnings from law enforcement—that
their employee Charles DiMaria, who among other things attended a
funeral for "Sam the Plumber" DeCavalcante, had reputed mob ties.
The wrecking company fired DiMaria just before Fedorko's ruling.

Fedorko's logic was the same in the Interstate case. He said
state lawyers, first under Attorney General John Farmer, and then
under Attorneys General David Samson and Peter Harvey, failed to

prove allegations against the company and its owners, brothers Frank and Peter DiTommaso. Fedorko filed an eighty-page report in April 2004 recommending the DiTommaso brothers' application be approved. He said any mob ties were "innocent" and "even inevitable" in the construction industry.[19]

New York disagreed. Its integrity commission said there were too many questionable contacts with the DiTommasos for them not to know whom they were dealing with.

Coauthor McClure wrote, "In July 2001, the New York State Dormitory Authority rejected the company for a contract and cited Interstate's acquisition of a stone company controlled by an alleged member of the Gambino family, the leasing of a transfer station from a company controlled by another Gambino associate and the employment of three persons with alleged organized crime or criminal backgrounds."

In New Jersey, Fedorko wasn't the only one praising the DiTommasos. Character witnesses for the brothers included former Democratic governor Florio and former Republican senate president Ray Bateman. Election records show the DiTommasos contributed to McGreevey's campaign, to Florio, and to Christopher Bateman, Ray's son, a state assembly member from Somerset County with eyes on a state senate seat.

Fedorko, however, was right about one thing. The state botched Interstate's hearing before the Casino Control Commission which lasted forty days and spanned thirteen months. It wasn't conducted by the experienced gaming division's licensing section, which usually handles such matters. Limits were placed on information gathered by investigators, prompting questions about how the case was handled. Incredibly, New Jersey used two people who claimed they were organized crime experts, but both said they never had heard of the DiTommaso brothers or their company. Perhaps New Jersey's "experts" should talk to the people who did the New York investigation and heard plenty. Two organized crime informants, including William Murtha, were eliminated at the state's request. The state's lawyer told Fedorko to ignore information from Murtha after he gave conflicting statements. Usually conflicting statements call for further investigation, not for trashing everything gathered.

Murtha, a former associate of the Gambino and Genovese families now in a witness protection program, said he met with a Genovese capo we have met before, John DiGilio, who stated he "owned" Interstate Industrial Corporation, according to a 2000 document filed by gaming authorities. "Murtha understood that statement to mean that DiGilio had an undocumented interest in and influence over Interstate Industrial," the document said.

Regardless of whether informer Murtha was telling the truth when he said DiGilio spoke of influence over Interstate, or whether DiGilio actually had any, and with the state disregarding what New York authorities did after their thorough investigations, Interstate's owners, the DiTommasos, were allowed to work in Atlantic City.[20] They also were contractors on the Marriott in Trenton.

New Jersey began to see the light of day on the DiTommasos only after another New York case—connecting Bernard Kerik to the brothers—drew national attention to them. Laid out for everyone to see was the New Jersey corruption that led to a shoddy investigation of Interstate, to praise for the brothers from high-ranking Jersey officials, and to statements by the state's mob "experts" who never heard of the brothers or their company.

A grand jury sitting in the Bronx, New York, for eighteen months heard testimony from Timothy Woods, a contractor who supervised a project to convert two apartments owned by Kerik—police commissioner under Mayor Rudolph Giuliani and President George W. Bush's pick in December 2004 to be homeland security secretary, until allegations of ethical lapses forced Kerik's withdrawal—into a single home.

(After Kerik's political demise, Bush turned to Michael Chertoff—another New Jersey connection. Chertoff as a private lawyer successfully defended Governor Whitman's Sports and Exposition Authority chairman, Michael Francis, when a grand jury charged him with trying to conceal alleged ties to organized crime from his boss, the governor, and with allegedly using his state position to get business for his private firm.[21] The employees of a potential Atlantic City client said they thought the man with Francis, convicted Teamsters official Anthony Rizzo, looked like a "thug, mobster type," which Chertoff maintained was stereotyping. Rizzo, who pleaded guilty to racketeering in 1997, was listed in a State Commission of Investigation report as a reputed associate of the Genovese crime family. He also pleaded guilty in 1983 and served half of a six-month sentence in a restraint of trade trash case.[22])

Concerning Kerik and Interstate Industrial, the Associated Press's Tom Hays reported in May 2006:[23] "In a civil complaint filed last year, New Jersey authorities now working with the Bronx prosecutors alleged that most of the $240,000 renovation was secretly paid for by a firm there with ties to the Mafia, Interstate Industrial Corp. In return, Kerik allegedly vouched for the company with city regulators . . . charges both he and the owners of the company . . . vehemently deny."

Kerik pleaded guilty to misdemeanor charges of breaking conflict-of-interest laws in June 2006 and was fined $221,000 but given no jail time. The next month the DiTommaso brothers were indicted for perjury in the Kerik investigation and pleaded innocent.[24]

The New Jersey Division of Gaming Enforcement filed court papers seeking to revoke Interstate Industrial's license to work on casinos, citing testimony from mob turncoats who said the DiTommasos were allied with the Gambino crime family.[25] When the gaming authorities sought answers from Kerik, he invoked his Fifth Amendment right against self-incrimination.

State gaming enforcement lawyer Gary Ehrlich said that Casino Control Commissioner Fedorko had a "see no evil" approach to the company's contacts with organized crime and that he ignored the conclusions of the New York agencies, which left little room for doubt: "The number and quality of the applicant's ties to organized crime over a period of many years renders unlikely in the extreme any innocent explanation in this case," the Business Integrity Commission of New York City said.

"It is likely the DiTommasos' meteoric success was partly attributable to the assistance of their connections to organized crime," said a footnote in the New York report. Former New Jersey Acting State Police Superintendent Fedorko, probably unaware of the double entendre, had attributed their success to being "part of a close-knit, loving and devoted family."[26]

Fedorko's warm and fuzzy feelings notwithstanding, New Jersey gaming regulators suspended the casino licenses for the DiTommaso brothers in August 2006.[27] The grand jury investigation of Kerik and the brothers' perjury indictment were cited.

In November 2007, Kerik was indicted and charged with accepting renovations to his apartment, including marble bathrooms, a whirlpool tub, and a grand marble rotunda, in return for helping an unnamed New Jersey construction firm with a mob reputation obtain New York City contracts, the *Washington Post* reported. Kerik pleaded not guilty and said he would fight to clear himself.

In addition to mob problems, governors, including Florio in the 1990s, have used Atlantic City as a cash cow for the state, through the revenue it generates; for their buddies, through the Casino Reinvestment Development Authority (CRDA); and for themselves, through campaign contributions from contractors who get work there.

"Interviews with local and state officials and other sources," coauthor McClure wrote for the *Trentonian*, "indicate the Florio administration had held up work on a new convention center and other improvements worth more than $300 million until they could make certain they controlled every element of the projects."[28]

A South Jersey Democrat told McClure it amounted to an unbelievable amount of power. "The Gambinos (crime family) would envy this situation."

Three weeks after Florio was elected in 1989, the Casino Control Commission was forced to pay an additional $15,840 per year, an 18 percent hike, for renting Atlantic City offices owned by Florio's soon-to-be chief of staff, Steven Perskie, who as a legislator authored New Jersey gaming legislation.[29] The rent hike letter was mailed by Perskie's agent when Perskie was on the state payroll as head of Florio's transition team. It demanded an extra three dollars per square foot by January 1.

In addition to Perskie, McClure found other ties to the gaming industry among those close to Florio:[30]

- Democratic State Committee Chairman Phil Keegan was a lobbyist for Resorts International and served as a consultant to Resorts International board chairman James Crosby, who built the first casino in Atlantic City.
- Harold Hodes, a key adviser to the Florio committee, was president of a public relations firm that represented the Casino Association of New Jersey.
- Attorney General Robert Del Tufo was a former member of the Hannoch Weisman law firm, which was hired to represent Donald Trump on gaming issues.

Republican Christie Whitman had her own headaches with the Atlantic City–Brigantine Connector, also called "the Tunnel" or "the Road to Nowhere." Whitman agreed to build the $330 million, 2.2-mile road and tunnel at the request of Mirage Resorts chairman Steve Wynn, a 1963 University of Pennsylvania grad who was no stranger to New Jersey or Atlantic City.

Brett Pulley wrote for the *New York Times* [31] that Wynn hated the heavy state regulation of New Jersey's casinos and sold the Golden Nugget in Atlantic City in 1980 for $180 million, vowing to never return. He reversed that stand after the industry convinced New Jersey officials to relax casino regulations. He then convinced the state to provide $220 million in public money to be combined with $110 million from Mirage for a roadway and tunnel to Le Jardin, a proposed $1 billion casino development.

Wynn pumped $31,000 into a U.S. Senate race in New Jersey— $17,000 to the eventual winner, Robert Torricelli, and $14,000 to his GOP opponent, Richard Zimmer. He also dined with Republican Christie Whitman at the governor's mansion.

There was widespread opposition to the tunnel from the residents of a black community that had to be disturbed because houses were razed for the project. Opposition also came from a group of mayors, who felt the use of $95 million from the state Transportation Trust Fund could be put to better use than a driveway for Wynn, and from Trump, owner of three casinos, who called New Jersey's underwriting of the project "corporate welfare" that favored out-of-state business over local companies.

Eventually, the black homeowners took $200,000 buyouts. A judge threw out the mayors' court case, saying there was a legitimate need for the tunnel even if there weren't plans for a casino. Trump changed his mind when the state agreed to build a special ramp to one of his casinos at a cost of $12 million, part of which was paid for by Trump.

Ironically, the guy who got nothing from it was Wynn. Mirage Resorts was bought by MGM, Inc., in a $6.7 billion merger. Wynn's project that started it all, Le Jardin, apparently is on hold some-where.

Not much changes in Atlantic City. Atlantic City Councilman Craig Callaway arrived at federal court in March 2007 and lifted his middle finger to the press. He was really flipping the bird to all of New Jersey, even though he said the bribes he took were "to help the people." Callaway said he accepted the $36,000 because the contractor who bribed him was hiring local people. "I tried to make my own rules to make things better for the people who have been left out."[32]

Caught in an FBI probe, Callaway agreed to help the feds by wearing a wire and recording more bad guys. But he couldn't resist a little revenge on the side. Callaway took a page from Charles Kushner's book and hired a hooker to lure a council opponent (also a minister) into sex that was quietly filmed and then sent to the press for all of New Jersey to see, prosecutors said he admit-ted.[33] Now that's something Kushner didn't think of—a broader audience. Callaway's goal was to blackmail his opponent into re-signing.

The FBI was none too happy with Callaway's moonlighting in the movies, and the federal judge didn't buy Callaway's excuse for the bribes or his lawyer's attempt to get Callaway credit for not try-ing to disguise the $36,000 as campaign contributions, the way many New Jersey pols do.

Looking at New Jersey's finest—a politician from Atlantic City—U.S. District Judge Joseph Rodriguez said, "Political corrup-tion is really a malignancy in the bloodstream of democracy." The judge sentenced Callaway to forty months in prison.[34]

About the same time Callaway was making his appearance in federal court, the younger Nicodemo Scarfo returned to the At-lantic City area. With his father still jailed on racketeering-murder charges, the younger Scarfo, according to the Philadelphia *In-quirer*'s George Anastasia, was believed to be skipper of a Lucchese crew in the Atlantic City area. Not so, according to Scarfo's lawyer, who told Anastasia the younger Scarfo moved to Atlantic County to get into the legit cement business. Seems like with his family history, he might have picked something else. But again, this is New Jersey, where things never change. By August 2007, Anastasia's sources were already telling him that young Scarfo and his associates were flexing their underworld muscles at Atlantic City clubs, strip joints and bars, a tactic reminiscent of his father.

Atlantic City drew international attention in October 2007. Once again, it wasn't for anything positive. It was because the mayor disappeared after finally admitting he lied about being a Green Beret during the Vietnam War. A decorated war hero with two Bronze Stars, Bob Levy apparently didn't think that was good enough. After an investigation into his war record by the *Press of Atlantic City*, he admitted he lied about being in the Special Forces, and according to the *Press*, the feds were probing whether he wrongfully boosted his military pension.

Longtime head of the city's beach patrol before becoming mayor, Levy disappeared on September 26 and went missing until October 9 when his lawyer announced Levy had spent a week in a clinic specializing in mental health and addiction. He resigned a day later. Less than a month later, Levy admitted in federal court that he lied—making up stories about his war record—to boost his veterans benefits. The feds said Levy, who claimed to have parachuted one hundred times, never parachuted from a military aircraft. He was sentenced to three years' probation and $30,000 in fines and restitution.

Jersey lawmaker James Whelan explained the whole situation to TV's Geraldo Rivera and to all his viewers: "The city is a national joke."

10

The Soviet Socialist Republic
of Jersey

Taxes in New Jersey remain a major headache mainly because there is too much government and an unholy alliance among public worker unions, the education establishment, and politicians on the take who see themselves as a cut above the average guy. They all but show their disgust for residents who pay huge sums in taxes to keep the state spending like a drunken sailor on shore leave, with much of the spending directed toward special interest groups that keep incumbents in office.

In all, 1,969 different entities can levy taxes. New Jersey's suburban school districts, which have a better track record of educating kids, must support their schools through the highest property taxes in the nation because about half the state's education budget goes to the thirty-one Abbott districts we discussed earlier. In most districts voters get their say at the ballot box on school budgets. But if voters turn those budgets down, the local municipality can reinstate them. In the rare instance when the local government backs the voters, the state education bureaucracy in Trenton can overturn voters and the municipality. Thus, in the twenty-first century, as the nation's men and women in uniform fight and sometimes die to instill democracies around the word, a legitimate vote of New Jersey people means nothing. During the Cold War, activity like that scared us into arming ourselves to the teeth lest the former Soviet Union bring such practices to our shores.

Author and urban affairs expert Steven Malanga, in his "Mob That Whacked Jersey," written for New York's *City Journal*, summed it up well:[1] "Increasingly muscular public-sector unions have won billions in outlandish benefits and wages from compliant officeholders. A powerful public education cartel has driven school spending skyward, making Jersey among the nation's biggest education spenders, even as student achievement lags. Inept, often corrupt, politicians have squandered yet more billions wrung from suburban taxpayers, supposedly to uplift the poor in the state's troubled cities, which have nevertheless continued to crumble despite the record spending. To fund the extravagance, the state has relentlessly raised taxes on both residents and businesses, while localities have jacked up property taxes furiously. Jersey's cost advantage over its free-spending neighbors has vanished. It is now among the nation's most heavily taxed places."

Residents pay an unreasonably high price for other things as well. Each year the Motor Vehicle Commission collects $202 million in traffic fines and surcharges. There is a long list of items you can have your driver's license suspended for that are not in any way related to driving. Some of them are draconian. Under Gov. Jim McGreevey, the state raised the fine for not having your license, registration, and proof of insurance available when a cop asks for it to $150 per document, or $450 for all three if you carry them in your wallet and accidentally leave it at home. The fines apply even if you have been issued the documents and they are current. If the agency suspends your license because someone lost track of a parking ticket you paid, it still charges fifty dollars for reinstatement although you did nothing wrong.

When did the people of New Jersey lose control of their government?

A former Wall Street businessman turned politician, multimillionaire Jon Corzine came into the governor's office in 2006 with a promise of getting things under control. After nine months he wasn't talking about rolling back property taxes or even holding them steady. The most optimistic Corzine would be was to say he *hoped* he could keep tax hikes to 4 percent a year. Taxes couldn't be cut, only increased. And yet other states provide services and get along fine on a lot less. Uncontrollable inflation is not the culprit. Lobbyist and political consultant John Torok's *In The Lobby* newsletter noted the state budget increased faster than inflation, zooming from $16.2 billion in 1997 to $30.8 billion for fiscal 2007.[2] During his first six months in office, Corzine raised taxes by almost $2 billion. That included a sales tax increase of one cent on the dollar that brings in $1.1 billion. At the same time, Corzine went along with fellow Democrats allocating more than $300 million in pork barrel spending for their districts. Assemblyman Richard Merkt, a Republican from Morris County, submitted an open public records request asking Corzine's Treasury which lawmakers requested which spending. Treasury responded the legislature exempted itself from such requests. The public be damned, in other words.

That's the attitude traditionally expressed by the committee established to hear ethics complaints against lawmakers. The Joint Legislative Committee on Ethical Standards originally consisted of only lawmakers hearing ethics complaints about fellow lawmakers, so the outcome was predictable. One critic said it should be named the "damage control committee." Legislators didn't take it too seriously, either. Its chairman, Assemblyman Anthony Impreveduto, told Gannett's Tom Baldwin in 2003 that the complaints heard by the committee—which reprimanded only two members and fined a fourth $200 in one hundred eleven cases it handled since 1972—generally didn't amount to "donkey dust."[3] One time the committee, under Impreveduto, claimed it dropped an ethics complaint because it couldn't find the accuser, an individual that a Gannett reporter found with ease.[4]

Ethics watchdog Impreveduto, a Democrat who represented corrupt Hudson County in the legislature for seventeen years while double-dipping as a teacher and administrator at Secaucus High School for thirty-three years, went from "donkey dust" to donkey doo. He resigned from the assembly and was forced to pay a $10,000 fine in a 2004 plea bargain with the attorney general after he was caught spending $50,000 in campaign donations on personal items such as a wedding, travel, eyeglasses, a hearing aid, and sports memorabilia.[5] He could have been sentenced to five years in jail and fined $25,000.

Coauthor Ingle quipped in his column, "Only in New Jersey would the former chairman of the Legislature's ethics committee plead guilty to misusing campaign funds and then have elected colleagues say they hope the criminal activity is not too much of a black mark on his record."[6] That was a reference to remarks by another Hudson County pol, then–Assembly Speaker Albio Sires, who went on to be a member of the U.S. House. Sires said, "I can only hope that many of his noteworthy accomplishments as a legislator and consumer advocate will not be overshadowed."

Ingle wrote, "If Sires and his colleagues really cared about ethics reform, they wouldn't be feeling sorry for Impreveduto. They would be calling for his head for confirming in the public's mind that being a New Jersey politician is tantamount to being shady."

For Sires's part, the New Jersey town hall where he was mayor for more than a decade—West New York—was handed subpoenas in April 2007 as part of the federal probe into the way discretionary state grants are handed out when lawmakers' votes are needed to pass the state budget. The subpoenas were served after the *Jersey Journal* reported that the lion's share of Hudson County grants, $7.2 million, went to West New York in 2005 while Sires was both its mayor and assembly Speaker.[7]

Impreveduto, incidentally, after the guilty plea, had his teacher's pension reduced from $58,000 to $40,000, but when he turns sixty he can apply for a pension from the legislative job.[8]

Following criticism that the "damage control committee" makeup was 100 percent lawmakers, the big thinkers under the Gold Dome in Trenton added four nonlawmakers and then four more so that eventually there were eight "public" members and eight legislators. Did that improve things? They can change the makeup, but it is still New Jersey.

Lawmakers dragged their feet before naming additional "public" members in July 2006. They didn't have a meeting until mid-October. After nearly a year and a half with no meetings, lawmakers fought for two hours over who should be chairman, eventually settling on a "public" member who was allied with the Democrats, Raymond Bramucci, who was labor commissioner under Gov. Jim Florio. That settled, they got into an argument about acceptance of the minutes of the last meeting, held seventeen months before. In the end, none of the pending complaints against lawmakers were heard that day.[9] For one thing, there were ethics complaints against five members of the ethics committee, who would have to recuse themselves. There also were complaints against Sen. Wayne Bryant, who was under state and federal investigation. The committee decided not to pursue the Bryant issues until it was clear whether doing so would interfere with U.S. Attorney Chris Christie's probe and until committee members had read a scathing report on Bryant issued more than a month earlier, a report most everyone else in the state had read or knew about from press coverage. Christie, who later indicted Bryant on thirteen counts in an ongoing case, wrote the committee a letter saying he had no objection to it investigating Bryant.

The new supposedly nonpolitical head of the ethics committee, Bramucci, prompted a call for his resignation when he said ethics complaints against lawmakers using the budget process to benefit their family members or employers amounted to just New Jersey doing what New Jersey does.

The "pork" or "Christmas tree" items are added to the budget at the last minute and give goodies to certain districts to entice lawmakers to vote for the budget. Bramucci said Republicans and Democrats alike enjoy the process and voters are wrong if they think something smells in Trenton. "Most voters think, 'Oh my God, they caught all of these people stealing money.' Well, they caught them mostly doing their job. . . . If you're helping a town beautify its downtown for example, why is that bad?"[10]

Bramucci resigned for another job a few months later. The man who was tone-deaf to ethical issues in the legislature landed a $120,000 post as director of the Prudential Business Ethics Center at Rutgers University's Business School.[11] That was right up there with Kean University hiring former governor McGreevey, whose administration was one of the most ethically challenged in state history, to teach ethics part-time for $17,500.[12] In doing so, McGreevey was jumping onto the bandwagon of college patronage jobs, as former governor Jim Florio was already teaching one course one day a week at Rutgers for $96,632 a year.[13] Those jobs kept the former governors in the state pension system, where, in McGreevey's case, his pension would be based on the three years he made $157,000 annually as governor. Meanwhile, McGreevey joined the Episcopal Church on a Sunday and decided the following Wednesday he wanted to be a priest.[14] And the *Star-Ledger* reported that he took home about ten boxes of state records to review for the New Jersey archives and sent nothing back because he threw out most of it.

Travelers crossing bridges or driving on the state's main arteries will continue to fork over money, not so much to maintain the facilities as to feed huge bureaucracies that create opportunities used to hire political hangers-on and former public officials who need more time on the overly generous state pension accompanied by fully paid health care for life. The projects these bureaucracies spin out are filled with money for lawyers and engineers and others who need to be rewarded for their monetary political contributions, which in New Jersey are seen as an investment, one that gives a much better return than any bank. After politicians have milked the state's assets for all they're worth, the self-serving pols want to sell them, the way Governor Florio sold a stretch of the Turnpike to another state agency to balance the state budget—a gimmick Governor Corzine picked up under the fancy name of "asset monetization."

Machine politics is not based on doing what's right for the state or in the long term. It's what's good for the party and getting candidates elected, and that usually means putting the faithful in jobs regardless of qualifications or whether the job is needed.

To show what can happen in one day in New Jersey, just before Thanksgiving 2006, coauthor Ingle's blog (http://bobingle.blogspot .com) had this litany of election, utility authority, state government, and school district corruption.[15] You couldn't make up this feast:

> First, Attorney General Stu Rabner today announced the first public corruption indictment of his state tenure. The mayor of Carneys Point in Salem County, John "Mack" Lake, is accused of trying to bribe his opponent in this year's election to drop out of the race by dangling municipal job offers for him . . . didn't work. Lake lost the election, and maybe much more.

Second, FBI and IRS agents today arrested Frank Abate, former head of the Western Monmouth Utilities Authority. He's been indicted for allegedly taking thousands of dollars of free or discounted home improvements and services from contractors and developers.

Third, there's [Assistant State Commissioner] Carolanne Kane-Cavaiola [at the Department of Human Services] accused in a report the state inspector general issued yesterday of steering $7.7 million in state grants to a group she's connected with, circumventing public bidding laws and eliminating financial oversight for how the money was spent—or misspent, as Mary Jane Cooper alleges.

Last, the Ledger's reporting that the former Paterson School District facilities director was sentenced to 43 months in prison this morning for taking more than $180,000 in kickbacks from vendors in return for helping them win millions of dollars in district contracts. "Corruption in this state is rampant," U.S. District Judge Jose Linares told the school official, James Cummings, during a hearing in Newark. "I sit in this court day after day and hear cases like this. There is a need for a specific deterrent."

Voters keep returning to office the people who support and maintain New Jersey's miserable setup, aided and abetted by election district lines drawn to make it easier to keep incumbents in power. So what's the incentive for incumbents to address the situation they created, past talking about the need for improvement?

Sometimes pols are returned to office with help from the great beyond. Former governor Brendan Byrne joked that when he died he wanted to be buried in Hudson County so he could continue to take part in the electoral process. But Mercer County

Superior Court Judge Linda R. Feinberg wasn't joking when she ordered the state to compile the names of all adult New Jersey residents who have died since 1985. That followed reports that an estimated 13,000 deceased people remained on voter registration lists and at least 4,755 of the more civic-minded corpses voted in the November 2003 election.[16]

Talk and promises from politicians who know damned well they won't change anything substantially are the only things in New Jersey that are cheap. Some residents, especially the elderly, have to choose between paying taxes and their phone bill or grocery bill. Frustrated citizens who can manage it are voting with their feet, with more people leaving the state than are coming in from other states. In 2006, 72,000 more people left the state than moved in. The U.S. Census Bureau estimated New Jersey had fallen out of the top ten states in population for the first time since 1910. As recently as 2000, it was ranked No. 9.

A healthy birth rate and foreign immigration kept the state's population growing, but at an ever slower rate. The Census Bureau's 2006 report said the population grew by only two-tenths of 1 percent. Were it not for immigrants, the Garden State population would be shrinking, but even the immigrants are looking elsewhere. The 2006 report showed New Jersey attracted almost 6 percent fewer immigrants than it had over the past five years on average.

That raises a question about what will happen after the baby boom generation retires. Should a large percentage of these folks decide to run for the border, the people coming in behind them, especially if they are mostly immigrants trying to start a new life, won't be able to make the same big contributions to the state treasury. Reduced income tax revenue and ever-rising state costs for pensions and operations could lead to state bankruptcy, which could be combined with a collapse of the housing market and a lot of empty mini-mansions on the market with no takers.

When people leave, they take their wealth and sometimes their businesses with them. "Jersey has blown a golden opportunity," magazine publisher Steve Forbes, a Jersey resident, told writer Steven Malanga. "It could have been like Hong Kong, a haven for wealth and industry among high-tax neighbors like New York. Instead, Jersey's now losing its own residents to places like North Carolina."[17]

Malanga observed that businesses are shown no more respect than hapless citizens. "McGreevey also chilled the state's already inhospitable business climate. He boosted corporate taxes and ended the ability of struggling companies to deduct losses from their tax bills—one of the most ruinous corporate tax schemes in the nation. When the head of Cincinnati-based Federated Department Stores, one of Jersey's biggest employers, noted that its state tax bill would more than double (to $10 million) and that it would reconsider any further expansion in the state, McGreevey attacked the company, challenging it to slash executive pay. His tax regime 'drastically alters New Jersey's corporate tax landscape, making it inhospitable to large corporations,' observed Glenn Newman, former deputy commissioner in New York City's Department of Finance."

During his first year in office, Corzine reversed McGreevey's policy that ended the ability of struggling companies to deduct losses, but most of the rest of McGreevey's tax increase remained.

And residents were hurting. By June 2007, a Monmouth University/New Jersey Monthly Poll found that 72 percent of the state's households earning below $50,000 a year and 64 percent of households earning between $50,000 and $100,000 said they could not keep pace with the cost of living. Forty-four percent of those earning more than $100,000 said the same.[18]

There is one huge drain not recorded in any Treasury document—the corruption tax. That's the price U.S. Attorney Christie says every New Jersey resident pays for jobs that are not needed and contracts that are padded and well-connected pols who are getting their slice of the pork. Investigation after investigation has discovered this. Fingers are pointed, and sometimes the guilty even get indicted. And yet it never stops. A new wave of well-connected crooks takes over. Lobbyist Alan Marcus told *New York* magazine, "In New Jersey, you contribute money not for access but results. Anybody who doesn't admit that is lying."[19]

"Corruption, both legal and illegal, is a hidden tax on the public," Christie told the *Record*'s Herb Jackson, who noted Christie's remarks were made "the same day more than a thousand lobbyists and politicians crammed together onto a chartered Amtrak train for the Chamber of Commerce's annual overnight schmoozefest in Washington."[20]

Christie explained the corruption to Jackson:

How big a tax? No one knows, Christie says, because there's no way to tell how many unnecessary contracts are given out or how many negotiated prices are inflated, either to repay contractors for past campaign contributions or to make sure they remain friendly and contribute in the future.

While this "pay to play" system does not happen everywhere, Christie says it is widespread in some parts of the state and appears to be spreading.

"There's this culture where people who are raised in public life somehow think 'now it's my turn to get extra benefits,'" he said. "There's no question the system in New Jersey is broken and is not operating in the best interests of the people in the state. The people who have a responsibility to do so should put a stop to it."

Christie said laws banning "pay to play" are needed because the practice falls into a "murky" area where prosecutors are powerless without evidence of an explicit promise of a contract in exchange for a contribution, or vice versa.

When it comes to cash bribes, no new laws to combat corruption are needed, he said, just enforcement of the existing laws. There have been laws against bribing public officials on the books for 175 years, but nearly all the cases he pursued as U.S. attorney involved officials caught with envelopes of cash.

New Jersey drew national attention in September 2007 when the feds rounded up eleven of the state's public officials like they do drug dealers in other states. The sting netted two mayors, three city council members, numerous school board members and two lawmakers—one a minister. They were taken into federal court in hand cuffs and leg shackles. Weysan Dun, special agent in charge of the FBI in New Jersey, said the case "paints a picture of a network of corruption . . . from one end of the state to the other." The elected officials were charged with taking cash bribes, ranging from as little as $5,000 to $35,800, from fake insurance and roofing firms. What New Jersey's finest offered the companies in return was help with winning public contracts. The two lawmakers, Democratic Assemblymen Mims Hackett Jr. and Alfred Steele, the minister, resigned.[21] Hackett Jr. and Steele later admitted to accepting a bribe from the fake company set up by the feds. By May 2008, all but two of the public officials either pleaded guilty or had been convicted. Awaiting trial were Keith O. Reid, former chief of staff to the Newark City Council President, and Jonathan Soto, former Passaic city council member.

But there is another side to political crime not as often discussed. "Corrupt politicians will steal your trust, your taxes and your hope," Christie said to a Seaside Park crowd.[22]

The culture of corruption is turning the public against all elected officials, even the honest ones. In the 1994 governor's race, 69 percent of the state's registered voters cast ballots. In the 2005 governor's race, only 46 percent did. Christie said the 23 percent decline over eleven years could be attributed to the loss of prestige in holding public office.

Perhaps it was that loss of prestige that contributed to so many officeholders deciding to call it quits. When spring of 2007 arrived, more than a quarter of the senate and others in the assembly had indicated they would not seek reelection in the fall. But it probably had more to do with Christie's sprinkling the legislature and the governor's office with federal subpoenas, and a growing movement to strip pensions from officeholders caught breaking the law, than it did prestige. By that time, Christie had nabbed more than a hundred people in public corruption cases, and the pols had learned he meant business. It was beginning to appear that Christie didn't feel the same way New Jersey's pols did about the longtime practice of trading lawmakers' votes for "Christmas tree" items in the state budget. Insiders speculated that what went on day to day in the halls under the Gold Dome wouldn't stand up to scrutiny if someone were wearing a wire. Maybe those dropping out thought the jig was up, the game was coming to a close.

But we have heard that before. There have been numerous attempts to fix what's wrong with New Jersey government, attempts that were mostly wasted efforts:

- In the old days lawmakers were able to run political action committees separate from their campaign funds. A 1993 law abolished PACs run by incumbents, other than the senate and assembly leaders, and put stricter limits on donations that rank-and-file candidates could receive from individuals, business, and interest groups. Far from being reform, the maneuver only concentrated power in legislative leaders, who can give unlimited donations from their PACs to legislative candidates and therefore hold more sway over how the lawmakers would vote after being elected.

- In 2001, after losing control of the legislature, Republicans in a lame-duck session (which in New Jersey can produce most anything) passed a law that reduced the size of the maximum contribution to leadership PACs and state party committees from $37,000 to $25,000. Once again, it was mostly for show, because it left out county party committees, which made those groups and their chairmen more powerful.

- When the legislature lowered the limit on how much in gifts lawmakers can accept, it decriminalized the acceptance of gifts, so offenders get a slap on the wrist.

- New Jersey began providing public financing for gubernatorial elections in 1977. It was rendered irrelevant in 2005 when rich guys Jon Corzine and Douglas Forrester spent $70 million of their own cash on the race.

- In 2005, the state began an experiment that provided public financing in two legislative districts. It flopped because only one of the five eligible pairs of candidates was able to raise the required matching donations in the cumbersome way mandated by the law. Some recommendations by a study commission to make it better were ignored when the program was renewed in 2007.

- The legislature partially banned wheeling—the process of sending contributions from one end of the state to another. But the rules applied only from January through June, leaving general election campaigns, where wheeling has the most corrupting influence, untouched.

- The proposal to ban officials from having more than one elected job at a time was signed into law by Corzine in September 2007, but it only affected those in the future. The current dual officeholders, including seventeen lawmakers, can swill at the public trough as long as they can keep getting elected.

- A law to force corrupt public officials to give up their pensions took effect in April 2007, but it was full of holes. For one thing, the pension that has to be forfeited is only the one attached to the job where the misdeed occurred. If a public official has seven jobs and gets nailed on job No. 4, that's the only pension he gives up. He keeps the pensions for the other six. Also, there is no grandfather clause, so it is only applicable to crooks in the future, not the crooks of the past and present, some of whom probably had a hand in framing the legislation complete with loopholes.

If the legislature wanted to make a difference, it could ban wheeling altogether. It also could do away with the "senatorial courtesy" that lets a senator block anything he wants for whatever reason, a system too often used as legalized blackmail. The practice is so archaic it isn't written anywhere, and it is one of the reasons, as we've seen, that party bosses will spend millions to get someone elected to a job that pays $49,000 a year.

Better and quicker disclosure of where campaign money comes from would do away with some of the more devious practices. And New Jersey would run cleaner and cheaper if there were a ban at all levels of government on the long-standing practice of handing out no-bid contracts to campaign contributors.

Another way to help U.S. Attorney Christie and his successors clean house would be to have an elected, rather than a governor-appointed, attorney general. That way the top law enforcement officer in the state would have to run on his record of criminal convictions and would be more likely to look under political rocks.

Elimination of pensions and health care for part-time government employees, including elected positions, would help cut the state deficit. Pensions should go only to full-time employees, and no one should have more than one public pension. Going forward, the overly generous public pensions that are out of step with the rest of the economy should be replaced with 401(k) plans, in which the employer makes a matching contribution. If the benefits packages continue to include health care for life, the insured should pay a market-rate copayment. And there should be no carrying over of allegedly unused sick leave and unused vacation from year to year so that at the end of a career some pol can claim hundreds of thousands of dollars' worth.

As we said at the start of this chapter, there is simply too much government in a relatively small state. There needs to be consolidation, especially of school districts and police departments. When the subject comes up, those with the most to lose yell that "Home Rule" is a long-standing tradition in the state. The truth is, New Jersey citizens have less control over their lives locally or otherwise than citizens of most other states. Home Rule is a myth perpetuated by pols living high on the hog off the status quo.

But the most valuable tool for returning government control to the people would be initiative and referendum (I&R) whereby citizens write a bill, and if they get enough signatures it goes on the ballot, and if it passes in an election it becomes law, without the legislature or the governor having anything to do with it. It works in twenty-four states. Former New Jersey governor and president Woodrow Wilson was an early supporter, saying this method of direct democracy "takes power from the boss and places it in the hands of the people."[23] The Initiative and Referendum Institute at the University of Southern California School of Law said the I&R movement started in the Garden State with the New Jersey Direct Legislation League, which gave up in 1907 after fourteen years of frustration.[24] Other unsuccessful attempts were made in 1947 and the 1970s. Efforts in 1981 and 1983 made it through the state senate only to get stalled by assembly Democrats. In 1986, it got through the assembly but lost in the senate.

Republicans promised the people I&R in the early '90s if they were put in power. They lied. Lobbyists and special interests, who saw their way of controlling government through donations coming to an end, panicked. They pulled out all the stops to kill it.

If the desire were there when voters went to the polls and enough "public servants" had the guts to stand up for the people, disinfecting the sewer that is New Jersey politics would be relatively easy. Will corruption ever be under control? It's doubtful, despite the best efforts of the men and women in Jersey journalism whose hard work keeps exposing the graft, and prosecutors like U.S. Attorney Christie who keep pursuing the crooks, and the efforts of whistle-blowers like Joe Potena, Ken Connolly, Michael Nappe, and Joseph Carruth, who spoke out for what's right and suffered the consequences.

Maybe there is something in the fabric of the body politic that can't be mended or something in the water that can't be filtered. Or maybe it's because New Jersey's destiny is to be the Soprano State.

EPILOGUE

At book signing after book signing, we explained to New Jersey taxpayers that this book connects the dots, like you did as a kid with those numbered connect-the-dots pictures. And the picture of New Jersey that emerges is not pretty.

Our book is called *The Soprano State* not just because the mob has muscled into New Jersey, but also because the government in New Jersey often acts like the mob. It beats up taxpayers and leaves them somewhere in an alley to fend for themselves.

And the taxpayer reaction to the book has been amazing—quickly making *The Soprano State* a *New York Times* bestseller.

At our first book signing in Bridgewater, the day the book came out, a man with a walker positioned himself in the front row long before the start. Another came with his oxygen tank. Another drove an hour and a half to get there. One woman sat on the floor and read the book during the signing. Others were reading it in the long lines while they waited for an autograph.

When stores and Amazon.com ran out of books, there were nightly readings, chapter by chapter, at the Irish Pub in Atlantic City.

And just when we thought the interest could be fading, more than one hundred and fifty people showed up for a signing outside

Trenton. One woman, who failed to get a book after trying three places, had a stroke before she could visit a fourth. A friend was buying her *The Soprano State* so she could read it in rehab, where she was learning to walk again. Another woman was buying the book for her soldier husband in Iraq. One middle-aged man said it was the first book he had read since high school. A number of those attending the signings said they had never attended a book signing before.

We worked long, hard hours on this book. But we are blessed. Lots of authors work long, hard hours and don't get the reaction we have received.

Investigative reporting is key to the democratic form of government, and it offers some hope for taxpayers.

What we wanted the most is happening. Taxpayers everywhere are getting a full view of New Jersey's culture of corruption. And some taxpayers are getting angry enough to ask, "How can I stop this?" or "How can I keep this from happening where I live?"

There is some good news on the corruption front in New Jersey. After six days of deliberation, a jury of six women and six men—hailing from six New Jersey counties and including school teachers, a computer programmer, and a postal worker—said to former Newark mayor Sharpe James: Even in New Jersey you can't steer city land worth $46,000 to your mistress so she can resell it for more than $600,000.

That's a start. But there is a long way to go before taxpayers claim what is rightfully theirs—honest government. We are constantly asked, "What needs to be done? How can that happen?"

This book is funny at times. But it is dead serious about the price taxpayers pay for such corruption. And the solutions are not easy. You can see some suggestions in chapter 10, but not a lot of hope. What it will take is another citizens group like the Hands Across New Jersey of the 1990s. Taxpayers are going to have to band together. They are going to need a handful of dedicated leaders, not aligned with a political party, but dedicated to what's right and fair for taxpayers and the tax dollars they have earned with hard work. Government needs to move from the hands of corrupt politicians and into the hands of taxpayers.

That's why we wanted you to come away from this book with your blood boiling and your heads shaking and your lips asking, "How can I change what I see?"

NOTES

Introduction

1. Josh Margolin and Kelly Heyboer, *Star-Ledger,* Dec. 30, 2005.
2. Josh Margolin and Ted Sherman, *Star-Ledger,* Nov. 7, 2006.
3. Margolin and Sherman, *Star-Ledger,* May 16, 2007.
4. Christie Whitman, U.S. Environmental Protection Agency press release, Sept. 18, 2001.
5. Robert Cohen, *Star-Ledger,* June 26, 2007.
6. Chip Scutari, *Trentonian,* Aug. 15, 1995.
7. Sandy McClure, *Asbury Park Press*, Sept. 23, 2003.
8. From www.city-data.com.
9. Paul Nussbaum, *Inquirer,* Feb. 8, 2007.
10. Sandy McClure, *Asbury Park Press*, Feb. 27, 2003.
11. State Commission of Investigation, *Society for the Prevention of Cruelty to Animals*, 2001.
12. Paul D'Ambrosio and Jason Method, *Asbury Park Press*, May 24, 2007.
13. Peter Applebome, *New York Times*, Nov. 2, 2005.
14. Chris Newmarker, Associated Press, Jan. 13, 2006.
15. Jeff Whelan, *Star-Ledger,* Jan. 13, 2006.

1. Deep in the Pits They Strike Gold

1. Josh Margolin and Ted Sherman, *Star-Ledger*, April 2, 2006.

2. Gregory J. Volpe, *Asbury Park Press*, April 25, 2006.

3. Volpe, *Asbury Park Press*, March 30, 2007.

4. Margolin and Sherman, Sept. 23, 2007.

5. Margolin and Sherman, *Star-Ledger*, Sept. 17, 2006.

6. Margolin and Sherman, *Star-Ledger*, June 6, 2006.

7. Margolin and Sherman, *Star-Ledger*, June 6, 2006.

8. Trish Braber, *Gloucester County Times*, June 21, 2006.

9. Margolin and Sherman, *Star-Ledger*, May 18, 2006.

10. Margolin and Sherman, *Star-Ledger*, July 26, 2006.

11. Margolin and Sherman, *Star-Ledger*, Nov. 7, 2006.

12. Margolin and Sherman, *Star-Ledger*, Nov. 14, 2006.

13. Ana M. Alaya, *Star-Ledger*, March 29, 2007.

14. Editorial, *Asbury Park Press*, Nov. 14, 2006.

15. Margolin and Sherman, *Star-Ledger*, May 16, 2006.

16. Margolin and Sherman, *Star-Ledger*, Feb. 16, 2007.

17. Jim O'Neill and Suleman Din, *Star-Ledger*, Oct. 6, 2006.

18. Ken Serrano, *Home News Tribune*, Feb. 2, 2007.

19. Jim O'Neill, *Star-Ledger*, March 2, 2007.

20. Serrano, *Home News Tribune*, Feb. 2, 2007.

21. Margolin and Sherman, *Star-Ledger*, July 28, 2006.

22. David Kocieniewski, *New York Times*, Aug. 9, 2006.

23. Jennifer Moroz, *Inquirer*, Aug. 10, 2006.

24. Margolin and Sherman, *Star-Ledger*, Nov. 29, 2006.

25. Margolin and Sherman, *Star-Ledger*, Dec. 1, 2006.

26. Sarah Greenblatt, *Asbury Park Press*, June 3, 2007.

2. Lots of Power, Less Common Sense

1. Sandy McClure, *Trentonian*, July 2, 1990.

2. McClure, *Trentonian*, Jan. 27–Feb. 3, 1993.

3. McClure, *Trentonian*, June 18, 1993.

4. McClure, *Trentonian*, June 10, 1993.

5. McClure, *Trentonian*, March 19, 1991.

6. Rowland Evans and Robert Novak, *Reader's Digest*, Oct. 1988, 113.

7. Dave Neese, *Trentonian*, Sept. 23, 1990.

8. Dennis M. Culnan, *Courier-Post*, Sept. 27–Oct. 1, 1987.

9. McClure, *Trentonian*, Dec. 20, 1990.

10. McClure, *Trentonian*, March 30, 1994.

11. Editorial, *New York Times*, 1995.

12. Mary Williams Walsh, *New York Times*, April 4, 2007.

13. Jonathan Tamari, Gannett State Bureau, June 1, 2007.

14. IntheLobby.net, May 31, 2007.

15. Alan Guenther, *Asbury Park Press*, April 16, 2000.

16. Jeff Tittle, *Asbury Park Press*, Aug. 10, 2006.

17. McClure, *Christie Whitman* (Amherst, NY: Prometheus Books, 1996).

18. State Commission of Investigation, *NJ Enhanced Motor Vehicle Inspection Contract*, 2002.

19. McClure, *Trentonian*, Jan. 31, 2000.

20. Dunstan McNichol, *Star-Ledger*, May 16, 2003.

21. Gregory J. Volpe, *Asbury Park Press*, Feb. 10, 2007.

22. Jeremy Olshan, *Press of Atlantic City*, Sept. 27, 2000.

23. McClure, *Asbury Park Press*, Feb. 13, 2001.

24. David M. Halbfinger, *New York Times*, April 17, 2001.

25. Halbfinger, *New York Times*, March 26, 2001.

26. McClure, *Asbury Park Press*, April 4, 2001.

27. McClure, Gannett State Bureau, April 24, 2001.

28. Dina Matos McGreevey, *Silent Partner* (New York: Hyperion, 2007).

29. Tom Turcol and Maureen Graham, *Inquirer*, June 1, 2003.

30. McClure and Tim Zatzariny Jr., *Asbury Park Press*, Jan. 1, 2003.

31. Josh Margolin, *Star-Ledger*, Nov. 23, 2004.

32. McClure, *Asbury Park Press*, Aug. 4, 2002.

33. Jim McGreevey, *The Confession* (New York: HarperCollins, 2006).

34. McGreevey, *Silent Partner* (New York: Hyperion, 2007).

35. McClure, Gannett State Bureau, May 5, 2001.

36. Rick Hepp, *Star-Ledger*, June 7, 2007.

37. Tom Moran, *Star-Ledger*, June 15, 2007.

38. Michael Rispoli, *Asbury Park Press*, July 31, 2007.

39. Margolin, *Star-Ledger*, Aug. 15, 2002.

40. McClure, *Aug. 4*, 2002.

41. Jeff Whelan, *Star-Ledger*, Nov. 27, 2002.

42. Laura Kaessinger, Gannett State Bureau, Dec. 3, 2002.

43. Jeff Pillets and Clint Riley, *Record*, Aug. 17, 2003.

44. McGreevey, *Confession*.

45. McGreevey, *Confession*.

46. *Asbury Park Press*, July 7, 2004.

47. *Asbury Park Press*, Jan 28, 2005.

48. McClure, Gannett State Bureau, Aug. 1, 2004.

49. David Noonan, *Daily News*, April 2, 2000.

50. McClure, *Trentonian*, Sept. 19, 2000.

51. David Kocieniewski and Patrick McGeehan, New York Times, Nov. 2, 2005.

52. Jeff Whelan and Josh Margolin, *Star-Ledger*, Nov. 5, 2005.

53. Ben Widdicombe, *Daily News*, Nov. 3, 2005.

54. Tom Baldwin, Gannett State Bureau, Aug. 14, 2005.

55. Deborah Howlett, *Star-Ledger*, March 7, 2007.

56. Baldwin, *Asbury Park Press*, April 8, 2007.

57. Moran, *Star-Ledger*, March 8, 2007.

58. Associated Press, *New York Post*, March 5, 2007.

59. Deborah Howlett, *Star-Ledger*, March 9, 2007.

60. Baldwin, Gannett State Bureau, March 12, 2007.

61. David Kocieniewski and Serge F. Kovaleski, *New York Times*, May 23, 2007.

62. Cindy Adams, *New York Post*, June 6, 2007.

63. Jonathan Tamari, Gannett State Bureau, June 19, 2007.

64. Whelan and Margolin, *Star-Ledger*, May 14, 2006.

65. Gregory J. Volpe, *Asbury Park Press*, Aug. 31, 2006.

66. Judith Lucas, *Star-Ledger*, March 6, 2007.

67. John P. Martin and Judith Lucas, *Star-Ledger*, April 3, 2007.

68. Volpe, *Asbury Park Press*, May 17, 2006.

69. Margolin and Amy Ellis Nutt, *Star-Ledger*, April 15, 2007.

70. Kocieniewski and David W. Chen, *New York Times*, April 30, 2007.

3. Like Days of Yore Minus the Shining Knights

1. Paul D'Ambrosio, *Asbury Park Press*, Oct. 24, 2004; Jim Walsh, Asbury Park Press, Oct. 25, 2004.

2. Deborah Howlett, *Star-Ledger*, July 30, 2006.

3. Jerry Gray, *New York Times*, May 28, 1992.

4. Tom Moran, *Star-Ledger*, Nov. 23, 2005.

5. Jeff Whelan and Josh Margolin, *Star-Ledger*, Sept. 8, 2006.

6. Jeff Whelan, *Star-Ledger*, Sept. 24, 2006.

7. Beth DeFalco, Associated Press, Sept. 8, 2006.

8. Joe Donohue and Jeff Whelan, *Star-Ledger*, Sept. 9, 2006.

9. Whelan and Margolin, *Star-Ledger*, Sept. 28, 2006.

10. Chris Mondics, *Inquirer*, Sept. 28, 2006.

11. Gregory J. Volpe, *Asbury Park Press*, Sept. 29, 2006.

12. Volpe, *Asbury Park Press*, Oct. 15, 2006.

13. Jennifer Liberto, *St. Petersburg Times*, Sept. 16, 2005.

14. David Futrelle, InTheseTimes.com, Jan. 22, 2001.

15. *New York Post*, March 2, 2002.

16. David Kocieniewski and Ray Rivera, *New York Times*, Oct. 29, 2006.

17. Jeffrey Gettleman, *New York Times*, July 17, 2005.

18. Donohue and Whelan, *Star-Ledger*, Oct. 31, 2006.

19. Rick Malwitz, *Asbury Park Press*, Oct. 24, 2004.

20. Suleman Din, *Star-Ledger*, June 12, 2006.

21. Din, *Star-Ledger*, June 12, 2006.

22. Bill Bowman, *Asbury Park Press*, May 7, 2006.

23. Bowman, *Asbury Park Press*, May 7, 2006.

24. Press release, Office of Attorney General, Oct. 6, 2006.

25. Kocieniewski, *New York Times*, Jan. 1, 2006.

26. Bowman, *Asbury Park Press*, Jan. 25, 2007.

27. Malwitz, *Home News Tribune*, Sept. 16, 2006.

28. McGreevey, *Confession*.

29. Kathy Barrett Carter and Josh Margolin, *Star-Ledger*, Nov. 30, 2003.

30. Carter and Margolin, *Star-Ledger*, Dec. 4, 2003.

31. *New York Daily News*, Feb. 23, 2006.

32. Bowman, *Asbury Park Press*, Jan. 25, 2007.

33. Diane C. Walsh, *Star-Ledger*, Dec. 24, 2006.

34. Malwitz, *Asbury Park Press*, Oct. 24, 2004.

35. Michael Rispoli, Gannett State Bureau, March 13, 2007.

36. Jason Method, *Asbury Park Press*, Sept. 17, 2006.

37. Richard Pearsall, *Courier-Post*, July 2, 2007.

38. Gannett NJ, *Courier-Post*, April 1, 2005.

39. Paul Mulshine, *Star-Ledger*, July 25, 2006.

40. Bob Ingle, Gannett State Bureau, May 22, 2005.

41. Pearsall, *Asbury Park Press*, July 6, 2005.

42. Pearsall, *Courier-Post*, Jan. 26, 2006.

43. Jim Walsh, *Courier-Post*, Oct. 25, 2004.

44. Jim Walsh, *Courier-Post*, Oct. 25, 2004.

45. Alan Guenther, *Courier-Post*, Feb. 17, 2003.

46. Guenther, *Asbury Park Press*, June 30, 2007.

47. Eileen Smith, *Asbury Park Press*, June 30, 2007.

48. Carol Loomis, CNNmoney.com, July 2, 2007.

49. Guenther, *Courier-Post*, Oct. 25, 2004.

50. Kathleen Hopkins, *Asbury Park Press*, Oct. 26, 2004.

51. Dina Matos McGreevey, *Silent Partner* (New York: Hyperion, 2007).

52. Chris Mondics and Patrick McGeehan, *Record*, Feb. 26, 1990.

53. McGreevey, *Confession*.

54. McGreevey, *Confession*.

4. All Aboard the Gravy Train

1. David Kocieniewski, *New York Times*, July 30, 2006.

2. Tom Moran, *Star-Ledger*, April 28, 2006.

3. Ian T. Shearn, *Star-Ledger*, Sept. 25, 2006.

4. Mike Kelly, *Record*, Aug. 24, 2006.

5. Dunstan McNichol, *Star-Ledger*, March 30, 2007.

6. Jeffrey C. Mays, *Star-Ledger*, July 17, 2006.

7. Mays, *Star-Ledger*, June 18, 2007.

8. Jonathan Tamari, *Asbury Park Press*, July 13, 2007.

9. Alan Guenther, *Courier-Post*, Sept. 21, 2003.

10. Alonso Heredia, *Courier-Post*, Oct. 11, 2006.

11. Rick Hepp, *Star-Ledger*, Feb. 8, 2007.

12. Gregory J. Volpe, Gannett State Bureau, Feb. 7, 2007.

13. Bob Ingle, *Asbury Park Press*, March 18, 2007.

14. Guenther, *Courier-Post*, April 14, 2006.

15. Sandy McClure, *Trentonian*, Oct. 14, 1992.

16. McClure, *Trentonian*, Feb. 28, 1992.

17. Volpe, Gannett State Bureau, March 30, 2007.

18. James W. Prado Roberts, *Asbury Park Press*, April 30, 2003.

19. Roberts, *Asbury Park Press*, April 30, 2003.

20. State Commission of Investigation, Pension and Benefit Abuses, 1998.

21. James A. Quirk and Kathy Matheson, *Asbury Park Press*, April 13, 2005.

22. Quirk, *Asbury Park Press*, April 13, 2005.

23. Roberts, *Asbury Park Press*, March 25, 2003.

24. Roberts, *Asbury Park Press*, March 25, 2003.

25. Roberts, *Asbury Park Press*, Sept. 21, 2003.

26. Wally Edge, PoliticsNJ.com, Jan. 10, 2005.

27. Jonathan Casiano, *Star-Ledger*, Feb. 3, 2006.

28. Sandy McClure, *Trentonian*, Jan. 16, 1992.

29. McClure, *Trentonian*, June 7, 1990.

30. McClure, *Trentonian*, March 26, 1990.

31. McClure, *Trentonian*, June 21, 1990.

32. McClure, *Trentonian*, June 6, 1990.

33. McClure, *Trentonian*, June 8, 1990.

34. McClure, *Trentonian*, June 18, 1990.

5. "See No Evil" Law Enforcement and Court Jesters

1. Sandy McClure, *Asbury Park Press*, Feb. 29, 2004.

2. McClure, *Asbury Park Press*, Nov. 23, 2003.

3. Wendy Ruderman, *Record*, March 1, 2002.

4. McClure, *Asbury Park Press*, April 12, 2003.

5. McClure, *Asbury Park Press*, May 15, 2005.

6. McClure, *Asbury Park Press*, April 23, 2003.

7. McClure, *Asbury Park Press*, Oct. 19, 2002.

8. McClure, *Asbury Park Press*, Oct. 8, 2002.

9. McClure, *Asbury Park Press*, Oct. 26, 2002.

10. Dina Matos McGreevey, *Silent Partner* (New York: Hyperion, 2007).

11. McClure, *Asbury Park Press*, April 25, 2003.

12. McClure, *Asbury Park Press*, April 14, 2004.

13. Maureen Graham and George Anastasia, *Inquirer*, June 9, 2004.

14. Graham and Anastasia, *Inquirer*, June 9, 2004.

15. McClure, *Asbury Park Press*, Oct. 12, 2003.

16. McClure, *Asbury Park Press*, March 18, 2004.

17. Gannett State Bureau, Feb. 11, 2004.

18. McClure, *Asbury Park Press*, Oct. 12, 2003.

19. Rick Reeno, BoxingScene.com, Nov. 10, 2003.

20. McClure, *Asbury Park Press*, Nov. 9, 2003.

21. McClure, *Asbury Park Press*, March 16, 2003.

22. McClure, *Asbury Park Press*, Feb. 29, 2004.

23. McClure, *Asbury Park Press*, Dec. 26, 2005.

24. Gregory J. Volpe, *Asbury Park Press*, April 2, 2007.

25. Nick Clunn, *Asbury Park Press*, May 8, 2007.

26. Bob Ingle, *Asbury Park Press*, July 9, 2006.

27. Rick Hepp, *Star-Ledger*, Aug. 17, 2006.

28. Hepp, *Star-Ledger*, July 13, 2006.

29. Kate Coscarelli, *Star-Ledger*, May 16, 2006.

30. Editorial, *Courier-Post*, May 24, 1999.

31. *Courier-Post*, May 3, 1999.

32. Editorial, *Courier-Post*, May 3, 1999.

33. Gannett State Bureau, April 22, 2004.

34. Jonathan Tamari, Gannett State Bureau, May 12, 2007.

35. Tamari, *Asbury Park Press*, July 12, 2007.

36. Melanie Burney, Frank Kummer, and Dwight Ott, *Inquirer*, March 26, 2006.

37. Sarah Greenblatt, *Courier-Post*, July 31, 2006.

38. Monica Yant Kinney, *Inquirer*, Aug. 3, 2006.

39. Burney, Kummer, and Ott, *Inquirer*, June 22, 2006.

40. Burney and Kummer, *Inquirer*, Aug. 7, 2006.

41. Kevin McArdle, Millennium Radio NJ, May 8, 2006.

42. Paul Mulshine, *Star-Ledger*, Jan. 14, 2007.

43. Mulshine, *Star-Ledger*, April 11, 2006.

44. David Kocieniewski, Tim Golden, and Carl Hulse, *New York Times*, July 31, 2002.

45. Golden and Kocieniewski, *New York Times*, Sept. 27, 2002.

46. Steve Kornacki, PoliticsNJ.com, Oct. 3, 2002.

47. Robert A. Levy, Cato Institute, Oct. 7, 2002.

48. Andrew Jacobs, *New York Times*, Aug. 1, 2006.

49. Kathleen Bird, *New Jersey Law Journal*, March 30, 1992.

50. Press release, U.S. Department of Justice, April 6, 2006.

51. Tony Wilson, *Trentonian*, Dec. 16, 2000.

52. *Courier-Post*, July 25, 2006.

53. Wilson, *Trentonian*, Dec. 16, 2000.

54. Wilson, *Trentonian*, Dec. 16, 2000.

55. *Courier-Post*, July 25, 2006.

56. Tom Hester, *Star-Ledger*, Sept. 23, 2006.

57. Jim O'Neill, *Star-Ledger*, Dec. 20, 2006.

58. Wally Edge, PoliticsNJ.com, July 24, 2006.

59. Edge, PoliticsNJ.com, July 24, 2006.

60. Edge, PoliticsNJ.com, July 24, 2006.

61. Linda Stein, *Trenton Times,* July 24, 2006.

62. Volpe, Gannett State Bureau, Dec. 1, 2006.

63. Robert G. Seidenstein, *New Jersey Lawyer,* June 13, 2007.

64. Jason Laughlin and Rennee Winkler, *Courier-Post,* Jan. 4, 2005.

65. Kristen A. Graham, *Inquirer,* Sept. 14, 2006.

66. NJ Office of Government Integrity, Camden Center Report, Sept. 13, 2006.

67. Ingle, Gannett State Bureau, Dec. 12, 2005.

6. The Run for the Roses Starts in the Boondocks

1. Bob Cullinane and Nina Rizzo, *Asbury Park Press,* Aug.7–8, 2005.

2. James A. Quirk and Karen Sudol, *Asbury Park Press,* June 6, 2006.

3. James Quirk, *Asbury Park Press,* April 25, 2006.

4. Quirk and James W. Prado Roberts, *Asbury Park Press,* Feb. 9, 2003.

5. Quirk, *Asbury Park Press,* April 13, 2005.

6. Loretta Weinberg and Michael Panter, press release, April 13, 2005.

7. *Asbury Park Press,* Sept. 20, 2006.

8. Tim Zatzariny Jr. and Sandy McClure, *Asbury Park Press,* July 8, 2003.

9. Josh Margolin, *Star-Ledger,* June 19, 2003.

10. Cullinane, *Asbury Park Press,* Oct. 29, 2006.

11. Erik Larsen, *Asbury Park Press,* Jan. 23, 2007.

12. Frank Kummer, Renee Winkler, and Kathy Matheson, *Courier-Post,* June 16, 2001.

13. U.S. attorney's office, news release, Dec. 16, 2003.

14. U.S. Attorney's Office, News release, July 8, 2003.

15. Diane C. Walsh and Nikita Stewart, *Star-Ledger,* Oct. 29, 2002.

16. Walsh and Stewart, *Star-Ledger,* Oct. 29, 2002.

17. John P. Martin, *Star-Ledger,* May 31, 2003.

18. Martin, *Star-Ledger,* April 13, 2005.

19. Martin, *Star-Ledger,* Oct. 29, 2002.

20. Wayne Parry, Associated Press, Dec. 17, 2000.

21. Martin, *Star-Ledger,* May 31, 2003.

22. Martin, *Star-Ledger,* Oct. 9, 2003.

23. Martin, *Star-Ledger,* Oct. 9, 2003.

24. Wally Edge, PoliticsNJ.com, June 11, 2007.

25. Martin, *Star-Ledger*, May 31, 2003.

26. *Jersey Journal*, June 24, 2003.

27. *Jersey Journal*, June 24, 2003.

28. *Jersey Journal*, June 24, 2003.

29. Al Sullivan, *Hudson Reporter*, Nov. 3, 2002.

30. Molly Bloom, *Jersey Journal*, Dec. 23, 2004.

31. Sullivan, *Hudson Reporter*, Dec. 21, 2003.

32. Tom Moran, *Star-Ledger*, June 1, 2007.

33. Sarah Greenblatt, *Courier-Post*, Oct. 8, 2006.

34. Rob Jennings, *Daily Record*, June 28, 2006.

35. Ian T. Shearn, *Star-Ledger*, July 26, 2006.

36. Paul J. Hendrie, *News Tribune*, May 26, 1993.

37. Hendrie, *Record*, Oct. 22, 1993.

38. Howard Gillette, *Camden After the Fall* (Philadelphia: Penn Press, 2005).

39. Alan Guenther, *Courier-Post*, Sept. 19, 2006.

40. Dwight Ott, *Inquirer*, Sept. 30, 2006.

41. Ott, *Inquirer*, Sept. 8, 2006.

42. Guenther, *Courier-Post*, Oct. 13, 2006.

43. *Courier-Post*, Sept. 21, 2003.

44. John McLaughlin, *Star-Ledger*, March 2, 2000.

45. Ivelisse DeJesus, *Star-Ledger*, Feb. 4, 2001.

46. Sandy McClure, *Trentonian*, Feb. 25, 2000.

47. Matt Katz and Sarah Greenblatt, *Courier-Post*, Jan. 31, 2007.

48. Katz, *Courier-Post*, March 27, 2007.

49. State Commission of Investigation, Taxpayers Beware, 2006.

50. Gregory J. Volpe, *Asbury Park Press*, Oct. 11, 2006.

51. Jonathan Tamari, *Asbury Park Press*, Oct. 11, 2006.

52. Tom Jennemann, *Hudson Reporter*, Oct. 22, 2006.

53. Dunstan McNichol, *Star-Ledger*, March 17, 2007.

54. Eileen Stilwell, *Courier-Post*, Sept. 9, 2006.

55. Stilwell, *Asbury Park Press*, Aug. 22, 2006.

56. Guenther, *Courier-Post*, June 15, 2003.

57. Guenther, *Courier-Post*, Sept. 26, 2006.

58. Guenther, *Courier-Post*, June 15, 2003.

59. Jason Laughlin, *Courier-Post*, Dec. 15, 2004.

60. Ted Sherman, *Star-Ledger*, Aug. 24, 2006.

7. Speaking Authoritatively: No Oversight

1. Jonathan Tamari, *Asbury Park Press*, Oct. 24, 2006.

2. Sandy McClure, *Asbury Park Press*, July 31, 2005.

3. McClure, *Asbury Park Press*, Sept. 18, 2005.

4. McClure, *Asbury Park Press*, Dec. 14, 2005.

5. Donald Wittkowski, The *Press of Atlantic City*, June 24, 2006.

6. Associated Press, March 13, 2007.

7. State of New Jersey, Office of Inspector General, New Jersey Schools Construction Corp., April 21, 2005.

8. Dunstan McNichol, *Star-Ledger*, Oct. 31, 2003.

9. Alan Guenther, *Courier-Post*, July 19, 2006.

10. Bob Ingle, *Courier-Post*, March 10, 1995.

11. Ingle, *Courier-Post*, Sept. 29, 1994.

12. Ingle, *Courier-Post*, June 20, 1995.

13. Ingle, *Courier-Post*, March 10, 1995.

14. Andrew Jacobs, *New York Times*, July 12, 2001.

15. Tom Baldwin, *Asbury Park Press*, June 14, 2003.

16. Ingle, Gannett State Bureau, June 17, 2007.

17. Sandy McClure, *Trentonian*, March 13, 1992.

18. James Fox, press release, July 11, 2002.

19. Editorial, *Courier-Post*, June 9, 2000.

20. Jim McGreevey, press release, May 28, 2002.

21. Tom Davis, *Record*, July 19, 2006.

22. Shannon D. Harrington, *Record*, Nov. 13, 2005.

23. Tom Baldwin, Gannett State Bureau, Jan. 17, 2007.

24. McClure, Gannett State Bureau, *Asbury Park Press*, March 12, 2006.

25. Ingle, Gannett State Bureau, June 25, 2006.

26. Baldwin and Gregory J. Volpe, Gannett State Bureau, July 26, 2006.

27. Baldwin, Gannett State Bureau, Jan. 17, 2007.

28. Kevin McArdle, Millennium Radio NJ, July 27, 2006.

29. Volpe, Gannett State Bureau, Aug. 2, 2006.

30. Alexander Lane, *Star-Ledger*, Aug. 25, 2006.

31. Baldwin, Gannett State Bureau, Aug. 24, 2006.

32. *Asbury Park Press*, Feb. 12, 2007.

33. Volpe, Gannett State Bureau, Nov. 26, 2006.

34. McClure, *Christie Whitman*.

35. McClure, *Trentonian*, Aug. 22, 1993.

36. McClure, *Trentonian*, Feb. 24, 1995.

37. McClure, *Trentonian*, Feb. 24, 1995.

38. McClure, *Trentonian*, Dec. 17, 1990.

39. McClure, *Trentonian*, Dec. 17, 1990.

40. McClure, *Trentonian*, May 19, 1993.

41. McClure, *Trentonian*, Dec. 18, 1990.

42. Jerry Gray, *New York Times*, May 4, 1993.

43. *New York Times*, June 5, 1996.

44. *New York Times*, Jan. 4, 1997.

45. Chip Scutari, *Trentonian*, Aug. 15, 1995.

46. Dave Neese, *Trentonian*, May 10, 1993.

47. Phyllis Plitch and McClure, *Trentonian*, Aug. 22, 1993.

48. Joe Donohue, *Star-Ledger*, May 2, 2004.

49. Donohue, *Star-Ledger*, March 11, 2007.

50. Guenther, *Courier-Post*, Nov. 19, 2005.

8. The Gospel According to the Mob

1. Thomas Hunt, "The Disappearance of Jimmy Hoffa," *The American Mafia* (www.onewal.com/maf-art08.html), 2005.

2. Charles Brandt, *I Heard You Paint Houses* (Hanover, NH: Steerforth Press, 2004).

3. Curt Anderson, Associated Press, Feb. 13, 2006.

4. Associated Press, Sept. 16, 2003.

5. George Anastasia, *Inquirer*, Oct. 20, 1998.

6. Jonathan Miller, *New York Times*, Nov. 3, 2002.

7. David Voreacos and Christopher Mumma, *Record*, March 22, 2000.

8. Sandy McClure, *Asbury Park Press*, April 14, 2004.

9. Eric Lipton, *New York Times*, Jan. 17, 2001.

10. Alex Philippidis, *Westchester County Business Journal*, Oct. 13, 1997.

11. Joe Strupp, *New Jersey Monthly*, May 2006.

12. Kathy Barrett Carter, *Star-Ledger*, March 9, 2003.

13. Carter, *Star-Ledger*, March 9, 2003.

14. Local Finance Board, Ethics Law Complaint, July 17, 2002.

15. McClure, *Asbury Park Press*, April 14, 2004.

16. Chris Baud, *Trentonian*, May 12, 2000.

17. Alfonso A. Narvaez, *New York Times*, March 7, 1981.

18. State Commission of Investigation, *The Changing Face of Organized Crime in NJ,* May 2004.

19. Guy Sterling, *Star-Ledger,* Dec. 28, 2001.

20. Associated Press, May 15, 1990.

21. CBS News, May 1, 2003.

22. Jerry Capeci, www.ganglandnews.com, June 29, 2000.

23. Robert Rudolph, *The Boys from New Jersey* (New Brunswick, NJ: Rutgers University Press, 1992).

24. Anthony Bruno, "Real Life Sopranos," www.crimelibrary.com, 2007.

25. Ana M. Alaya, *Star-Ledger,* Feb. 10, 2006.

26. Jeffrey Gettleman, *New York Times,* Aug. 18, 2005.

27. Chad Hemenway, *Courier News,* March 13, 2007.

28. Guy Sterling, *Star-Ledger,* March 12, 2007.

29. Carol Gorga Williams, *Asbury Park Press,* June 20, 1998.

30. Steve Scholfield and Michael Rafferty, *Asbury Park Press,* Sept. 30, 1994.

31. Robert Schwanberg, *Star-Ledger,* Oct. 7, 2006.

32. McClure, Gannett State Bureau, *Asbury Park Press,* Feb. 27, 2003.

33. McClure, *Asbury Park Press,* March 5, 2003.

34. McClure, *Asbury Park Press,* Aug. 28, 2005.

35. McClure, *Asbury Park Press,* Feb. 27, 2003.

36. McClure, *Asbury Park Press,* Aug. 28, 2005.

37. McClure, *Asbury Park Press,* July 19, 2003.

38. Tom Baldwin, Gannett State Bureau, June 15, 2006.

39. Donald Scarinci, deposition, Oct. 27, 2005.

40. McClure, *Asbury Park Press,* June 8, 2003.

41. Lilo H. Stainton, Gannett State Bureau, March 3, 2004.

42. McClure, *Asbury Park Press,* May 4, 2003.

43. Susan K. Livio, *Star-Ledger,* April 12, 2006.

44. State Commission of Investigation, *The Changing Face of Organized Crime in NJ,* May 2004.

45. McClure, *Asbury Park Press,* May 14, 2004.

46. *Ocean County Observer,* Feb. 13, 2005.

47. U.S. attorney's office, press release, March 7, 2006.

48. *Star-Ledger,* April 23, 2006.

49. Paul Lieberman, *Los Angeles Times,* Feb. 12, 2003.

50. McClure, *Asbury Park Press*, Aug. 28, 2005.
51. National Legal and Policy Center, Union Corruption Update, Aug. 4, 2003.
52. John P. Martin, *Star-Ledger*, Oct. 14, 2004.
53. *Shipping Digest*, March 6, 2006.
54. Anthony M. Destefano, *Newsday*, Dec. 7, 2005.
55. McClure, *Asbury Park Press*, July 22, 2003.
56. Michael Rispoli, Gannett State Bureau, April 13, 2007.
57. Nick Clunn, *Asbury Park Press*, May 8, 2007.
58. Tom Baldwin, *Asbury Park Press*, May 18, 2007.
59. Thomas Zolper, *Record*, May 11, 2000.
60. Zolper, *Record*, May 11, 2000.
61. Dan Weissman, *Star-Ledger*, June 17, 1989.
62. Zolper, *Record*, June 11, 2000.
63. Zolper, *Record*, June 11, 2000.
64. Brian Donohue, *Star-Ledger*, Oct. 1, 2000.
65. Zolper, *Record*, June 11, 2000.
66. Donohue, *Star-Ledger*, Oct. 1, 2000.
67. Zolper, *Record*, May 11, 2000.
68. Zolper, *Record*, June 23, 2000.
69. Donohue, *Star-Ledger*, Oct. 1, 2000.
70. Donohue, *Star-Ledger*, Oct. 1, 2000.
71. Donohue, *Star-Ledger*, Sept. 22, 2000.
72. Guy Sterling, *Star-Ledger*, April 4, 2002.
73. Jonathan Tamari, *Asbury Park Press*, April 1, 2007.

9. On the Boardwalk: Sand, Sea, Sun, and Scandal

1. State of New Jersey, budget, fiscal year 2007.
2. George Anastasia, *Inquirer*, July 2, 1989.
3. Frank Lentino, interview, 1993.
4. Philip Leonetti, U.S. District Court, affidavit, Dec. 7, 1990.
5. Rudy Larini and David Schwab, *Star-Ledger*, Dec. 20, 1990.
6. Associated Press, 1985.
7. *Press of Atlantic City*, Dec. 20, 1984.
8. Fen Montaigne, *Inquirer*, Jan. 1, 1985.
9. Joseph Tanfani, *Press of Atlantic City*, July 28, 1989.
10. Derek Harper, *Press of Atlantic City*, Aug. 8, 2006.

11. U.S. Office of Special Counsel, Merit Systems Protection Board, March 24, 2006.

12. Associated Press, April 20, 1985.

13. Ovid Demaris, *The Boardwalk Jungle*, (New York: Bantam Books, 1986).

14. Demaris, *Boardwalk Jungle*.

15. Bob Ingle, Gannett State Bureau, June 20, 2005.

16. Sandy McClure, *Asbury Park Press*, June 12, 2005.

17. James Ridgway de Szigethy, Rick Porrello's AmericanMafia.com, Dec. 2004.

18. Judy DeHaven, *Star-Ledger*, March 27, 2003.

19. McClure, *Asbury Park Press*, July 4, 2004.

20. *Asbury Park Press*, July 22, 2004.

21. Robert Schwanberg, *Star-Ledger*, Jan 10, 2000.

22. Guy Sterling, *Star-Ledger*, July 25, 1996.

23. Tom Hays, Associated Press, May 26, 2006.

24. Hays, Associated Press, July 19, 2006.

25. *Asbury Park Press*, Nov. 16, 2005.

26. McClure, *Asbury Park Press*, July 4, 2004.

27. Donald Wittkowski, *Press of Atlantic City*, Aug. 3, 2006.

28. McClure, *Trentonian*, July 26, 1992.

29. McClure, *Trentonian*, March 5, 1990.

30. McClure, *Trentonian*, March 5, 1990.

31. Brett Pulley, *New York Times*, Dec. 6, 1998.

32. Associated Press, March 14, 2007.

33. Jeff Whelan, *Star-Ledger*, March 14, 2007.

34. Associated Press, March 14, 2007.

10. The Soviet Socialist Republic of Jersey

1. Steven Malanga, "The Mob That Whacked Jersey," *City Journal*, Spring 2006.

2. *In the Lobby*, vol. 1, no. 4, July 2006.

3. Tom Baldwin, *Asbury Park Press*, Sept. 22, 2003.

4. *Asbury Park Press*, Dec. 6, 2003.

5. Dunstan McNichol, *Star-Ledger*, Jan. 25, 2005.

6. Bob Ingle, Gannett State Bureau, Nov. 29, 2004.

7. Jarrett Renshaw, *Jersey Journal*, April 19, 2007.

8. *Asbury Park Press*, April 8, 2005.

9. *Asbury Park Press*, Oct. 24, 2006.

10. Kevin McArdle, Millennium Radio NJ, Nov. 27, 2006.

11. Gregory J. Volpe, Gannett State Bureau, Jan. 18, 2007.

12. Josh Margolin, *Star-Ledger*, April 19, 2007.

13. Tom Baldwin, *Asbury Park Press*, Dec. 3, 2006.

14. Patti Sapone, *Star-Ledger*, May 2, 2007.

15. Bob Ingle blog, Gannett State Bureau, Nov. 21, 2006.

16. Michelle Malkin, www.michellemalkin.com, Nov. 6, 2005.

17. Malanga, "The Mob That Whacked Jersey,"

18. Associated Press, June 26, 2007.

19. Craig Horowitz, *New York*, Sept. 20, 2004.

20. Herb Jackson, *Record*, Feb. 2, 2004.

21. Tom Baldwin and Jonathan Tamari, Gannett State Bureau, Sept. 7, 2007.

22. Carolynne Van Houten, *Asbury Park Press*, March 22, 2007.

23. Election Central, Constitutional Rights Foundation, 2007.

24. Initiative & Referendum Institute, http://www.iandrinstitute.org/New%20Jersey.htm, USC School of Law, 2006.

INDEX

THE SOPRANO STATE

NEW JERSEY'S CULTURE OF CORRUPTION

by Bob Ingle and Sandy McClure

In Their Own Words

- About the Authors
- Ask the Authors

Keep on Reading

- Discussion Questions

A
Reading
Group
Guide

For more reading group suggestions
visit www.readinggroupgold.com

 ST. MARTIN'S GRIFFIN

St. Martin's
Griffin

INTRODUCTION

The Soprano State details the you-couldn't-make-this-up true story of the corruption that has pervaded New Jersey politics, government, and business for the past thirty years. From Jimmy Hoffa purportedly being buried somewhere beneath the end zone in Giants Stadium in the Meadowlands, through allegations of a corrupt medical and dental university, through Mafia influence at all levels, to a governor who suddenly declares himself a "gay American" and resigns, the Garden State might indeed be better named after the HBO mobsters.

Where else would: A state attorney general show up after police pulled over her boyfriend for driving with his seatbelt unfastened? A state senator and mayor of Newark (the same guy) spend thousands of dollars of taxpayers' money on a junket to Rio days before leaving office? A politically connected developer hire a prostitute to tape sex acts with his own brother-in-law and then send the tape to his sister? A U.S. senator about to run for governor break up with his union-leader girlfriend then give her a reported $6 million parting gift? Only in *The Soprano State*. It's real, but it reads like fiction. And makes everywhere else seem downright normal.

But *The Soprano State* is more than just a litany of strange New Jersey events. The book is a call to arms for taxpayers interested in cleaning up government wherever political expediency has pushed ethical behavior into a darkened corner.

ABOUT THE AUTHORS

Whether it is news, editorial, or column writing, **BOB INGLE** is known for his straightforward, no-holds-barred style. A veteran reporter and editor who has won numerous journalism awards over a thirty-year career, he is bureau chief for Gannett New Jersey Newspapers in Trenton, the state capital. He also is a part of The Jersey Guys program on 101.5 FM radio and writes a widely read blog.

SANDY McCLURE is a multiple award–winning veteran reporter whose New Jersey statehouse stories, first for *The Trentonian* and then for the Gannett State Bureau, span three decades from Republican Gov. Tom Kean to Democrat Gov. Jon Corzine. She also worked two stints in Pennsylvania covering government and corruption for five newspapers.

ASK THE AUTHORS

Q. How long did it take to write *The Soprano State*?

A. It took two years from the writing of the book proposal to publication. But the news reporting spans three decades.

Q. How can two people write a book?

A. Some of it was written by both of us, as the research also was shared, but Bob wrote more of the book and Sandy did more of the research.

Q. Whose hands are on the cover?

A. That's a secret known only to St. Martin's Press.

Q. What was the hardest part?

A. The documentation, making sure all the i's were dotted and the t's crossed.

Q. Why do you have footnotes?

A. They're there in case someone thinks we made it up. It reads like fiction.

Q. What has been the best part of the experience after the book came out?

A. All the people we met at book signings and in interviews— some really wonderful folks.

Q. Did you have to leave anything out?

A. The book is about 30 percent less copy than the manuscript.

Q. Why was the manuscript cut?

A. The book had to be affordable and a size that wouldn't cause a hernia when you carry it around.

Q. How can I know what happens next?

A. Check out the authors' Web site, www.thesopranostate.com, for updates on the people in the book.

A
Reading
Group
Guide

St. Martin's
Griffin

DISCUSSION QUESTIONS

1. In *The Soprano State*, Bob Ingle and Sandy McClure explain why New Jersey is the most corrupt state in the nation. What do you think makes New Jersey the worst? Or do you disagree? What similar problems do other states have?

2. People who see political and government corruption at a state level often believe their own government representative is exempt from the corruption. Is that the way you feel? Does that contribute to the problem in New Jersey and other states?

3. Because of his dramatic announcement, Jim McGreevey is probably the best known New Jersey governor. Do you believe what he said? If not, why did he resign? What was the worst thing he did during his tenure as governor?

4. If you could be the judge and the jury, how many years in jail—if any—would you give John Lynch and Sharpe James? Who else in the book do you think should go to jail? For how long?

5. In most states citizens look to law enforcement and the courts to protect their interests. In chapter 5, the authors discuss the people named to the bench and to the post of attorney general. Do you think the New Jersey system is designed to look the other way when there is political corruption? What is the rational explanation for so many ill-equipped people in such jobs? Do appointments reflect badly on the people of New Jersey or the governor and state senate?

6. Political bosses are the puppet masters behind the scenes, in effect choosing which candidates the voters get to vote for or against. Thus, an important decision is made before ballots are drawn. Is this something unique to New Jersey?

7. After reading the chapter on Atlantic City and its mob influence, do you think gambling contributed to the corruption? If there were no gambling, would the mob still be there?

8. What is the single worst example of corruption in New Jersey? Who could have stepped up to prevent it? Can it be prevented from happening again?

9. In chapter 10, the authors propose solutions to New Jersey's corruption. Are they realistic? Can the problem ever be cured? What do you think will curb corruption?

10. People are fleeing New Jersey. Is that the answer? Should they stay and fight for better, cleaner government? Will they take New Jersey's corrupt system with them to other states?

A Reading Group Guide

MORE ABOUT *THE SOPRANO STATE*

Stay up to date with the latest news on New Jersey corruption by visiting Bob Ingle and Sandy McClure's Web site: www.thesopranostate.com.

To see what Bob Ingle has to say and what Gannett New Jersey is reporting today on the state's corruption, visit bobingle.blogspot.com.

For more reading group suggestions, visit
www.readinggroupgold.com

St. Martin's
Griffin